School of Interpersonal
Communication
102 Lasher Hall
Athens, OH 45701

RHETORIC IN AN
ORGANIZATIONAL SOCIETY

School of Interpersonal
Communication
102 Lasher Hall
Athens, OH 45701

STUDIES IN RHETORIC/COMMUNICATION
Thomas W. Benson, Series Editor

Richard B. Gregg
Symbolic Inducement and Knowing:
A Study in the Foundations of Rhetoric

Richard A. Cherwitz and James W. Hikins
Communication and Knowledge:
An Investigation in Rhetorical Epistemology

Herbert W. Simons and Aram A. Aghazarian, Editors
Form, Genre, and the Study of Political Discourse

Walter R. Fisher
Human Communication as Narration:
Toward a Philosophy of Reason, Value, and Action

David Payne
Coping with Failure:
The Therapeutic Uses of Rhetoric

David Bartine
Early English Reading Theory:
Origins of Current Debates

Craig R. Smith
Freedom of Expression and
Partisan Politics

Lawrence J. Prelli
A Rhetoric of Science
Inventing Scientific Discourse

Rhetoric in an Organizational Society

Managing Multiple Identities

George Cheney

University of South Carolina Press

To those around the world who are trying to build a better society:

"The point is to work where we are without at the same time regretting that those who struggle elsewhere may never hear our voice."

Frank Lentricchia, *Criticism and Social Change*

Copyright © 1991 University of South Carolina

Published in Columbia, South Carolina, by the University of South Carolina Press

Manufactured in the United States of America

Library of Congress Cataloging-in-Publication Data

Cheney, George.
  Rhetoric in an organizational society : managing multiple
identities / George Cheney.
    p.   cm. — (Studies in rhetoric/communication)
  Includes bibliographical references and indexes.
  ISBN 0-87249-733-X (hard back : alk. paper)
  1. Catholic Church—United States.   2. Communication in
organizations.   3. Catholic Church—Government.   4. Catholic Church—
Doctrines.   I. Title.   II. Series.
BX1406.2.C43   1990
282'.73'014—dc20   90-20305

CONTENTS

Foreword   vii
Preface   ix
Acknowledgments   xi

1. **Rhetoric, Identity, and Organization**   1
    Rhetoric as Organizational, Organizations as Rhetorical   2
    Identity as a Central Term in the Study of Social Life   10
    Identity, Rhetoric, and Organization   13
    The Management of Multiple Identities: A Framework
        for Analysis   15
    Analyzing Organizational Rhetoric   20

2. **The Roman Catholic Church, Organizational Structure,
    and Social Change**   34
    The Church as an Organization   34
    The Church in the United States   37
    Challenges to U.S. Catholicism   40

3. **Historical, Organizational, and Rhetorical Contexts for
    the Case**   47
    Catholic Social Teaching   48
    Catholic Peace Activism   52
    The U.S. Catholic Bishops on Peace   54
    The Challenge of Peace: A Selective Chronology   60

4. **Managing Identities While Addressing Issues**   82
    The Levels of Management   83
    The Catholic Church and the World: What Kind of
        Relationship?   84
    The United States and the World: A Big "We," or "Us"
        and "Them"?   89

Contents

The Church in the United States: American–Catholic or
  Catholic–American?   95
The National Conference of Catholic Bishops: An
  Organization within an Organization   110

5.   **Creating Crucial Rhetorical Connections**   124
The Bishops and the Individual Catholic: Collegiality,
  Community, Communication   125
Trying to Forge Connections across Issues: Peace,
  Justice, Life   132
The Practical Challenge: Managing Multiple Interests
  and Multiple Groups   140
Conclusion   155

6.   **Conclusions, Lessons, Implications**   163
Appendixes   186
  A. Record of Elite Interviews and Contacts   186
  B. Composite Interview Schedule   193
Index of Names   196
Index of Subjects   199

FOREWORD

This is a book of wide significance for students of rhetoric and communication in general. It addresses concerns of all who study communication, especially within and from organizations, and it will be of special interest to students of church–state relations.

In his analysis of how "corporate" rhetoric is created George Cheney (1) freshly applies a major Burkean concept to the study of corporate rhetoric; (2) illustrates the many kinds of interrelated constraints that influence formulation of "authoritative" rhetoric composed on behalf of organizations; (3) illustrates how official "constitutive" or "sacred" organizational traditions must be specially interwoven with pragmatic concerns; and (4) provides a fascinating, detailed narrative of the rhetorical travail through which the National Conference of Catholic Bishops went for more than two years in formulating their famous *The Challenge of Peace: God's Promise and Our Response,* released in 1983. This account in itself will be of major interest to students of religion, especially those who are concerned with how religious bodies justify "intervention" in secular affairs within a society where separation of church and state is a "constitutive" or "sacred" doctrine.

In answer to the question "What do you consider your most important contribution to modern rhetorical theory?" Kenneth Burke once replied, "I hope my concept of *identification* will stand as an important contribution." Making extensive use of this important concept, Professor Cheney offers one of today's few intensive case studies of organizational rhetoric. Burke's notions of "identification" and of divergent "identities" have special value in analyses of persuasion and argument because they avoid confining, two-valued concepts such as conversion, acceptance–rejection, agree–disagree, and up-or-down communication in organizations. Like Chaim Perelman's concept of "adherence," Burke's concept of identification forces observers to focus on (1) types and degrees of sharing and difference among those who communicate and (2) the identifying characteristics of audiences necessarily addressed in public communication by organizations. Using this point of view Cheney recognizes that identification or adherence is never total in situations where rhetoric is necessary.

vii

Rather, in Burke's language, identification is "petitioned" for, and petitions are refused or granted, in part or in full, without the grantors' ever identifying totally with—becoming wholly subservient to—the petitioners. Cheney's detailed exploration of decisions the Catholic bishops made in order to address secular issues *without abandoning their identities as authoritative-persuasive-corporate* "voices" is based on extensive communication with participants in the project and on detailed study of relevant documents. His exposition and analysis lay open the complex rhetorical decisions that face all organizational spokespersons presuming to speak for, from, and to their colleagues while at the same time addressing the affairs of "outsiders." The general principles illustrated by the case study are suggested throughout the book and are treated in detail in the final chapter.

A reviewer of the manuscript for this book observed that the work should be of great interest to scholars in organizational communication, rhetorical criticism, organizational behavior, sociology, public relations, and political science. It will also be of value to scholars concerned with the issue of church-state relationships and to students of the Roman Catholic Church.

Carroll C. Arnold

PREFACE

Well, the guy that comes aroun' talked as nice as pie. "You got to get off [the land]. It ain't my fault." "Well," I says, "whose fault is it? I'll go an' I'll nut the fella." "It's the Shawnee Lan' an' Cattle Company. I jus' got orders." "Who's the Shawnee Lan' an' Cattle Company?" "It ain't nobody. It's a company." Got a fella crazy. There wasn't nobody you could lay for.

John Steinbeck, *The Grapes of Wrath*

This book examines the phenomenon of *organizational rhetoric*—how it is that organizations "speak" to and enlist the "voices" of individual persons. In this connection organizations are treated as being fundamentally rhetorical in nature; that is, organizations are systems of communication which necessarily involve the persuasion of individuals and groups. Further, much of contemporary rhetoric is organizational in that many of the messages which individuals "hear" are from "corporate" or collective sources. Today individuals do much of their speaking to one another through the auspices of corporate or organizational "persons"; much of public—and even private—discourse is in this way "organized." Organizational rhetoric is understood here in terms of "managing" multiple identities, for this is the rhetorical challenge ever facing individuals and organizations in a complex postindustrial society.

In this book I present a variety of examples to illustrate the perspective on organizational rhetoric as the management of multiple identities. I explore in particular a case with historical, political, and religious significance: the development of the U.S. Catholic bishops' 1983 pastoral letter, *The Challenge of Peace*. The bishops acted in a very real sense as "managers" of their identities, individually and as a corporate body; managers of multiple interests and multiple groups, both inside and outside of the Roman Catholic Church; and managers of the various audiences they sought to affect: U.S. Catholics, the Reagan Administration, the public at large, the United States, and the Soviet Union. Indeed, the bishops' challenge in these respects was as profound as *The Challenge of Peace* is itself.

Through a detailed analysis of this complex case I shall show how many of the issues that confronted the bishops do in fact confront all "producers" and "consumers" of organizational rhetoric. For example, how to adapt to outside audiences without jeopardizing established authority with insiders is a problem that faces any organization that seeks to maintain a traditional identity while adapting to changing times and circumstances. By focusing on the intersection of three key terms—identity, organization, and rhetoric—I hope to provide an understanding of how the bishops moved from "I's" to "we" in constructing a constitutional document and to provide a framework for analyzing how corporate "we's" of all sorts are constructed.

ACKNOWLEDGMENTS

This book, while an account of complex organizational relations, is also about *people*. I want to thank all those whose names are listed in Appendix A for their information, insight, and encouragement. I mention especially the late Bishop George A. Fulcher, a man of peace, who offered me vital support during the early days of my project when the bishops had just completed theirs.

I also thank my doctoral committee at Purdue University, where this book was offered in its initial form in exchange for a Ph.D. in 1985. I am grateful especially to Phil Tompkins, my Purdue-adviser-turned-Colorado-colleague, for his encouragement, for his valuable suggestions, and for our many moments of shared intellectual discovery.

I mention next the Speech Communication Association and its awards committee for presenting me "Dissertation of the Year" recognition in 1986. This award was important to me, both for acknowledging my past work and for encouraging my future effort: this book. The award helped me to rediscover my own project after it had been interrupted by a move to the University of Illinois in 1985 and a move to the University of Colorado in 1986.

Too, I express gratitude to the people in Colorado, my adopted home, who helped to produce this work. The Council on Research and Creative Work at the University of Colorado at Boulder, by offering me a Junior Faculty Development Grant for 1987–88, had a generous hand in making this work possible. And my typist, Ann Underwood, used her care and expertise to prepare the work for publication.

Carroll Arnold merits great praise and appreciation from me. This book shows the benefits of his guidance, insight, and extraordinary ability to take the perspective of the author. Robert Doolittle and Jim Brancato deserve my gratitude for their careful reviews of the penultimate and ultimate drafts, respectively.

I thank my parents for their love and their lasting interest in my work. Finally, I thank Sally for her love, her support, and for not taking me too seriously.

RHETORIC IN AN
ORGANIZATIONAL SOCIETY

RHETORIC, IDENTITY, AND ORGANIZATION

[The phrase] "to identify with" constitutes a logical bridge between an individual identity and a shared social identity, and it harks back to the classical tradition of rhetoric, how an orator should handle an audience. This is very well worked out by Kenneth Burke in A Rhetoric of Motives: *when should the orator slip from "I" to "we" and how is he to bring it off?*

W. J. M. Mackenzie, *Political Identity*

No matter how effusive their rhetoric to the contrary, most Americans cannot bring themselves to trust the unaffiliated individual. They prefer to repose their confidence in institutions—in a brand name, a corporation, or a bank.

Lewis H. Lapham, "Brand Names," *Harper's*, February 1986

Through the drafting process the peace pastoral came to be owned by the bishops. . . . And now The Challenge of Peace *is becoming the possession of the whole U.S. Church. It is becoming part of who we are.*

Interview with Fr. Richard Warner, a representative to the bishops' peace committee

What does it mean to speak with a collective voice? As animals who rely heavily on the use of symbols to understand and influence one another, we know a great deal about what it means to speak *as* an individual, *to* an individual. However, in today's postindustrial, information-oriented, and perhaps "postmodern" society, many of the voices we hear are ostensibly those of organizations, institutions, collectivities of considerable size, resources, and power. And in our jobs and avocations we contribute to those voices as well, communicating in, by, and for collectivities; we become parts of the conversation of organizations. Although all messages are in some way the products of individual efforts, many voices we hear speak for organizations, representing organizational interests. Yet both citizens and scholars find this dimension of communication perplexing; we are left to ponder what it means to speak with a collective voice and how to interpret a collective or "corporate" message.

This book addresses these general questions. Specifically, it explores the nature of *organizational rhetoric* (or organized persuasion) as *the management of multiple identities*. From this perspective much of what organizations do is rhetorical. Further, much of contemporary rhetorical practice is organizational, within complex organizational settings. Thus, organizational and rhetorical theory converge.[1] The nature of organizational rhetoric is explained here as the management of multiple identities, both individual and collective. I shall illustrate such management with an in-depth analysis of the development of a historic document, the U.S. Catholic bishops' pastoral letter on nuclear arms, *The Challenge of Peace: God's Promise and Our Response* (1983).[2] This opening chapter outlines my historical and theoretical perspective.

RHETORIC AS ORGANIZATIONAL, ORGANIZATIONS AS RHETORICAL

It is a truism that we live in an organizational society. This term, suggested in the 1950s by Kenneth Boulding,[3] may be applied to the wide range of activities performed by, within, and for organizations. Most adults in contemporary Western society work for organizations. Many employees are also members of labor or professional associations, illustrating how it is that there are many more member*ships* than organizational members. Government, at least in theory, is a highly organized activity. So too, in many instances, are religion, health care, sports, education, entertainment, the news media, social action, lobbying, and even leisure. Many of the dominant organizations within which we participate and with which we cope are of the bureaucratic type that Max Weber described, celebrated, and feared early in this century.[4] But there are other varieties of organizations around us as well: some, such as the "mom-and-pop shop," now seem anachronisms from a simpler organizational world; others, such as lean, high-tech firms, are touted as promising alternatives to bureaucracy.

All types of organizations, however, fit the definition of organization offered by Chester Barnard in 1938: "a system of consciously coordinated activities or forces of two of more persons."[5] This conception of organization recognizes communication as *constitutive* of organization; moreover, it avoids the reification of organizations—the temptation to treat them as being concrete and removed from individual action—that characterizes everyday discourse. In Barnard's view, when we remove the physical environment of an organization and take away the parts of its members' lives that are not included within the organizational context, what we have left is a communicative system as the essence of the organization. This view has become widely accepted and broadly influential in the trans-disciplinary field of organizational studies where, for example, leadership is now commonly understood in terms of interaction, language, and persuasion.[6]

Despite the taken-for-granted nature of organizational life and scholars' tendencies to explain it in terms of communication, we know surprisingly little about messages by, from, and for organizations. We are perplexed by the practical and theoretical aspects of messages that cannot be easily identified with individual persons. Put another way, we have difficulty in coping with and in understanding "corporate" messages, even though we are subject to communications from corporate bodies all of the time. How should we "read" a message by a large organization—a corporation's policy statement, a religious pronouncement, a United Nations resolution? How do we interpret a message from Exxon's chairman? *Whom* do his words represent? When the AFL-CIO speaks, just *who* is doing the talking? How should AT&T's regular sponsorship of television news programming on PBS be understood? What does *Time* magazine mean when it quotes "a top official in the White House?" When political leaders use "we," just how embracing is that pronoun? Corporate messages take the forms of memos, announcements, policy statements, advertising, public relations, treaties, image management, doctrines, issue advocacy, lobbying efforts, resolutions, annual reports, declarations, surveys, and so on. And many of these messages purport to represent entire organizations. These messages cannot be treated simply as though they were from one individual to another; corporate messages have corporate sources, corporate purposes, and corporate audiences (although, of course, individuals may shape or dominate any of these).

I choose the word "corporate" because of its origins in reference to a body (of persons): the Latin *corpus* to corporate to corporation.[7] I wish to highlight the broad meaning of the term as referring to any group or collectivity, while also acknowledging the specific legal sense of "corporation," which allows for limited liability. The term "corporate" is significant in its legal sense because Western, capitalist legal systems accord certain rights and responsibilities (usually more of the former than of the latter) to corporate or juristic or legal "persons," entities that transcend natural persons in time, space, and resources. In the United States an 1886 Supreme Court ruling recognizes corporations as "persons" that are entitled to protection of the equal protection clause of the Fourteenth Amendment to the Constitution. And a series of Supreme Court decisions since the 1960s has expanded protection over corporate free speech by making explicit appeals to First Amendment rights.[8] Thus, the metaphor of the organization-as-person has important implications in our legal system and in our everyday thinking, although we know but sometimes forget that the metaphor should not be taken literally. It is instructive that among the corresponding terms for "Inc." in French and in Spanish are "S.A.," *société anonyme* or *sociedad anónima,* respectively; that is, anonymous society. The corporation or the anonymous society allows individuals to speak with a collective voice while retaining anonymity and symbolic detachment, if the individuals who are doing the speaking wish it so and are legally and rhetorically successful. This complicates issues of responsibility and accountability. On the other hand, a corporate message can be identified with everyone who is part of the organization, whether some members like it or not. Hence, our legal system finds the criminal prosecution of corporate persons to be slippery and difficult. Moreover, relatively little progress has been made toward the development of guidelines for holding corporations responsible for actions harmful to society.[9] The corporate "we" is an ambiguous but powerful term; it is employed not only by legal corporations but also by nonincorporated cities, businesses, schools, governmental agencies, churches, unions, and so forth. But what does a corporate "we" mean in theory and in practice? And how does one analyze corporate or organizational rhetoric?

To answer these questions requires that we keep in mind the subtleties and complexities of "rhetorical situations." We need to consider aspects related to the messages, the audiences, and the sources. First, consider the nature of the *corporate message.* Because of the ways in which corporate or organizational messages are often presented, assessment of who specifically authored a message, how it was constructed, and where it originated is exceedingly difficult. Many corporate messages appear to us as if from "above," often without identifying place of origin or creator. A good example is much of the advocacy advertising on behalf of nuclear power which regularly appears in U.S. news magazines. Such ads, which offer a variety of strongly worded arguments to promote greater reliance on nuclear power, typically include as their sole by-line "Committee on Energy Awareness." The committee does not acknowledge its composition, which is agents of the nuclear power industry, or its primary activity, lobbying in Washington, D.C. Another case points up the puzzling nature of many corporate messages. In 1980 Kaiser Aluminum responded to media attacks on the quality and safety of its products with an aggressive ad campaign. The ads argued not only that Kaiser *did not act* as its accusers claimed, but also that it *could not act* that way because such action would not be in keeping with its nature or character as a corporate agent.[10] Thus, the persona (or "mask") of the organization became reified as a personal, individual agent; the organization became in effect a *natural* person. In these cases and others, organizational messages take on a relatively placeless, nameless, omniscient quality, even when a corporate identity is assumed and declared. And this mystery which surrounds corporate rhetoric often obscures its workings, its effects. In the language of contemporary philosophy and literary criticism, corporate messages tend to "de-center" the self, the individual, the acting subject.[11]

Another aspect of corporate messages that complicates analysis is the way many messages are structured. The grammar of organizational pronouncements is such that they are frequently expressed in the passive voice; for example, "It has been decided that. . . ."[12] And when the active voice is used, so is the powerfully ambiguous corporate "we," as in "We Catholics believe. . . ."[13] A synecdoche, or personification, may be used: "The White House said today"; "The Pentagon reacted"; "Ma Bell decided." These conventions make the analysis of corporate messages decidedly complex. Observers are often left wondering, "Decided by whom?" or "Who are 'we'?" or "Which officials in the White House?" The problem of assigning responsibility became visible and acute in the case of the Exxon-Valdez oil spill in 1989; while the disaster spread across Alaska's Prince William Sound, the news media struggled to pinpoint blame on specific individuals within the corporation, the Coast Guard, the government of Alaska, and the Bush Administration, along with pursuing some discussion of wider institutional responsibility.

One more important aspect of corporate messages is how they are shaped and constrained by the media in which they are presented. Many corporate messages, particularly those addressed to mass audiences, take on the characteristics of the medium through which they are communicated. Thus, both political commentary (sometimes called "advertorials") and traditional advertising material are likely to be given the forms of brief magazine copy or short spots on television. Consider as examples the almost ubiquitous advocacy advertising of Mobil, AT&T, and United Technologies. All three corporations offer brief statements (usually less than a page) to advocate such positions as unrestrained technological development and limited governmental regulation. Typical corporate messages feature colorful images and appeal to the "logic" of feelings more than to cold reason. Such was the case, for example, with Philip Morris Corporation's 1989–90 television ads which commemorated the two hundreth anniversary of the U.S. Bill of Rights: after the words and images of freedom, the corporate logo appeared, implicitly linking the Bill of Rights with Philip Morris's well-known smokers' rights campaign. Needless to say, the charge about *pathos,* or emotionalism, has been leveled against much of the content of contemporary television and popular periodicals.[14] Whether or not such constraints are inherent to media in the age of television is surely debatable, but that today's media lend themselves to content which minimizes the role of reasoned discourse (or *logos*) is clear. The widely criticized U.S. presidential campaign of 1988, in which "sound bite" became a household phrase, further illustrated the prevalence of tailoring discourse for the media of mass communication. Such is, in any case, the rhetorical environment within which corporate messages are crafted and presented, even those of a complex nature. In sum, by condensing, coloring, and pictorializing content for modern mass media, communications from corporations (and other organizations) displace or suppress details and connections that would be required for carefully reasoned analysis of whatever subject is considered.[15]

A second basic element in the rhetorical situation for corporate rhetoric is the *audience*. Corporate rhetors today face multiple, differing, yet often overlapping audiences. In U.S. business the term "stakeholder" is now accepted and used to refer to the various groups that have a stake in the company's activities, those groups that are in any way affected by what an organization does. For a typical corporation its stakeholders include shareholders, employees (and their families), consumers and clients, competitors, Congress, the general public, and even federal regulatory agencies. These stakeholding groups function rhetorically as audiences or publics of the organization. Major corporations today pursue comprehensive communications policies that seek to bring together "internal" and "external" communications practices.[16] General Motors, for example, now considers its tens of thousands of employees all to be potential advocates for the corporation's welfare.[17] These trends embrace other types of organizations in the public and independent sectors. Organizations of many stripes—including unions, churches, hospitals, and social action groups—are now pursuing and persuading multiple audiences. To adapt their rhetoric to this multi-organizational, multi-public, contemporary setting, corporate communications work to "adjust organizations [or rather, their messages] to environments and environments to organizations."[18] And such "environments" are commonly understood to include aspects internal to the organization and aspects outside of it, though the boundaries are often unclear (as is the case for many service organizations in particular).

The third basic element of the rhetorical situation for organizational rhetoric is the *source* of the message, the corporate rhetor itself. In particular we must consider how corporate communication has moved toward a proactive role in shaping values, issues, and identities. To understand this development fully, however, a historical perspective is needed.

James Coleman explains how the corporate person was first established in the late Middle Ages by individuals who formed craft guilds in order to increase their power vis-à-vis the two most powerful institutions of the day, the church and the state. However, while the sum total of power exercised in the industrialized world has expanded enormously over the centuries, the actual proportion of power held by individuals has decreased relative to that held by organizations. Today organized individuals loom large and powerful.[19] This development, of course, has important implications for our legal system (which attempts to hold organizations responsible and accountable), for our economic system (where corporate persons often join or merge), and for our society as a whole (where individuals who speak for organizations are generally seen as more credible than those who do not). In fact, the celebration of organization as an end in itself has come to typify advanced industrial society.[20]

Related to this transfer of power, particularly in the twentieth century, is the seemingly unstoppable march of bureaucracy. Weber was profoundly ambivalent about the rise of bureaucratic organization that he observed and analyzed during the first two decades of this century. He saw benefits in the rational coordination of large-scale efforts and dangers in the excessive centralization of power, threats to individuality, and the elevation of calculated means over ultimate ends (i.e., *doing* things being seen as more important than systematic and collective reflection on *what* is being done). What bureaucratic organization has done, according to Richard Edwards, is to shift the locus of control in the organization from direct supervision (as in the mom-and-pop shop) and technical direction (as in assembly-line technologies) to shared goals, rules, regulations, and procedures.[21] The modern bureaucratic organization is held together in precisely this manner, by communicating and "inculcating"[22] premises for decisions inside the organization and to other publics outside the organization. As Herbert A. Simon explains: When premises of value (e.g., relating to quality, or growth , or efficiency, or cost, or power) are internalized by an audience of an organization, its members can be depended upon to act in the best interests of the organization, as they understand them.[23] Thus, the loyal employee will seek to trace out the implications of a premise communicated by the organization—say, "Always make decisions by the book"—through employing that rule-oriented premise in his or her decisions, thereby supporting the System.[24]

In this sense the contemporary bureaucratic organization is fundamentally a rhetorical enterprise. The organization seeks to establish or reinforce certain value premises in the minds of its audiences so that the members of the audience will make decisions in accord with the preferences of the controlling members of the organization. As Tompkins and Cheney explain, this is a modern variant of Aristotle's *enthymeme:* the rhetorical syllogism, the deductive building block of persuasion.[25] The enthymeme works because it draws upon premises already held by the audience. Thus, a rhetor today who seeks to persuade an audience to give blood might appeal to the commonly held premise, "It is good to help other people," and then work toward a conclusion that becomes an action by the audience. In the relatively homogeneous society of ancient Greece, Aristotle did not need to specify the origin of major premises; they were generally shared throughout the *polis,* the privileged sociopolitical community of Athens. Today we find corporate rhetors of many types vying to persuade mass audiences by supporting particular organizational value premises which may or may not coincide with others held in the wider society. If many people share the premise that government is too big, they will be likely to vote for candidates who vow to shrink it. If many share the premise that youth is beautiful, they will be likely to buy products which help them to look young. If many share the premise that owning a gun is a fundamental right, they will be likely to support pro-gun lobbies. And, of course, a particular message—say, one for cosmetics designed to emphasize youthfulness—may not need to *state* the major premise, "Looking youthful is good," because the audience already accepts it as a cultural "fact." These are types of rhetorical connections that various corporate rhetors hope their audiences will make.

Corporate communications today are powerful, expensive, and wide-ranging activities. In the words of Barry Bozeman, many organizations in every sector have "gone public."[26] Such activity is of course not new (the advertising industry is well over a hundred years old). But it has been noticeably stepped up since the mid-1970s. In reaction to the early 1970s—years when public confidence in American institutions seemed quite low—corporations and other organizations began adopting more aggressive and decidedly political postures in their communications. Thus emerged the "corporate advocacy" model, in which an organization seeks to foster a more favorable environment for itself by addressing various publics who will in turn support particular candidates and policies.[27] The presumed circle of influence runs thus: organization to public to public policy makers to organization. This model of communication was adopted explicitly by Mobil Oil, which in the 1970s began publishing a series of essays: "Observations" on such matters as governmental regulation, trade relations, and "American common sense." Encouraged by Mobil's economic recovery, other organizations followed the lead. Today we find diverse organizations engaged in "packaging" premises and images for their various publics. Such corporate advocates in the United States include AT&T, General Dynamics, United Technologies, the National Rifle Association, the Committee on Energy Awareness, Greenpeace, the Sierra Club, the Roman Catholic Church, and the National Council of Churches.

Thus, there are profound senses in which *organizations are rhetorical and rhetoric is organizational* in the late twentieth-century United States. This observation, which is both historically and theoretically grounded, can be generalized for the entire industrialized world.[28]

The third term of importance in this book, in addition to "organization" and "rhetoric," is "identity." Contemporary organizations do more than manage issues by inculcating values; they also manage identities. In fact, it can be said that *the nature of organizational rhetoric in the industrialized world in the late twentieth century is the management of multiple identities.* That is the central point of this book. The term "management" suggests control, a primary concern of most organizations. But "management" also evokes the idea of coping, as in the case of individuals who must balance multiple commitments and deal with an increasingly organized society. I shall illustrate my thesis through a detailed examination of corporate rhetoric by part of the oldest, largest bureaucracy (or, for that matter, formal organization) in the world: the Roman Catholic Church. Specifically, I shall consider a particularly controversial and important piece of advocacy by the National Conference of Catholic Bishops (NCCB): their 1983 pastoral letter on nuclear arms, *The Challenge of Peace: God's Promise and Our Response.* By focusing on this historic document and the process of its development, we shall be able to explore the nature of organizational rhetoric as the management of identities. The analysis will help us to understand complex organizational relationships, subtle rhetorical adaptations by a corporate rhetor, and the shaping of individual and collective identities. "Identity" is perhaps *the* central term in this analysis because of the ways in which the bishops spoke of who they were—as organized individuals within a larger organization—while they developed their statement on the issue of nuclear arms control. The bishops simultaneously worked through the issue of individual identity and the matter of collective identity, their identity as a conference of bishops. Moreover, they had to take into account and in a very real sense manage the identities of their many audiences: U.S. Catholics, the Vatican, the Reagan Administration, nuclear pacifists, the public at large. Thus, we must look carefully at the term "identity," its central role in the study of organizational rhetoric, and its importance for the study of social life in general.

IDENTITY AS A CENTRAL TERM
IN THE STUDY OF SOCIAL LIFE

In the twentieth century identity has in various terminological and conceptual forms become a focal point of inquiry across the social sciences and the humanities. From the philosophically inclined psychology of William James[29] at the turn of the century to the critical post-structuralism of Michel Foucault and others recently,[30] questions about what it means to be an individual in society have been vigorously pursued. Identity as a category has been rooted in unconscious processes and emotional attachments (e.g., by Sigmund Freud[31]), socialized (e.g., by George H. Mead[32]), celebrated (e.g., by Erik Erikson[33]), culturally situated (e.g., by Margaret Mead[34]), and politicized (e.g., by Harold Lasswell[35]). Across all of these treatments of identity, the self, and related concepts we find consensus on the general assumption that one's identity is somehow related to the larger social order. However, these theorists and others disagree substantially on what kind of relationship this entails.

Kenneth Burke sees most social questions as "coming to a head" in the

10

problem of identity. Burke's key term for the study of rhetoric is "identification." By using it Burke incorporates Aristotle's conception of persuasion; he also draws upon and connects with the theories of Marx, Freud, James, G. H. Mead, and Lasswell. Burke extends the common notion of identity as a strictly individual matter to include the collective, yet he still allows for the individual, acting subject.[36] He reminds us, for example, that "however much the individual . . . may transform language for his special purposes, the resources with which he begins are 'traditional,' that is: *social*."[37] Thus, the question of identity, which we in Western society are so prone to conceive in exclusively individual terms, is actually a social matter. American individualism, for instance, is not a primordial condition but an ideology—a taken-for-granted set of beliefs—with a particular history. In fact, U.S. society has been called "identitarian" for its tendency, particularly through the homogeneity of the popular media, to justify and reinforce its own *self*-indulgence, individually and collectively.[38] In the contemporary West identity naturally becomes the concern of organizations as well as of individuals. The question of what it means to be an individual preoccupies both natural and corporate persons. This development in the history of "identity" can be more fully appreciated through a brief etymological and historical analysis.

Surprisingly, the notion of identity as distinctiveness—as something one "has" to set him or her apart from others—had a relatively recent introduction into the history of systematic Western thought. W. J. M. Mackenzie, in his enlightening essay *Political Identity*, explains that "the word 'identity' appears to mirror a Latin word *identitas*." It was Aristotle, it seems, who coined the abstract term *tautotes*, "rendered exactly into Latin by *identitas*, except that the Latin is a word simply for 'sameness' without any aura of 'self-hood.' "[39] In *Nicomachean Ethics*, for example, Aristotle wrote that "brothers love each other as being born of the same parents; for their *identity* with them makes them *identical* with each other (which is the reason why people talk of 'the same blood,' 'the same stock,' and so on)." Thus Aristotle appeared to treat identity in terms of an almost complete sharing. In the same passage he continued: "[The brothers], are, therefore, in a sense the same thing, though in separate individuals."[40]

From this classical point of departure Mackenzie traces the term "identity" through late Roman and medieval thought, where a great deal of speculative energy was applied to the trinitarian conception of God: three persons who are identifiable yet share the same substance. Debate centered on whether the members of the Trinity are the same or simply alike in substance.[41]

According to Mackenzie it was the romantic poets who gave us the first written examples of identity *as essence,* though this Western notion can be traced at least back through the Enlightenment to the Italian Renaissance. So, for example, William Blake wrote, "States change, but individual identities never change nor cease." John Keats penned: "His identity presses upon me." And by 1820 the *Oxford English Dictionary* quoted from Washington Irving a totally modern use of identity: "He doubted his own identity and whether he was himself or another man." In addition, Mackenzie reports early uses of the verb "to identify" which suggest the modern usage. In his speech on "economical reform" of 1780 Edmund Burke proclaimed, "Let us identify, let us incorporate ourselves with the people."[42]

As Mackenzie notes, the terms "identity," "identification," and "to identify" acquired a "bureaucratic colour" around 1900. Mackenzie observes that society's penchant for classification became much stronger with the maturing of the bureaucratic state and the organizational society.

> There are two grim cases from that period; the need to register and identify motor cars; the need to register and identify each soldier in the mass armies of the First World War, so that his mutilated and rotting corpse could be identified by imperishable disc or tag.[43]

Thus it became more common to identify individuals by their papers, files, numbers, fingerprints, etc., and the classificatory techniques took on even greater sophistication with the computer age. With such a shift came inevitably greater reliance for self-definition on various bureaucratic organizations and positions. Hence, Kenneth Burke's observation as early as 1937 made sense: "In America, it is *natural* for a man to identify himself with the business corporation he serves."[44] And this comment is strikingly relevant more than a half-century later.

The preceding discussion uncovers the historical roots of the methods of identification we now take for granted in their individualized and institutionalized pervasiveness. Today there are myriad ways in which we tell others "who we are," with organizational membership or affiliation being a primary indicator.[45] Moreover, others often tell *us* by insisting, "It says right here in *your* file (or your job description) that. . . ." Categories (or "classes"), of course, make organization possible, and they carry with them powerful implications for shaping attitudes and beliefs. Thus, even in its simplest form identity points us toward organizational and rhetorical concerns.

IDENTITY, RHETORIC, AND ORGANIZATION

Surely one of the most penetrating observations made by Mackenzie in his review is that there has been a transformation of the term "identity" from its "sameness" meaning to its "essence" meaning. This shift is important not just because it represents the partial replacement of one conception with another, but because it puts us in touch with the profound ambiguity surrounding "identity": we are able to express our uniqueness (our individuality) principally by aligning ourselves with *other* individuals, collectivities, or social categories. Just as estrangement or alienation from one social unit often implies identification with another, so does individual difference with respect to some other person imply sameness with regard to a third party. Thus, similarity and difference mutually implicate one another, exist in ongoing dialectical tension, and provide the formative context for what we call our "identity." We are in this way charged with building our differences out of unique combinations of "samenesses," linking ourselves with some groups and organizations and distancing ourselves from others. This is the basis of both consensus and conflict in social life; in Kenneth Burke's terms, the grounds for rhetoric are in the conditions of "congregation" and "segregation."[46]

Moreover, the paradox of identity—making differences out of samenesses and vice versa—opens the theoretical door into the meaningful and realistic treatment of collective as well as individual identity. Mackenzie bemoans the "murder of a word" in that "identity" has been loosely applied to a variety of referents and analytical levels in social thought. For example, in criticizing some comparative research in political science,[47] Mackenzie argues that it is inappropriate to speak of "Burma's search for identity" or South Africa's "identity crisis" because it assumes that a nation, as a collective "agent," actually has or ought to have an identity. Such unreflective theorizing, continues Mackenzie, pervades the social sciences and the humanities. For him, reasonable resolution of the problem lies in the treatment of identity *in terms of shared interests or interests that are perceived to be shared.* After all, he explains, it is through symbolic means—means common to some group—that individual "uniqueness" is constructed of "samenesses." By logical extension, then, we can speak of collective (e.g., organizational) identity: "Those who share an interest share an identity; the interest of each requires the collaboration of all." Mackenzie continues: "The community of communicators, vague though it is, is yet sharper in definition than community of interest or contiguity of space."[48] Appropriately, Mackenzie credits Kenneth Burke for inspiration here and invites the reader to explore Burke's rhetoric of identification as a way of systematically relating "I" and "we," individual identity and collective identity. As Mackenzie explains, Burke builds "a logical bridge between [the] individual identity and [the] shared social identity . . . [and his formulation] harks back to the classical tradition of rhetoric."[49]

To speak of collective identity is to speak of collective or shared interests—or at least of how the interests of a collective are represented and understood. This is a fundamental concern of contemporary organizations. Large bureaucratic organizations are in the business of identity management; their controlling members must be concerned about how to (re)present the organization as a whole *and* how to connect the individual identities of many members to that embracing collective identity. Ironically, in the individualistic West, "the ethic of organization clearly encourages reliance on the collective rather than on the individual for self-definition."[50] So, for example, some corporations maintain the name, logo, and symbols of an acquired firm; they are sensitive to the importance of the traditional corporate identity for employees and others. A similar concern undergirds IBM's ongoing campaign to present itself as being about customer service, to establish in the minds of both employees and customers a clear identity which they can share and promote.[51] And during the Reagan era the Administration in Washington sought the identification of the U.S. public by paradoxically attacking "big goverment," all the while expanding the defense establishment (and the federal deficit).

Resource-rich organizations are in particularly strong positions to manage their corporate identities, their corporate "we's." The National Rifle Association (NRA) is often described as the single most powerful lobby in the United States. In the 1980s the NRA pursued a vigorous, image-oriented campaign, featuring full-page ads in major magazines. The ads displayed Americans from all walks of life sporting rifles and declaring, "I'm the NRA." These ads presented a highly personalized identity of the organization, beckoning readers (members and prospective members of the lobby) to "locate" themselves within the symbolic reach of the corporate "we."[52] A similarly "personal" strategy was pursued by both the Carter and the Reagan Administrations through televised attempts to show that the President was "one of us." However, this "just folks" image was more effective for Hollywood-trained Reagan than it was for businessman Carter. In both cases, though, an effort was made to manage the identity of an ordinarily impersonal office and thereby solicit the identifications of millions.

In a way the Roman Catholic Church, as a transnational bureaucratic organization, has been fundamentally engaged in the management of identities throughout most of its history. "As St. Bernard of Clairvaux wrote perceptively to the Pope in 1150: 'Your power is not in possessions, but in the hearts of men.' "[53] Continually the Church has sought to balance its universal, or catholic, identity with local and particular concerns while encouraging individuals, the faithful, to derive a sense of self from allegiance to the Church. Indeed, the Church may be seen as "a multinational mass communication organization,"[54] which has at many points over the centuries exhibited Donald Bryant's dual function of rhetoric: "adjusting ideas to people and people to ideas."[55] Because of the Church's central role in the history of the West, much of that adjustment has directly involved or affected identities, both individual and collective.

THE MANAGEMENT OF MULTIPLE IDENTITIES: A FRAMEWORK FOR ANALYSIS

With "identification" as a key term, Kenneth Burke's theory of human relations offers a basis for treating organizational rhetoric as the management of identities. Burke offers an overarching perspective on social relations that he calls "Dramatism," a method and a theory which "helps us discover what the implications of the terms 'act' and 'person' *really are*."[56] Just as an act requires an actor, so "belonging" is fundamentally rhetorical, says Burke. The challenges of achieving, maintaining, and transforming identity bring one simultaneously into the realms of persuasion and organization—both with respect to others and in reference to one's self. To understand and analyze organizational rhetoric, then, we must begin with Burke's conception of rhetoric as identification and then complicate it for application to complex organizations.

Initially Burke maintains that identification is necessary to compensate for the "mystery" or estrangement built into the division of labor and other ordered domains of human experience.[57] Order and hierarchy are natural, says Burke; they are bound up with the human ability to use language to abstract categories.[58] But in labeling and categorizing, we both unite and divide. As Burke puts it, "There are two kinds of terms: terms that put things together, and terms that take them apart. Otherwise put, A can feel himself identified with B, or he can think of himself as dissociated from B."[59] In these words we find one of the simplest yet most powerful insights about human relations in all of Burke's works. He is saying that *associations between terms reveal much about associations between people.* In a very real sense, here is the heart of Burke's theory of human communication.

As our terms are applied to different social scenes, they create classes and divisions. With so much emphasis on distinctions and differences (consider social strata, the corporate ladder, and elitism as just a few examples), "*identification* arises as a communicative, cooperative response."[60] Burke expresses this necessary, social function of identification succinctly: "Identification is affirmed with earnestness precisely because there is division. Identification is compensatory to division." Of course, as he also notes, there is "a wavering line between identification and division," one that never ceases to complicate social relations.[61]

Names function both as terms of description and terms for action. With reference to ourselves we use terms of identification to say not only "who we are" but also "how well we're doing." Many terms contribute to self-enhancement, including but not restricted to the ways they place us in social hierarchies. This point in Burke's analysis is especially relevant to the study of corporate management of identities. One person may say smugly, "*I'm* a New Yorker," but another may say with equal smugness, "*I* work for Xerox," or "*Our* company is IBM, the largest producer of business computers." As Burke explains in vivid terms:

> [One] identifies himself with some corporate unit (church, guild, company, lodge, party, team, college, city, nation, etc.)—and by profuse praise of this unit he praises himself. For he "owns shares" in the corporate unit—and by "rigging the market" for the value of the stock as a whole, he runs up the value of his personal holdings.[62]

According to Burke, as a necessary, individual response to the divisions of society a person acts to identify with some target(s)—persons, groups, and so forth. "Thus, a person may think of himself as 'belonging' to some special body more or less clearly defined . . . or to various combinations of these." Through these associations an individual comes to have a variety of "corporate identities" that are sometimes concentric and sometimes in conflict.[63] "For instance, one may have a job in some large financial corporation, while at the same time being a member of a party opposed to its policies."[64] Our corporate identities are vital because they grant us personal meaning and because they place us in the matrix of the social order. Burke explains: "The so-called 'I' is merely a unique combination of partially conflicting 'corporate we's,' "[65] thus emphasizing the necessarily social aspects of individual identity.

Burke notes that an "identity" is continually in a state of flux, though we may speak of something's "uniqueness as an entity in itself and by itself, a demarcated unit having its own particular structure."[66] "Identity involves 'change of identity' insofar as any given structure of society calls forth conflict among our 'corporate we's.' "[67] It is thus through encountering and managing conflicting elements of "self"—and, by implication, their social referents—that we experience both continuity and change. As Norman Holland puts it, "One can think of a person as a sameness in relation to differences and as differences in relation to a sameness."[68] Similarly, Peter du Preez writes: "A coherent style, sense of integrity and continuity do not depend on the abolition of our different identities. That would be reverting to personae. What is required is that identities be coordinated as the words of a language are coordinated in the expression of a particular message."[69] In this way messages "locate" a person with respect to various social units as expressed in the network of symbols that is social life.[70] The coordination of identities in expression becomes complicated in proportion to the multiplicity of identities for which and to which a collectivity such as a corporation must speak, including both members and outsiders. In developing *The Challenge of Peace* the U.S. Catholic bishops had to expend much effort to achieve language that would effectively speak for the many differing identities represented in their Church and in the audiences they sought to address.

Identifications, for Burke, are the bases of social roles. In fact, he insists, "one's participation in a collective, social role cannot be obtained in any other way. . . . 'Identification' is hardly other than a name for the *function of sociality*."[71] Thus, to act in a role is also to be identified with certain activities or interests, even when those concerns are not viewed by the individual as central to self-definition. Such is the case for many employees of organizations who see their work as "just a job." Thus, Burke finds it appropriate to speak of partial or role-related identifications—"for one's identification as a member of a group *is* a role."[72] However, such "partial inclusion" of the individual within the organization[73] often extends toward total inclusion, particularly today for professionals in the United States and in Japan.

It is precisely because of the shared nature of identity—and the impossibility of divorcing the individual from the social—that Burke insists on treating individuals as members of a group rather than considering a group as an aggregate of individuals. Burke is not lapsing into an uncompromising collectivism here but simply asserting the way our sociality defines in a substantial way "who we are": sociality, for Burke, is our shared "substance."[74] As Nelson Foote explains in a comment consistent with Burke's theory, "It is only through identification as the sharing of identity that individual motives become social values and social values become individual motives."[75]

As individuals who form groups, what we share are *interests*—interests that are expressed in one way or another. To echo Burke's oft-quoted passage: "Insofar as their interests are joined, A is *identified* with B. Or he may *identify himself* with B even when their interests are not joined, if he assumes that they are, or is persuaded to believe so."[76] And the joining of interests, of course, takes place primarily through the transcendent power of language.[77] The failure of such a merger is at the root of racism, nationalism, sexism, and ethnocentrism. Acknowledging the contribution of Burke's theory of identification, Mackenzie stresses that

> at least in complex societies, the use of "we" depends on context; "we" the family, "we" the local community, "we" the craftsmen, the teachers, the medical profession, and so on. One "I" can have many "we's"; but perhaps "I" also is to some extent context dependent. There may or may not be a unique and persistent identity resident somewhere in each of us: but certainly our individuality shifts a little according to context, chooses different words and gestures, *gives priority to different interests,* according to the "we" which temporarily has the upper hand in the social context. "I" is certainly not fixed and external, "we" subsidiary and fleeting.[78]

Wayne Booth summarizes eloquently the wavering line between "I" and "we": "When I assent to your thought (or symphony or novel or account of your divorce) the line between us grows dim; in the ideal case it in a sense disappears."[79] "We" works and cooperation occurs because individuals symbolically express their shared interests.

This line of argument helps us to come to terms with collective identity and at the same time to understand individual identity better. Pursuing this argument, then, I choose not to posit anything like a collective mind or even a truly collective agent, but rather the shared identity that comes with the sharing of interests—although that sharing may be insincere or deceptive from the point of view of one or more parties.[80]

In contemporary Western society the key sources of identity include formal, identifiable organizations. Herbert A. Simon stresses the importance of members' identification in organizational settings. For Simon, the link between identification and decision making is crucial: the act of identifying leads the decision maker to select a particular alternative, to choose one course of action over another. Viewed in this sense, identification reduces the "range" of decision: the decision maker is confined largely to the alternative(s) "seen" or associated with his or her personal targets of identification,[81] in seeking to do "what's best" for the organization. Thus, Simon adopts an administrative perspective, treating identification as an internal means by which an individual allows herself or himself to be influenced by the organization. At the same time, of course, the organization seeks the identification of the individual so that she or he will take the organization's interests as her or his own, perhaps even adopting an "organizational personality."[82]

Socialization is both an individual and a collective process; it allows for the person to acquire and to use the cultural symbols available (often in idiosyncratic ways) while enabling the social order to reproduce itself (albeit often with significant distortions, transformations, even breaks). Thus, it makes sense to speak not just of how society is composed of different people but also of how people are composed of different "societies." We make social bonds which are both enabling and constraining: bonds connect us with something larger than the self but at the same time limit our autonomy.[83] As individual persons we "muddle through" with the symbolic resources at our disposal and align ourselves to varying degrees with particular "targets," many of these being key symbolic loci which organize society. In fact we "choose" (though sometimes unconsciously) to identify with some organizations, accepting their value premises and in some cases their authority (*ultimate* authority in organizational defenses used by many war criminals), while distancing ourselves from other potential sources for allegiance. Our identities in this sense are unique composites of multiple identifications, along with implicit and explicit alienations.[84] And to the extent that these composites overlap— for example, in that a group of persons all express themselves in terms of the same interests—we may speak meaningfully of collective identity and, on a broader level, social structure. Identity, in short, is a term that is commonly used to represent an individual or group;[85] identification is the process by which identity is "appropriated."[86] Organization, generally speaking, is the coordination of individual interests; it is the mobilization of energies (symbolic and material) toward selective goals and values, including the value of organization *in itself* and the goal of its maintenance. Rhetoric infuses both processes—identification and organization—because symbolic means are necessary to bring about what Burke

19

called "congregation" and "segregation," whether for the individuals who comprise the society or the societal elements that comprise the identities of the individuals.

All types of rhetoric involve some appeal to the identifications, the associations, of human beings; organizational rhetoric involves the management of multiple identifications, multiple interests. As I have shown above, "identity" is a term traditionally associated with the individual that must draw upon social and collective resources for its meaning. "Organization," a term originally derived from the individual body *(organ)*, usually is applied to the collectivity; yet it is equally relevant to the process by which individuals come together and are themselves organized. "Rhetoric," then, is the arbiter of "congregation" and "segregation"; it makes possible the moves from "I" to "we" and "we" to "I."

ANALYZING ORGANIZATIONAL RHETORIC

Human attitudes and behaviors would be rather predictable if we all lived in a simple society where everyone belonged to only one social group; however, this is not the case, as William James recognized and commented on a century ago.[87] When we make decisions about which friend deserves our loyalty, or how best to serve an employer, or what club to join, or which candidate to support in an election, the relevance of the management of multiple identities is apparent. But the management of multiple identities is just as relevant, though not as obvious, when we delegate authority to subordinates, or account for deviant behavior, or disagree with a critic's interpretation of a film's central character, or acquire the manner and trappings of a desired social status or group. We are constantly aligning ourselves with the interests of some persons and distancing ourselves from the interests of other persons.

A formal organization must manage a variety of interests, though certain interests will surely take precedence or become dominant over others. In *The Functions of the Executive* Chester Barnard explains the key functions of organization: the administrator, the executive, the policy-maker must be concerned with (1) maintaining a system of communication, (2) creating a sense of common purpose, and (3) securing essential contributions or services from organizational members. In the modern bureaucratic organization these processes necessarily entail the management of multiple identities—the identities of members, of "publics," of audiences, of the whole organization itself.

The corporate voice, which speaks so loudly and so frequently in contemporary society, needs to be examined for how it speaks as well as for what it says. We need to learn how to "read" and "listen to" the organizational rhetoric that is all around us. This requires a somewhat non-traditional conception of rhetoric. For centuries rhetoric has been thought of as created by *someone*. As my discussion of identities has shown, this is not strictly the case with what I have been calling corporate, collective voices. While all messages in fact originate with individuals, many present themselves otherwise, as the voices of corporate or artificial persons. As Weber observed, to the extent that organizations are understood in practice as entities or even as persons, they *are* those things. The rhetorical theory that is required in an organizational age therefore cannot be exclusively a theory of the "good *person* speaking well."[88] Rhetorical analysis of *organizational* rhetoric requires simultaneous conceptualizations of individually and collectively created discourse. We need to examine the (good) organization speaking (well).

In examining specific cases or campaigns in organizational rhetoric, we must assess the interrelationships of identity, organization, and rhetoric. The nature of the organization—its structure, values, practices, and categories—reveals important features of its persuasive strategies and possibilities. Conversely, from the rhetoric of an organization features of the organization can be inferred or "read." And both rhetoric and organization necessarily lead us toward the study of identity. As the coordinator and mobilizer of biases or interests,[89] an organization must manage identities, both individual and collective. This is the definition of the rhetorical situation from an organizational point of view. From an individual's standpoint the organization of his or her identity reveals how he or she is "located" with respect to social groups, organizations, and institutions. The individual manages multiple identities while participating in an organizational world. For many people this balancing act is challenging if not overwhelming, as a 1989 *Time* cover story on "The Rat Race" explained.[90] None of this is to say, of course, that for an individual or for an organization all identities are treated equally. In U.S. society, for example, a prevailing orientation is, unfortunately, to produce and consume as much as possible. In the process of managing identities, particular ones become influential or even dominant for individuals and organizations.

As a guiding concept, the management of multiple identities can be used to understand and evaluate all types of organizations and rhetorical situations.[91] For example, the recent trend toward personalizing otherwise impersonal institutions is clearly an effort to encourage the identification of large audiences. The Reagan Administration was immensely successful in "connecting" with the everyday and emotional sensibilities of the American public, even to the point of obscuring fundamental policy disagreements between the people and President Reagan. That Reagan became the embodiment of U.S. national identity and that the average American could identify with him became all-important to Reagan's popularity and endurance in the office. Lee Iacocca's persuasive accomplishments at the leadership of Chrysler Corporation displayed a similar rhetorical pattern. Iacocca used his own personal characteristics and the power of multiple media to establish an identificational coalition with Chrysler's many thousands of employees. He enlisted their energies and their sacrifices by appealing to them as individuals and linking Chrysler's cause to the American Dream. In this way Iacocca managed the identities of multiple audiences, both inside and outside the corporation. AT&T's nostalgic, sentimental ads worked toward the same end, albeit in a less direct manner. This trend toward personalization and personification represents a confluence of organizational strategy and public need to see organizations *as people*. The public thus reponds to efforts to overcome or obscure the necessarily impersonal aspects of large bureaucratic organizations. And much contemporary rhetoric in the public, private, and other sectors reflects and reveals the trend.

Since the mid-1970s a group of corporate consulting firms has emerged which specialize in "image" or "identity management." The folk wisdom in many of these organizations is that they *give* identities to organizations and to people. At one internationally prominent consulting firm the employees speak of "selecting," "creating," "handling," and "presenting" identities. When they design an "identity package" for an organization or a city, they aim to establish an identity that will *become* what internal and external publics perceive as the organization. They do this through architecture, graphics, copy, and like symbolic processes. Their preoccupation with identity and its management necessarily involves these professionals in contemporary organizational rhetoric.

Of course, the management of multiple identities is also relevant to complex organizational situations where "identity" is not explicitly discussed. The advocacy of the NRA is a vivid example: it attempts to link the possession of firearms with the very idea of being "American." And until the debate over semi-automatic assault rifles in 1989, the lobbying organization was almost universally successful. IBM's ongoing management of an image and aspects of its employees' identities is long standing, well documented, and commonly known. Job-seeking undergraduates nationwide are familiar with the "IBMers," their "look," and their common dedication to service. In the arenas of mass media, advertising, and public relations, efforts to define and sell audiences, using sophisticated techniques of psychographics, have become commonplace. Such communication-based organizations now target highly specific market segments with messages designed to address "who you are."[92] Typically, of course, these messages attempt to link specific images to specific patterns of consumption (e.g., the packaging of environmental awareness), and these attempts are often enormously effective. The popular wearing of corporate logos (e.g., the Status City Polo Club) by today's young people is but one obvious case in point: these symbols celebrate the corporate symbol writ large (i.e., "Corporate America").

On the international level we can see the relevance of the management of multiple identifications in the European Economic Community's move toward 1992, when most trade and legal barriers between and among member nations will be eliminated. This drive toward unity (in fact, toward a single market, a single identity) suggests that various national, ethnic, and cultural identities will be "managed" in one way or another. Businesses from the member nation with the most powerful banks and industries, West Germany, were already in the late 1980s luring their Southern Italian counterparts to accept an efficient, fast-paced, and siesta-free model of work life, showing how apparently "global" or broad-based interests can be defined, shaped, or dominated by "local" ones.[93]

And at the same time that regional trading blocs are coalescing in North America, Europe, and the Far East, essentially "stateless" corporations are "learning how to juggle multiple identities and multiple loyalties." Dozens of multinational corporations now derive forty percent or more of their sales from countries other than their home nations. These corporations "are developing chameleon-like abilities to resemble insiders no matter where they operate."[94]

The management of multiple identities is therefore pursued vigorously by individuals and by organizations, often in cooperation with one another. *Identity* is a preoccupation of contemporary Western society, and the *management of multiple identities* is a preoccupation of contemporary organizational life.

From my perspective, much of what organizations do is rhetorical or persuasive and much of what is rhetorical in contemporary Western society is organized. The rhetoric of organizational life is conceived in terms of how identity is managed on the individual and collective levels. All of these theoretical and practical considerations aim at understanding the meaning of messages which come from "corporate" persons or collective bodies.

In the following chapters I shall give careful consideration to an important case and to a complex historical-political-rhetorical process, the drafting of the U.S. Catholic bishops' 1983 pastoral letter, *The Challenge of Peace.* This document, created within the traditional constraints, the hierarchical structure, and with at least partial authority of the global Church, was a product of and a testimony to the ways in which multiple identities are managed by organizations. The bishops themselves expressed concern about such issues as the interests with which members of the drafting committee were identified, their collective identity as a national conference, and how best to identify their peace advocacy with positions on other life-related issues. As a national hierarchy within a global structure and as pastoral leaders of one country's Catholic faithful, the National Conference of Catholic Bishops faced complex rhetorical problems in trying to clarify their own authority while tackling the controversial topics of defense and arms control for their several audiences. The bishops were conscious (even self-conscious) about their several audiences—both inside and outside the religious and organizational boundaries of the Roman Catholic Church. These challenges in the bishops' rhetorical situation make their case a fascinating and illuminating one for study. In the formation of their peace pastoral we can see a developing organization-within-an-organization struggling to be persuasive by managing a variety of identities, both individual and collective. And from this case—as explored through Church documents, selective interviews, and media commentary[95]—we can learn much about the interwoven processes of identification, rhetorical influence, and social organization.

NOTES

1. See, e.g., George Cheney, "The Corporate Person (Re)presents Itself," in *Rhetorical and Critical Approaches to Public Relations,* ed. Elizabeth L. Toth and Robert L. Heath (Hillsdale, NJ: Erlbaum, in press); George Cheney, "The Rhetoric of Identification and the Study of Organizational Communication," *Quarterly Journal of Speech* 69 (1983): 143–58; George Cheney and George N. Dionisopoulos, "Public Relations? No, Relations with Publics: A Rhetorical-Organizational Approach to Contemporary Corporate Communications," in *Public Relations Theory,* ed. Carl Botan and Vince Hazleton (Hillsdale, NJ: Erlbaum, 1989), 135–57; George Cheney and Jill J. McMillan, "Organizational Rhetoric and the Practice of Criticism," *Journal of Applied Communication Research,* in press; George Cheney and Steven L. Vibbert, "Corporate Discourse:

Public Relations and Issue Management," in *Handbook of Organizational Communication: An Interdisciplinary Perspective* (Newbury Park, CA: Sage), pp. 165–94; Charles Conrad, "Identity, Structure and Communicative Action in Church Decision-Making," *Journal for the Scientific Study of Religion* 27 (1988): 345–61; Richard E. Crable, "The Organizational 'System' of Rhetoric: The Influence of Megatrends into the Twenty-first Century," in *Rhetorical Studies Honoring James L. Golden,* ed. Lawrence W. Hugenberg (Dubuque, IA: Kendall/Hunt, 1986), 57–68; Carol J. Jablonski, "Rhetoric, Paradox, and the Movement for Women's Ordination in the Roman Catholic Church," *Quarterly Journal of Speech* 74 (1988): 164–83; Jill J. McMillan, "In Search of the Organizational Persona: A Rationale for Studying Organizations Rhetorically," in *Organization—Communication: Emerging Perspectives II,* ed. Lee Thayer (Norwood, NJ: Ablex, 1987), 21–45; Phillip K. Tompkins, Jeanne Y. Fisher, Dominic A. Infante, and Elaine V. B. Tompkins, "Kenneth Burke and the Inherent Characteristics of Formal Organizations: A Field Study," *Speech Monographs* 42 (1975): 135–42; Phillip K. Tompkins, "Translating Organizational Theory: Symbolism over Substance," in *Handbook of Organizational Communication: An Interdisciplinary Perspective,* ed. Fredric M. Jablin, Linda L. Putnam, Karlene H. Roberts, and Lyman W. Porter (Newbury Park, CA: Sage, 1987), 70–96; Phillip K. Tompkins and George Cheney, "Communication and Unobtrusive Control in Contemporary Organizations," in *Organizational Communication: Traditional Themes and New Directions,* ed. Robert D. McPhee and Phillip K. Tompkins (Sage, 1985), 179–210.

2. National Conference of Catholic Bishops—United States Catholic Conference, *The Challenge of Peace: God's Promise and Our Response* (Washington: USCC, 1983). Hereafter this organization is abbreviated as NCCB–USCC. The NCCB is the primary hierarchical structure of the U.S. Catholic Church; the USCC is its operational secretariat and a civil corporation.

3. Kenneth E. Boulding, *The Organizational Revolution* (1953; rpt., Chicago: Quadrangle Books, 1968).

4. Max Weber, *Economy and Society,* 2 vols., trans. Guenther Roth and Claus Wittich (Berkeley: University of California Press, 1978).

5. Chester I. Barnard, *The Functions of the Executive,* 30th anniversary ed. (Cambridge, MA: Harvard University Press, 1968), 73.

6. See, e.g., Louis Pondy, "Leadership Is a Language Game," in *Leadership: Where Else Can We Go?* ed. M. McCall and M. Lombardo (Durham, NC: Duke University Press, 1978), 87–99; Linda Smircich and Gareth Morgan, "Leadership: The Management of Meaning," *Journal of Applied Behavioral Science* 18 (1982): 257–73; Elaine V. B. Tompkins, Phillip K. Tompkins, and George Cheney, "Organizations as Arguments: Discovering, Expressing, and Analyzing the Premises for Decisions," *Journal of Management Systems* 1 (1989): 35–48; Karl E. Weick, *The Social Psychology of Organizing,* 2nd ed. (Reading, MA: Addison-Wesley, 1979).

7. See the *Oxford English Dictionary* (Oxford: Oxford University Press, 1988); see also the history of the rise of the corporate or juristic or legal "person" in James Coleman, *Power and the Structure of Society* (New York: Norton, 1974).

8. Herbert I. Schiller, *Culture, Inc.: The Corporate Takeover of Public*

Expression (New York: Oxford University Press, 1989), 46–65; Marjorie Kelly, "Revolution in the Marketplace," *Utne Reader,* Jan./Feb. 1989: 56–57. An interesting discussion of the power of the corporation-as-person metaphor is found in Phillip K. Tompkins and Michael A. Lampert, "Conspiracies, Corporations, Communication" (Paper delivered at the annual meeting of the Speech Communication Association, New York, Nov. 1980).

9. See the extended discussion of this problem in Russell Mokhiber, *Corporate Crime and Violence: Big Business Power and the Abuse of the Public Trust* (San Francisco: Sierra Club Books, 1989). Cf. Charles Redding, various papers.

10. A fuller discussion is found in George N. Dionisopoulos and Steven L. Vibbert, "Organizational Apologia: 'Corporate' Public Discourse and the Genre of Self-Defense" (Paper delivered at the annual meeting of the Speech Communication Association, Washington, Nov. 1983).

11. See, e.g., Todd Gitlin, "Postmodernism Defined, at Last!" *Utne Reader,* July/Aug. 1989: 52–61. Cf. the central argument of Joshua Meyrowitz, *No Sense of Place: The Impact of Electronic Media on Social Behavior* (New York: Oxford University Press, 1985). Also see Cheney, "The Corporate Person."

12. Richard Sennett, *Authority* (New York: Random House, 1980).

13. Cheney, "Rhetoric of Identification."

14. Neil Postman, *Amusing Ourselves to Death: Public Discourse in the Age of Show Business* (New York: Penguin, 1985); J. Michael Sproule, "The New Managerial Rhetoric and the Old Criticism," *Quarterly Journal of Speech* 74 (1988): 468–86.

15. See, e.g., Kathleen Hall Jamieson, *Eloquence in an Electronic Age: The Transformation of Political Speechmaking* (New York: Oxford University Press, 1988); and Cheney, "The Corporate Person."

16. George Cheney and Steven L. Vibbert, "Corporate Discourse," 165–94.

17. Karen Paonessa, "Corporate Advocacy and Organizational Member Identification: A Case Study of General Motors" (M.A. thesis, Purdue University, 1983). Of course, this expectation became increasingly problematic in the late 1980s when the corporation closed some of its U.S. plants and laid off thousands of workers while expanding its operations overseas.

18. This perspective is articulated and elaborated in Richard E. Crable and Steven L. Vibbert, *Public Relations as Communication Management* (Edina, MN: Bellweather Press, 1986).

19. Coleman, *Power and the Structure of Society;* see also Alfred Kieser, "Organizational, Institutional, and Societal Evolution: Medieval Craft Guilds and the Genesis of Formal Organizations," *Administrative Science Quarterly* 34 (1989): 540–64.

20. See William G. Scott and David K. Hart, *Organizational America* (Boston: Houghton Mifflin, 1979).

21. Richard Edwards, *Contested Terrain: The Transformation of the Workplace in the Twentieth Century* (New York: Basic Books, 1979); see also Tompkins and Cheney, "Communication and Unobtrusive Control."

22. See Barnard, *Functions of the Executive.*

23. Herbert A. Simon, *Adminstrative Behavior,* 3rd ed. (New York: Free Press, 1976).

24. Tompkins and Cheney, "Communication and Unobtrusive Control."

25. Tompkins and Cheney, "Communication and Unobtrusive Control."

26. Barry Bozeman, *All Organizations Are Public (San Francisco: Jossey-Bass, 1987).*

27. See, e.g., Cheney and Vibbert, "Corporate Discourse"; Richard E. Crable and Steven L. Vibbert, "Managing Issues and Influencing Public Policy," *Public Relations Review* 11 (1985): 3–16; Robert L. Heath and R. A. Nelson, *Issues Management: Corporate Public Policymaking in an Information Society* (Newbury Park, CA: Sage, 1986); S. Prakhash Sethi, *Advocacy Advertising and Large Corporations* (Lexington, MA: Heath, 1977).

28. See, e.g., Crable, "The Organizational 'System.' "

29. William James, *The Principles of Psychology,* vol. 1 (1890; rpt., New York: Dover, 1950), esp. 291.

30. See, e.g., Michel Foucault, *The Foucault Reader,* ed. Paul Rabinow (New York: Pantheon, 1984); Foucault, "The Subject and Power," *Critical Inquiry* 8 (1982): 777–95; and Mario J. Valdés and Owen Miller, eds., *Identity of the Literary Text* (Toronto: University of Toronto Press, 1985).

31. See Sigmund Freud, *Group Psychology and the Analysis of the Ego* (1922; rpt., New York: Norton, 1959).

32. See George Herbert Mead, *Mind, Self, and Society,* ed. Charles W. Morris (1934; rpt., Chicago: University of Chicago Press, 1962).

33. See Erik H. Erikson, *Childhood and Society,* 2nd ed. (New York: Norton, 1963).

34. See Margaret Mead, *Soviet Attitudes toward Authority* (New York: McGraw-Hill, 1951).

35. See Harold Lasswell, *World Politics and Personal Insecurity* (1935; rpt., New York: Free Press, 1965).

36. See, e.g., Christine Oravec, "Kenneth Burke's Concept of Association and the Complexity of Identity," in *The Legacy of Kenneth Burke,* ed. Herbert W. Simons and Trevor Melia (Madison: University of Wisconsin Press, 1989), 174–95; see also George Cheney, "Speaking of Who 'We' Are: The U.S. Catholic Bishops' Pastoral Letter *The Challenge of Peace* as a Case Study in Identity, Organization and Rhetoric" (Ph.D. diss., Purdue University, 1985). What has been called "post-structuralist" thought tends to deny the possibility of truly individual identity. See, e.g., Anthony Giddens, "Structuralism, Post-structuralism and the Production of Culture," in *Social Theory Today,* ed. Anthony Giddens and Jonathan Turner (Stanford: Stanford University Press, 1987), 195–223.

37. Kenneth Burke, *Permanence and Change: An Anatomy of Purpose,* 3rd ed. (1935; rpt., Berkeley: University of California Press, 1984), liii; see also Burke, *Attitudes toward History* (New York: New Republic, 1937), 2: 138.

38. John W. Meyer, "Myths of Socialization and of Personality," in *Reconstructing Individualism*, ed. T. C. Heller, M. Sosna, and D. E. Wellbery (Stanford: Stanford University Press, 1986), 208–21; Martin Jay, *The Dialectical Imagination* (Boston: Little, Brown, 1973). Cf. Carol Gilligan, *In a Different Voice* (Cambridge, MA: Harvard University Press, 1982), for an interpretation of myths about identity in terms of sex roles.

39. W. J. M. Mackenzie, *Political Identity* (New York: St. Martin's Press, 1978), 19–20. Cf. Marcel Mauss, "A Category of the Human Mind: The Notion of Person, the Notion of Self," in *The Category of the Person: Anthropology, Philosophy, History,* ed. Michael Carrithers, Steven Collins, and Steven Lukes (Cambridge: Cambridge University Press, 1985), 1–25. See the overview of the idea of identity in Robert C. Solomon, *Continental Philosophy Since 1750: The Rise and Fall of the Self* (Oxford: Oxford University Press, 1988).

40. Aristotle, *Nicomachean Ethics,* trans. David Ross (Oxford: Oxford University Press, 1980), 1161b. emphasis added.

41. Mackenzie, *Political Identity*, 20. See also Kenneth Burke, *The Rhetoric of Religion* (Berkeley: University of California Press, 1961).

42. Blake, Keats, Irving, and Burke, as quoted in Mackenzie, *Political Identity,* 23–25.

43. Mackenzie, *Political Identity*, 25.

44. Burke, *Attitudes toward History*, 2: 140.

45. Manford H. Kuhn and Thomas S. McPartland, "An Empirical Investigation of Self-Attitudes," *American Sociological Review* 19 (1954): 68–76. Frank Lentricchia, in *Criticism and Social Change* (Chicago: University of Chicago Press, 1983), reminds us to consider both identification *of* and identification *with*.

46. Burke, "The Rhetorical Situation," in *Communication: Ethical and Moral Issues,* ed. Lee Thayer (London: Gordon & Breach, 1973), 263–75.

47. Lucian W. Pye, *Politics, Personality, and Nation-Building: Burma's Search for Identity* (New Haven: Yale University Press, 1962).

48. Mackenzie, *Political Identity*, 124, 165.

49. Mackenzie, *Political Identity*, 24.

50. Robert B. Denhardt, *In the Shadow of Organization* (Lawrence: University Press of Kansas, 1981), 53. See also George Cheney, "On the Various and Changing Meanings of Organizational Membership: A Field Study of Organizational Identification," *Communication Monographs* 50 (1983): 342–63.

51. Thomas J. Watson, Jr., *A Business and Its Beliefs: The Ideas That Helped Build IBM* (New York: McGraw-Hill, 1963).

52. See the fuller discussion of this example in Cheney and Vibbert, "Corporate Discourse."

53. Quoted by James Curran, "Communication, Power, and Social Order," in *Culture, Society, and the Media,* ed. James Curran, Michael Gurevitch, and Janet Woollacott (London: Methuen, 1982), 204.

54. Phillip K. Tompkins and George Cheney, "Mass Communication: Studying the Roman Catholic Church Yields Some Important Information about

Organizations for Communication Researchers," *The Purdue Alumnus,* Mar. 1985: 10.

55. Donald C. Bryant, *Rhetoric: Its Functions and Its Scope,*" 1953; rpt. in *Contemporary Rhetoric: A Reader's Coursebook,* ed. Douglas Ehninger (Glenview, IL: Scott, Foresman, 1972), 26, emphasis deleted.

56. Burke, "Dramatism," in *Drama in Life: The Uses of Communication in Society,* ed. James E. Combs and M. W. Mansfield (New York: Hastings House, 1976), 11.

57. Burke, *A Rhetoric of Motives* (1950; rpt., Berkeley: University of California Press, 1969). See also Tompkins et al., "Kenneth Burke and Inherent Characteristics."

58. Burke, *Permanence and Change,* 184–85, n. 1.

59. Burke, *Language as Symbolic Action: Essays on Life, Literature, and Method* (Berkeley: University of California Press, 1966), 49.

60. Cheney, "Rhetoric of Identification," 145.

61. Burke, *Rhetoric of Motives,* 22, 45.

62. Burke, *Attitudes toward History,* 2: 144–45. See also Jean-Claude Deschamps, "Social Identity and the Relations of Power between Groups," in *Social Identity and Intergroup Relations,* ed. Henri Tajfel (Cambridge, MA: Harvard University Press, 1982), 85–98; Tajfel, *Human Groups and Social Categories* (Harvard University Press, 1981).

63. Burke, "The Rhetorical Situation," 268.

64. Burke, "Twelve Propositions by Kenneth Burke on the Relation between Economics and Psychology," *Science and Society* 2 (1938): 243.

65. Burke, *Attitudes toward History,* 2: 140; see also Erving Goffman, *The Presentation of Self in Everyday Life* (Garden City, NY: Doubleday, 1959).

66. Burke, *Rhetoric of Motives,* 21.

67. Burke, *Attitudes toward History,* 2: 147.

68. Norman N. Holland, "Human Identity," *Critical Inquiry* 4 (1978): 452. Cf. Henry W. Johnstone, Jr., *The Problem of the Self* (University Park: Pennsylvania State University Press, 1970).

69. Peter du Preez, *The Politics of Identity: Ideology and the Human Image* (New York: St. Martin's Press, 1984), 7.

70. See, e.g., Phillip K. Tompkins and George Cheney, "On the Facts of the 'Text' as the Basis of Human Communication Research," in *Communication Yearbook 11,* ed. James A. Anderson (Newbury Park, CA: Sage, 1988), 455–81. See also the thorough discussion of textuality in Richard Harvey Brown, *Society as Text: Essays on Rhetoric, Reason, and Reality* (Chicago: University of Chicago Press, 1987), and the discussions of identity and textuality in John Shotter and Kenneth J. Gergen, eds., *Texts of Identity* (London: Sage, 1989).

71. Burke, *Attitudes toward History,* 2: 144.

72. Burke "Twelve Propositions," 246, emphasis added.

73. See, e.g., F. H. Allport, "A Structuronomic Conception of Behavior:

Individual and Collective," *Journal of Abnormal and Social Psychology* 64 (1962): 3–30; cf. Talcott Parsons and Edward A. Shils, eds., *Toward a General Theory of Action* (Cambridge, MA: Harvard University Press, 1967); Barnard, *Functions of the Executive;* Weick, *Social Psychology of Organizing.*

74. Burke, *The Philosophy of Literary Form* (1941; rpt., Berkeley: University of California Press, 1973), 226; Burke, *A Grammar of Motives* (1945; rpt., University of California Press, 1969).

75. Nelson N. Foote, "Identification as the Basis of a Theory of Motivation," *American Sociological Review* 16 (1951): 20.

76. Burke, *Rhetoric of Motives,* 20. Both Burke's and Mackenzie's formulations about "interests" allow for the notion of a "class" in that its members may experience a common interest, a class "consciousness"; or an outsider may group them that way by recognizing their common interests. Here again is the dialectic of "self"-representation and representation of the "self" by others. See also Jürgen Habermas, *Legitimation Crisis,* trans. Thomas McCarthy (Boston: Beacon Press, 1973), esp. 38–39.

77. Mackenzie, *Political Identity,* 124; Burke, "The Rhetorical Situation."

78. Mackenzie, *Political Identity,* 116, emphasis added.

79. Wayne C. Booth, *Modern Dogma and the Rhetoric of Assent* (Chicago: University of Chicago Press, 1974), xvi.

80. Du Preez, in *The Politics of Identity,* posits and reifies a "collective agent." But I would argue that only natural persons are capable of authentic social action, though people often act together.

81. Simon, *Administrative Behavior,* 192–219; for an elaboration and modification of Simon's model see Tompkins and Cheney, "Communication and Unobtrusive Control."

82. See George Cheney and Phillip K. Tompkins, "Coming to Terms with Organizational Identification and Commitment," *Central States Speech Journal* 38 (1987): 1–15; Barnard, *Functions of the Executive;* Simon, *Administrative Behavior.* See also Robert Presthus, *The Organizational Society* (New York: Vintage, 1962), and William H. Whyte, *The Organization Man* (New York: Simon and Schuster, 1956). Of course, at the same time we find that many individuals feel alienated from and dispossessed by the major institutions of advanced industrial society.

83. Sennett, *Authority,* esp. p. 4.

84. See Burke, *Attitudes toward History,* 2: 52. See also Elaine V. B. Tompkins, "Alienation," unpublished manuscript, University of Iowa, 1983.

85. This definition is adopted in Cheney and Tompkins, "Coming to Terms." Cf. Rom Harré, *Personal Being: A Theory for Social Psychology* (Totowa, NJ: Littlefield, Adams, 1980), where he describes identity as "a chief unifying concept."

86. This definition, using the strategically ambiguous verb "to appropriate," is adapted from the one used by Foote ("Identification as the Basis") in his account of motivation. A complete rationale for this definition is offered in Cheney and Tompkins, "Coming to Terms."

87. James, *Principles;* see also Vernon L. Allen, David A. Wilder, and Michael L. Atkinson, "Multiple Group Membership and Social Identity," in *Studies in Social Identity,* ed. Theodore S. Sarbin and Karl E. Scheibe (New York: Praeger, 1983), 92–115.

88. This point was inspired by the discussions between Jill McMillan and the author as we prepared and interpreted two day-long seminars on "Organizational Rhetoric" at the annual conferences of the Speech Communication Association, Nov. 1988 in New Orleans and Nov. 1989 in San Francisco. Jill J. McMillan, in "The Rhetoric of the Modern Organization" (Ph.D. diss., University of Texas at Austin, 1982), argues that the rhetorical study of social movements represented a step along the way to the full consideration of organizations and institutions as rhetorical enterprises; see also Cheney, "The Corporate Person"; Cheney and McMillan, "Organization Rhetoric." See also the related discussion of an individualistic bias in American criticism in general (artistic, literary, social, and rhetorical) by Giles Gunn, *The Culture of Criticism* (New York: Oxford University Press, 1987), 25–26. Finally, see James F. Klumpp and Thomas A. Hollihan, "Rhetorical Criticism as Moral Action," *Quarterly Journal of Speech* 75 (1989): 84–97, esp. 88.

89. See, e.g., E. E. Schattschneider, *The Semi-Sovereign People: A Realist's View of Democracy in America* (New York: Holt, Rinehart & Winston, 1960), where he uses the term "mobilization of bias" to describe the functioning of political organizations.

90. Nancy Gibbs, "How America Has Run Out of Time," *Time,* 24 Apr. 1989: 58–61, 64, 67. One problem identified in this article is the challenge of managing multiple roles and commitments. Researchers are beginning to examine multiple roles, goals, identities, and commitments. See, e.g., Mark Abrahamson and William P. Anderson, "People's Commitments to Institutions," *Social Psychology Quarterly* 47 (1984): 371–81; Connie A. Bullis and Phillip K. Tompkins, "The Forest Ranger Revisited: A Study of Control Practices and Identification," *Communication Monographs* 56 (1989): 287–306; Carl F. Graumann, "On Multiple Identities," *International Social Science Journal* 35 (1983): 309–21; E. Spreitzer, E. E. Snyder, and D. L. Larson, "Multiple Roles and Psychological Well-Being," *Sociological Focus* 12 (1979): 141–46; Cynthia Stohl, "Bridging the Parallel Organization: A Study of Quality Circle Effectiveness," in *Communication Yearbook 10,* ed. Margaret L. McLaughlin (Newbury Park, CA: Sage, 1987), 416–30; Elaine V. B. Tompkins, "Possible Antecedents and Outcomes of Identification with a Parturient Organization" (Ph.D. diss., University of Iowa, 1986) and Karen Tracy and Nik Coupland, eds., *Multiple Goals in Discourse* (Clevedon, England: Multilingual Matters, in press).

91. The term "management" is used deliberately here, for it readily suggests *control,* a central concern of organizational life that has been recognized at least since Weber. Of course, related ethical questions arise: Control by whom? By how many? For what purpose? In whose interests? Through what means? With what effect? It is of course ironic that pursuing "individuality" can lead to social control.

92. See, e.g., Stuart Ewen, *All Consuming Images: The Politics of Style in Contemporary Culture* (New York: Basic Books, 1988).

93. A detailed discussion of this and related issues in European unification can be found in George Cheney, "Issues in European Unification: Equality, Hegemony, Identity, and Their Communicative Implications" (Paper delivered at the annual conference of the International Communication Association, Dublin, June 1990).

94. Amy Borrus, Wendy Zellner, and William J. Holstein, "The Stateless Corporation," *Business Week*, 14 May 1990, 98.

95. The resources used for this study were both numerous and diverse. They included the several drafts of the peace pastoral itself; papal, conciliar, and other major Catholic documents; articles from the popular religious press, especially five national Catholic weekly newspapers (*Catholic Twin Circle, National Catholic Register, National Catholic Reporter, Our Sunday Visitor,* and *The Wanderer*) and three general interest Catholic magazines *(America, Catholicism in Crisis, Commonweal);* articles from scholarly religious publications (such as *Chicago Studies, Communio, Journal for the Scientific Study of Religion, New Review of Books and Religion, Review of Religious Research, Sociological Analysis, Theological Studies,* and *This World*); *Origins,* the U.S. Catholic Conference news service; audiocassettes from the National Catholic Education Association; articles from the popular secular press, especially the *New York Times* and the three major news weeklies *(Newsweek, Time, U.S. News and World Report);* several editorial magazines *(Commentary, The Nation, National Review, New Republic, New York Review of Books, New Yorker);* articles from journals on public and foreign policy (including *American Political Science Review, Bulletin of the Atomic Scientists, Bulletin of Peace Proposals, Foreign Affairs, Journal of Peace Research,* and *World Politics*); the several books and journal issues devoted exclusively to the peace pastoral—e.g., Jim Castelli's *The Bishops and the Bomb: Waging Peace in a Nuclear Age* (Garden City, NY: Doubleday, 1983); written input to the drafting committee; and finally, and most important, interviews with principal actors, critics, and observers.

The libraries explored included those of Purdue University, the University of Illinois, the University of Notre Dame, and St. Louis University. This array of resources enabled me to consider the various religious, political, and social "voices" that in some way contributed to the development of the bishops' document. Sources pertaining directly to the case were consulted primarily for the period 1980–84. This time period was appropriate because the bishops' interest in nuclear arms control became most apparent with the campaign and first election of Ronald Reagan. Further, with the appearance of the first draft of the bishops' pastoral on the American economy in November 1984, public attention was diverted to a great extent away from the peace pastoral. Relevant sources for the period 1984–89 were reviewed to consider the impact of the peace pastoral.

Between July 1983 and February 1985 I conducted "elite-style," moderately structured interviews with 30 persons who had various kinds of expertise. When possible, the interviews were conducted in person; however, many were done by telephone. The interviews ranged in length from 25 minutes to one hour and 50 minutes. When interviews were not possible, written correspondence was obtained.

The interviews may be described as "moderately structured" in that prepared schedules included major topical questions and some probes; however, substantial flexibility allowed for topic shifts and specific follow-up questions. The interviews may be called "elite-style" because questions were adapted, deleted, and added with respect to the "core" list and according to the specific expertise of the interviewee and the constraints of the situation (notably, time limitations).

Each interviewee is listed in Appendix A, along with the nature and approximate length of the interview, the participant's position, and his or her relevance to the study. The entries are presented in order by date of interview. Also included are several items of written correspondence used in cases where interviews were not possible.

At the outset of each interview the interviewee was informed of the general nature of the research and encouraged to ask questions of the researcher. The opportunity for inquiry was offered again at the close of each interview. With the permission of the interviewee, seven sessions were audiotape recorded. During others the researcher took careful notes which were reconstructed following the interviews. The interview schedule is shown in Appendix B.

Questions were designed to be both broad-ranging and direct, exploring issues related to the management of multiple identities. The questions touched on such matters as the bishops' recognition of various interest groups, the stance of the bishops toward the nation and the Reagan Administration, consideration for other Church hierarchies and the Vatican, levels of moral authority, and role conceptions of the bishops for themselves, the laity, and the U.S. Church as a whole.

2

THE ROMAN CATHOLIC CHURCH, ORGANIZATIONAL STRUCTURE, AND SOCIAL CHANGE

The current demand for prophets in the Church is due in part to the revolutionary changes of our time. . . . Scrutinizing the signs of the time, Christianity must reinterpret its own doctrine and goals in terms of the world of today. To effect this transposition without loss of substance is a task calling for prophetic insight.

Avery Dulles, *The Survival of Dogma*

[Pope] John saw the [Second Vatican] council itself as the beginning of a transfer of power from the papal monarchy to the Church as a whole. It was a parliament of the episcopate and he was a constitutional sovereign. He wished to reverse the process whereby, during the nineteenth century, the bishops had been deprived of their independence and had become mere functionaries of a populist papacy.

Paul Johnson, *A History of Christianity*

[The Roman Catholic Church] is committed both to spiritual and temporal goals and its normative system must reflect a proportionate balance between these two different priorities, the former more perduring and transcendent and the latter subject to change and development.

Brian H. Smith, *The Church and Politics in Chile: Challenges to Modern Catholicism*

THE CHURCH AS AN ORGANIZATION

Whatever else it may be, the Roman Catholic Church is a complex organization: "It is doubtful that anyone fully understands this complex organization, so it is necessary before studying it, or any part of it, to develop some common base from which to proceed."[1] The Church is bureaucratic and hierarchical; it is steeped in tradition. The Roman Catholic Church is not only "the oldest significant organization in western civilization," but "endures as a self-correcting, living system,"[2] an institution which has adapted to an amazing array of cultures and historical circumstances.

We should take note of the dynamics of what often appear to be strictly static hierarchical relationships. Historically and currently there have appeared shifting movements and coalitions within the Catholic Church organization, changes that help the Church adapt to and affect its various internal and external audiences. For example, the Society of Jesus (the Jesuits), an influential worldwide order of Catholic priests, was founded from a papal-priestly coalition in direct response to the forces of the Reformation. A second case comes from post-war France, where French priests tried to ally themselves closely with the working people and thereby temper anti-clerical sentiments throughout the country. A further example, of course, may be seen in the actions of the U.S. bishops since the early 1980s: growing numbers have been taking public steps to reduce the "distance" between themselves and the laity.

I raise these issues and examples to point up some important aspects of the Roman Catholic Church organization. It is not as monolithic or unchanging as is commonly assumed. This judgment is shared in various ways by Peter Nichols, who describes the Church as "the Pope's divisions";[3] Richard McBrien, who argues that "just as the world is pluralistic in character, so too is the Catholic Church";[4] and Mary Hanna, who quotes an editor of a Catholic magazine: "The Church is like a barge. It seems to move so slowly but somehow it always gets there and always keeps moving."[5]

Moreover, the Catholic Church, which most certainly qualifies as an institution, is an organization of organizations (and subpopulations); or seen yet another way, an organization of interest groups and movements. For example, Murray Stedman writes that "the churches are social organizations. Of course, they are and claim to be a good deal more than that. But they are, in fact, social organizations. They seek to control people, and they are both actual and potential interest groups."[6] This statement implicitly addresses the three key terms of the present study: identity (in the form of interest groups), rhetoric, and organization (the latter two terms relating to control). In the worldly order the Catholic Church transcends national borders, economic systems, and innumerable cultures and subcultures. Within the Church's boundaries are the offices of the

Roman Curia; national and regional episcopal (bishops') conferences; councils of priests; religious orders of men and women; many and varied media organizations; lobby groups; social welfare associations; schools; diocesan offices; and, of course, individual parishes or congregations. Thus it is hardly surprising that Kenneth Boulding, even before the Second Vatican Council (or Vatican II, 1962–65), declared: "To the most casual observer . . . it is clear that the Catholic Church in different parts of the world represents a quite astonishing diversity, not only of social structure, but even of religious experiences and images."[7] Within the Roman Catholic Church, perhaps more than in any other formal organization, unity and diversity exist in a remarkable dialectical synthesis.

Finally, Catholic clerical, religious, and lay leaders often confront a multiplicity of audiences—both within and outside the Church, organizationally understood. Traditionally, much of this communication has been "top-down" in the form of dogma, doctrine, and directives pertaining to theology, ecclesiology (institutional structure), and morality. Today, however, with the stimulated increase in dialogue at all levels of the Church since Vatican II, the growing involvement of the hierarchy in political affairs, and the many grass-roots movements afoot in areas such as Latin America, this communication matrix has become much more complex.

With such a scene in mind Brian Smith articulates four challenges for the Church in this period of pronounced change, the late twentieth century: (1) to integrate new social commitments into the Church without detracting from its essential mission; (2) to implement values of collegiality and pluralism without undermining hierarchical authority; (3) to develop widespread acceptance of its social emphases while allowing for a range of responses from different types of Catholics; and (4) to balance concerns of national Church groups with those of the transnational Church.[8] These are essentially rhetorical challenges, according to Goldzwig and Cheney, who used modifications of them to frame their preliminary analysis of the NCCB's peace pastoral.[9] The relevance of these challenges to the present discussion is that, not unlike other giant organizations, pressures on the Church make it necessary to construct and express very carefully messages of concern to members, and to a lesser extent non-members, while sustaining an institutional and historical status. Such rhetorical obligations involve the Roman Catholic Church, perhaps more than any other organization, in the business of managing multiple identities. Thus, the Roman Catholic Church offers rich opportunities for the study of enduring institutions' adaptations to and adaptations of their internal and external audiences.[10]

THE CHURCH IN THE UNITED STATES

The U.S. Catholic Church is subject to diverse cultural influences, displays a relatively pluralistic character, and owns a history of controversy over its posture with respect to American culture. It has always managed multiple identities; history has required that it do so. As Dorothy Dohen explains, "One desperate need of the Church at every moment of her history has been the need to distinguish that which is essential to the faith, and that which is its transitory, cultural, historical, or national expression."[11] The Catholic Church in the United States has from the beginning faced troubling and persistent problems in trying to maintain allegiance to centralized transnational authority and to universal symbols while developing within a society that is officially pluralistic and occasionally prone to great nationalistic fervor. As William Bausch notes in a historical overview:

> Catholics in America were always somehow "foreign." After all, they were not democratic but still operated under the old clerical hierarchical structure. This smacked of the old European royalism. Then too, unlike the Protestants, doctrine mattered very much to the Catholics, and there was a strict canon of Catholic doctrinal positions on every question whatever. No wonder Protestants thought that Catholics could never adapt to "their country."[12]

Indeed, this is the type of problem faced by any group—religious, political, or ethnic—which maintains allegiance to an authority outside the borders which contain it. For example, multinational corporations struggle to preserve their organizational allegiance over and above the allegiances of their employees to specific countries or divisions.

The early history of the Church in this country was forged in large part by Protestant fear, national reaction against waves of immigration from Europe, and popular response to an often unsupportive and centralized "Rome." In *Catholic America* John Cogley says:

> What American Catholics themselves now good-naturedly refer to as their "ghetto culture" (which all seem to agree is dying) actually marked a departure from Archbishop Carroll's [the first U.S. bishop] notion of a Church comfortably integrated into American life. The ghetto culture was not deliberately planned. It developed as an early defense measure, and as the years went on it matured into a whole set of institutions paralleling some of the basic structures of American life. In time it became the best organized and most powerful of the nation's subcultures—a source of both alienation and enrichment for those born within it and an object of bafflement or uneasiness for others.[13]

This "uneasiness" over the years took the forms of legal challenges to bishops' rights in the early 1800s, occasional questions about the confidentiality of statements made in confession, and disputes over the status of parochial schools—which persist today in issues about state aid to education. Unfortunately, at several points in U.S. history there emerged strong and violent anti-Catholic sentiment manifesting itself in the campaigns of the nativist groups of the 1820s and '30s, the "Know-Nothing" party of the 1850s and '60s, the American Protective Association of the 1880s and '90s, and the Ku Klux Klan of the 1920s and '30s.

Nevertheless, as the dean of Catholic historians, John Tracy Ellis, observed in 1956, "The very real differences between Catholics and their countrymen in no sense need imply a war to the death, for the fundamental principle of separation of church and state has always been accepted by the American [Catholic] hierarchy."[14] Moreover, by the end of the nineteenth century the mainline approach of American Catholicism under the direction of such spokesmen as James Cardinal Gibbons of Baltimore, Archbishop John Ireland of St. Paul, and Bishop John Lancaster Spalding of Peoria was a position known as "American Catholic liberalism." Notes Charles Curran: "This position saw no basic incompatibility between being Catholic and being American, urging strong Catholic participation in American life and espousing cooperation with non-Catholics in areas of political, social, and economic life."[15]

Such liberalism did not go unopposed, however; in 1899 Pope Leo XIII issued a letter sharply criticizing "Religious Americanism" as dangerous and hostile to Catholic doctrine and discipline.[16] The movement had enemies as well within the American community, setting the stage for the "Romanization" of the American hierarchy through carefully orchestrated episcopal appointments during the first two decades of this century. Not until the "liberal" cause was taken up by the eloquent Jesuit spokesman John Courtney Murray in the two decades following World War II and many of his ideas on religious freedom were incorporated into the documents of Vatican II did this tension dissipate.

In light of this history it is both ironic and understandable how many Catholic leaders and faithful have embraced American nationalism. Indeed, nationalism has been a persistent and public feature of the Church in the United States, as Dorothy Dohen explains in *Nationalism and American Catholicism*. She observes, among other things, that a sense of American "destiny" coupled with the desire (particularly among bishops of Irish descent) to fuse nationalism and religion, led many in the Church to be virulently pro-American, pro-military, and anti-communist. Mary Hanna says, "The bishops . . . have been the biggest hawks in our skies,"[17] accepting and promoting a powerful and embracing national identity.

With the election of Catholic John F. Kennedy, the implementation of numerous Vatican II–related reforms, and the social upheaval of the 1960s and '70s, changes have been remarkably rapid and diverse in American Catholicism. Beginning with late but vocal criticism of U.S. involvement in Vietnam, some groups within the Church and some members of the hierarchy began to voice opposition to particular governmental policies. Bausch notes the irony here: "After finally getting recognized as a genuine part of American life and their right to be full, accredited Americans—suddenly their own members and many of their most revered leaders . . . began raising questions about America itself."[18]

Organizationally, this irony makes sense. A group must be accepted as part of a larger body before its criticisms of that larger body can be heard and perhaps make a difference. Only "insiders" are privileged to criticize *their* organization or *their* country. That is why individuals at the boundaries of organizations often have difficulty in getting their voices heard; only those persons at the "centers" of the organizations, after having proven their loyalty, are able to voice opposition and be accorded attention and respect.[19] Nearly everyone who has ever served in a "boundary-role position" (e.g., as a sales representative, as a diplomatic negotiator, or as a public relations officer) understands this problem deeply.

Today we witness a Catholic Church in the United States which is marked by independence and pluralism—independence in the sense of the hierarchy's stance vis-à-vis Washington (and to some extent Rome) and pluralism in the sense of the variety of ways Catholics define their own religiosity. Commentators and observers describe this situation variously. Vincent Yzermans, former information director for the U.S. Catholic Conference (the administrative adjunct to the NCCB), writes of "the Catholic Revolution" in terms of Church conflict with the federal government;[20] George A. Kelly characterizes "the battle" within a Church which is deviating more and more from the Roman path;[21] John H. Whyte refers to the "decay of closed Catholicism" in the West;[22] Greeley and Durkin examine the rise of "selective Catholics" who choose from among doctrinal and religious tenets as they would make selections in a cafeteria;[23] and Richard McBrien dramatically portrays current pluralism as a situation where "there are sometimes sharper divisions *within* [American

Catholicism] than there are between certain Catholics and certain Protestants."[24]

CHALLENGES TO U.S. CATHOLICISM

Whether one views the current phase in U.S. Catholic history as a crisis, an opportunity, an omen, or an awakening, he or she must acknowledge the justification for systematic study and reflection on it. David O'Brien sees contemporary Catholicism in terms of a confluence of factors, some grounded in the past and others springing from the present. It is against this background, says O'Brien, that "many Catholics are looking for a clearer understanding of the relationship between their Catholicism and their Americanness, and a more hopeful vision of the mission of the Church in the United States."[25] Thus, the individual Catholic today is well aware of the need to manage his or her own identities.

The four challenges to the Roman Catholic Church that Brian Smith outlines in *The Church and Politics in Chile* merit special attention here. Although he applies them specifically to the Church in Chile, the challenges are strikingly relevant to the Church in the United States, and for that matter to contemporary Catholicism in general. The challenges suggest ways in which the experience of the U.S. Catholic Church today parallels that of other groups or organizations struggling with social change. Finally and relatedly, the challenges connect with the concerns of social movements as examined by rhetorical scholars. Each challenge helps to explain the dilemmas of the contemporary U.S. Catholic Church and yields generalizable insights.

The first challenge is *to integrate new social commitments into the Church without detracting from its essential mission.* This challenge is particularly difficult for an organization which relies heavily on tradition for its institutional authority. The challenge is relevant to any organization that seeks to maintain a coherent identity. As a corporation takes on new subsidiaries, for example, it risks a loss of identity and a diffusion of its mission. In response to such a situation, many corporations (e.g., Beatrice, TRW, General Foods) remind their many audiences, internal and external, of who and what the organization *is*.

Today the U.S. Catholic Church, in the form of the NCCB, is attempting to take on new social commitments by engaging socio-political issues more directly and by issuing pastoral letters and other statements on issues as diverse as the U.S. economy, Central America, racism, and women. The 1983 peace pastoral was the first of these statements to become front-page news. The peace pastoral's emergence was a dramatic example of what William McSweeney calls "political Catholicism"[26] and it typified what Martin Marty terms "the public church"[27] or the church as public speaker—specifically in an effort to transform the organization into a movement for the elimination of social injustice. One of the challenges for the bishops is to become more "catholic" without becoming less "Catholic." Put another way, the bishops, as representatives of a larger hierarchy, must engage secular political discussions without losing touch with Catholic tradition.

As Simons, Mechling, and Schreier note, this dilemma also faces social change groups when they seek to update themselves or adapt to new circumstances.[28] Change *within* the organization must be effected with special care so that no constituencies are lost in the process. In sum, this first challenge lies at the nexus of the three key terms for this book: rhetoric, identity, and organization.

The second challenge to Catholicism is *to implement values of collegiality and pluralism without undermining hierarchical authority*. This problem is, of course, especially relevant to the U.S. Catholic Church. An ongoing problem for the Church in the United States is to balance the cultural pluralism of the nation with the absolute, transnational authority of the universal Church. In fact, this has plagued U.S. Catholicism since its first bishop, John Carroll, argued to the American colonists and to the Vatican that the Church had to be adapted fully to the American context, particularly in terms of structure.[29] And the problem persists today as U.S. bishops attempt to defend the pluralism of U.S. Catholicism to a sometimes unsympathetic Pope John Paul II. They did this, for example, at a March 1989 meeting in Rome at the Pope's request.

The same problem faces any group, organization, or nation that attempts to allow diversity of views and open discussion while holding to an authoritarian or a distinctly hierarchical power structure. In June of 1989 the Chinese government's brutal response to the student demonstrations for democracy provided a tragic example of how poorly such tensions can be managed.

In a less acute way corporations that seek to foster widespread employee participation experience these tensions. Corporate leaders, policy makers, and bureaucrats frequently initiate participation programs such as quality circles only to tighten the reins when discussion becomes too open or criticism too vocal; that is, when centralized control is threatened.

For an organization actively seeking social change, the same problem surfaces. Social movements often succumb to pressures for hierarchy and institutionalization while struggling to preserve equality, diversity, and spontaneity.[30] A movement within a larger organization, such as the peace movement within the Catholic Church, must simultaneously adapt to the egalitarian principles which undergird it in the larger society and enlist the hierarchical authority of the Church. This requires a delicate balance, indeed: it calls for sensitivity to different organizational structures, a concern for identity and the possibilities for being coopted, and the use of sophisticated rhetorical strategies.

The third challenge for Catholicism is *to develop widespread acceptance of the Church's social emphases while allowing for a range of responses from different types of Catholics.* This challenge too is a difficult one to meet. What it means for the U.S. Church is that the bishops must promote *their* positions on social and political issues but still allow for a diversity of responses from the Catholic faithful. To celebrate openness, dialogue, and collegiality is also to invite free and open discussion with and among the "flock." To allow for less would be noticeably hypocritical. However, with open discussion comes disagreement. So the bishops must be careful to preserve the integrity and the authority of their positions without simply falling back on the authorial stamp of the institutional Church.

Again we see a challenge relevant in other organizational and institutional contexts. To compete in the marketplace of ideas (a limited but widely used metaphor today) an interest group must make its voice heard while allowing for other voices to speak. The temptation for any group, regardless of its commitment to democracy and consensus, is to assert its own position in such a way as to silence other groups. This has been the unhappy and ironic fate of some organizations within the peace movement: they have become authoritarian and domineering in their dealings with similarly committed groups, often because of the intensity of their own commitment to a cause and their determination to "win." To speak with conviction and to allow others to do the same is as extraordinarily challenging for organizations as it is for individuals.[31]

The fourth challenge that Smith articulates is *to balance concerns of national Church groups with those of the transnational Church.* Clearly, this challenge is most pertinent to organizations and institutions with global reach, the Catholic Church being perhaps the best example. The universal Church has always tried to balance its essential mission, which transcends national boundaries, with the specific concerns of different cultures and nationalities. Much of the *aggiornamento* (or bringing up to date) that characterized the Second Vatican Council aimed to allow for fuller national and ethnic expression within the transnational institution of the Church.

A similar problem faces intergovernmental organizations, multinational corporations, other kinds of international organizations, and, of course, nations. The French multinational Schlumberger has been exceptionally successful at allowing substantial autonomy to its units around the world while maintaining a common and overarching vision. Italian-based Benetton uses a unity-in-diversity theme throughout its ubiquitous and highly successful ad campaign to bring together many types of consumers, "The United Colors."

As a transnational political system the Soviet Union has experienced the rise of ethnic and national tensions with the implementation of Mikhail Gorbachev's *glasnost* (openness) and *perestroika* (restructuring). As various groups and republics assert their autonomy and identity, general policies are and will be seriously tested and strained. The management of multiple identities presents a formidable challenge to an autocratic political system that is seeking to allow greater diversity of expression by its subunits: nations and ethnic groups.

For the Catholic Church in the United States the issue centers on the order of the words in the hyphenated term: Catholic–American or American–Catholic. As I will show, this matter was of no small importance for the NCCB as it drafted and disseminated *The Challenge of Peace*. The order of the terms struck to the very heart of issues concerning the bishops' identities as individuals, as a conference, and as political advocates. As an organization–within–an–organization, a national conference of bishops in a transnational Church, the NCCB faced multiple challenges.

On a broader level an understanding of the Roman Catholic Church as an organization is important, not only for analysis of the Church from the outside but also because of implications for members. As Franz-Xaver Kaufmann explains, the breakdown of a strong Catholic subculture in the West has led Catholics to consider the Church increasingly in *organizational* terms. "As long as Catholic sub-culture was intact, as long as Catholics gravitated to fellow Catholics in other than religious connections because of their denominational allegiance, the predominantly organizational character of the modern structures of the Church was not apparent to believers." With a cohesive social substratum, argues Kaufmann, "The Church could still be regarded as the 'holy mother' and not as a bureaucratic organization, and the pope as the 'holy father' and not as the hierocratic leader of a multi-national organization."[32] For many Catholics, particularly those in multi-vocal, pluralistic democracies, the hierarchical, centralized structure of the Church seems increasingly inappropriate and even implausible. Meanwhile, others within the Church defend its current structure as morally proper and pragmatically necessary. These and related organizational issues must be considered as we examine the case of the bishops; that is, we must ask what the key terms of this study—identity, rhetoric, and organization—*mean* for the Roman Catholic Church as a whole during this period of profound social change.

NOTES

1. Scott R. Safranski, *Managing God's Organization: The Catholic Church in Society* (Ann Arbor, MI: UMI Research Press, 1985), 43.

2. Phillip K. Tompkins and George Cheney, "Mass Communication: Studying the Roman Catholic Church Yields Some Important Information about Organizations for Communication Researchers," *The Purdue Alumnus*, Mar. 1985: 10.

3. Peter Nichols, *The Pope's Divisions: The Roman Catholic Church Today* (Harmondsworth, England: Penguin, 1982).

4. Richard P. McBrien, "Roman Catholicism: *E Pluribus Unum*," in *Religion in America: Spirituality in a Secular Age,* ed. Mary Douglas and Steven M. Tipton (Boston: Beacon Press, 1982), 179.

5. Mary T. Hanna, *Catholics and American Politics* (Cambridge, MA: Harvard University Press, 1979), 11.

6. Murray S. Stedman, Jr., *Religion and Politics in America* (New York: Harcourt, Brace, 1964), 62–63. See also Gotthold Hasenhuttl, "Church and Institution," in *The Church as Institution,* ed. Gregory Baum and Andrew Greeley (New York: Herder, 1964), 11–21; and Andrew Greeley, *The American Catholic: A Social Portrait* (New York: Basic Books, 1977).

7. Kenneth E. Boulding, *The Image: Knowledge in Life and Society* (Ann Arbor: University of Michigan Press, 1961), 141–42.

8. Brian H. Smith, *The Church and Politics in Chile: Challenges to Modern Catholicism* (Princeton, NJ: Princeton University Press, 1982), 20–21.

9. Steve Goldzwig and George Cheney, "The U.S. Catholic Bishops on Nuclear Arms: Corporate Advocacy, Role Redefinition and Rhetorical Adaptation," *Central States Speech Journal* 35 (1984): 8–23.

10. Phillip K. Tompkins, George Cheney, and Elaine V. B. Tompkins, "Permanence and Change in the Roman Catholic Church: Communication, Coalitions, Conscience" (Paper delivered at the annual meeting of the Speech Communication Association, Louisville, KY, Nov. 1982).

11. Dorothy Dohen, *Nationalism and American Catholicism* (New York: Sheed and Ward, 1967), xi.

12. William J. Bausch, *Pilgrim Church: A Popular History of Catholic Christianity* (Mystic, CT: Twenty-third Publications, 1981), 483.

13. John Cogley, *Catholic America* (Garden City, NY: Doubleday, 1973), 135. See also James Hennesey, *American Catholics: A History of the Roman Catholic Community in the United States* (New York: Oxford University Press, 1981), 69–100.

14. John Tracy Ellis, *American Catholicism*, 2nd ed. (Chicago: University of Chicago Press, 1969), 157.

15. Charles E. Curran, *American Catholic Social Ethics: Twentieth-Century Approaches* (Notre Dame, IN: University of Notre Dame Press, 1982), 5.

16. Pope Leo XIII, as quoted in Gerald P. Fogarty, *The Vatican and the American Hierarchy from 1870 to 1965* (Stuttgart: Anton Hiersemann, 1982), 178.

17. Mary Hanna, "From Civil Religion to Prophetic Church: American Bishops and the Bomb," *Humanities in Society* 6 (1983): 41.

18. Bausch, *Pilgrim Church*, 515–16.

19. J. Stacy Adams, "The Structure and Dynamics of Organizational Boundary Roles," in *Handbook of Industrial and Organizational Psychology*, ed. Marvin D. Dunnette (Chicago: Rand McNally, 1976), 1175–99.

20. Vincent A. Yzermans, "The Catholic Revolution," *Christianity and Crisis*, 1 Mar. 1982: 39.

21. George A. Kelly, *The Battle for the American Church* (Garden City, NY: Doubleday, 1981).

22. John H. Whyte, *Catholics in Western Democracies: A Study in Political Behavior* (New York: St. Martin's Press, 1981).

23. Andrew M. Greeley and Mary Greeley Durkin, *How to Save the Catholic Church* (New York: Viking, 1984).

24. McBrien, "Roman Catholicism," 181.

25. David O'Brien, "Toward an American Catholic Church," *Cross Currents* 31 (1981–82), 472.

26. William McSweeney, *Roman Catholicism: The Search for Relevance* (New York: St. Martin's Press, 1980).

27. Martin E. Marty, *The Public Church: Mainline, Evangelical, Catholic* (New York: Crossroad, 1981).

28. Herbert W. Simons, Elizabeth W. Mechling, and Howard N. Schreier, "The Functions of Human Communication in Mobilizing for Action from the Bottom Up: The Rhetoric of Social Movements," in *Handbook of Rhetorical and Communication Theory*, ed. Carroll C. Arnold and John Waite Bowers (Boston: Allyn and Bacon, 1984), 792–867. Cf. John Waite Bowers and Donovan Ochs, *The Rhetoric of Agitation and Control* (Reading, MA: Addison-Wesley, 1971).

29. Hennesey, *American Catholics* 69–100.

30. See Simons, Mechling, and Schreier, "Functions of Human Communication"; see also Max Weber's discussion of the routinization of charisma in *Economy and Society,* vol. 1, trans. Guenther Roth and Claus Wittich (Berkeley: University of California Press, 1978).

31. Craig R. Smith's *Freedom of Expression and Partisan Politics* (Columbia: University of South Carolina Press, 1989) treats American political and regulatory agencies' varied difficulties in facing this challenge since colonial times. George Cheney and Phillip K. Tompkins, "Toward an Ethics of Identification" (Paper delivered at the Burke Conference, Philadelphia, Mar. 1984), discuss generally the tension between persuasiveness and persuasibility.

32. Franz-Xaver Kaufmann, "The Church as a Religious Organization," in *The Church as Institution,* ed. Baum and Greeley, 70–82. See also Whyte, *Catholics in Western Democracies.*

3

HISTORICAL, ORGANIZATIONAL, AND RHETORICAL CONTEXTS FOR THE CASE

Something is stirring in the Roman Catholic church in the United States that portends an explosion between church and state that will make the abortion issue, the school-aid controversy and the tax-exempt status of churches look like a child's sparkler on the Fourth of July. Stated simply, the church in the United States is becoming a "peace" church.

Vincent Yzermans, "The Catholic Revolution,"
Christianity and Crisis, March 1982

In the wake of the peace pastoral, the bishops must weigh to what extent they want to be reconcilers and to what extent they want to be dividers. . . . The justification that the bishops have been giving for more political action is that it's wrong to remain silent or to stay on a high level of generalization. But they haven't thought sufficiently about the dangers on the other side—in getting too specific on political matters.

Telephone interview with Michael Novak, Research
Associate at the American Enterprise Institute.

The very root of the word religion means to "rebind" or to "bind together." . . . At bottom, religion, like the public life, has to do with unity, with the overcoming of brokenness and fragmentation, and with the reconciling of that which has been estranged.

Parker J. Palmer, *The Company of Strangers:
Christians and the Renewal of America's Public Life*

47

CATHOLIC SOCIAL TEACHING

The claim by Vincent Yzermans cited above was probably overstated, particularly for a time when the U.S. Catholic bishops' peace pastoral was not even in its final form. Nevertheless, that any informed observer would make such a statement publicly early in the 1980s dramatized that important changes had occurred in the U.S. Catholic Church *qua* organization. The peace pastoral (and its evolution) symbolized many of these.

In this chapter I shall offer an interpretive, historical account of (1) Catholic teaching on peace and social justice; (2) Catholic peace activism in the United States; (3) the U.S. Catholic bishops' statements on peace; and (4) key events in the development of the peace pastoral itself, especially the nuclear "freeze" movement of the early 1980s. Against this background I shall consider the Church's new problems in managing identities.

The Roman Catholic Church always has displayed an active interest in the social order; in fact, from the time of the Holy Roman Empire to the Reformation, the Church *was* in a very real sense the social order of the Western world.

The comprehensive vision of the world articulated by St. Thomas Aquinas (1225–74), in which the individual person seeks God through the inherent goodness of creation, continues to motivate Catholic moral teaching.[1] What has been added over the years, particularly in the past century, is a concern that the Church has a responsibility to improve society as a whole while also guiding individuals along a path of personal salvation. This "new" view was clearly articulated and institutionalized in Pope Leo XIII's famous encyclical *Rerum Novarum* (The Condition of Labor) in 1891. This proclamation formally launched the Catholic Church's direct engagement with key social, economic, and political issues of the day.

As Joseph Gremillion points out in his comprehensive study *The Gospel of Peace and Justice,* there were just two documents that guided the Catholic social apostolate before 1960—*Rerum Novarum* and Pope Pius XI's 1931 encyclical *Quadragesimo Anno* (On Reconstructing the Social Order), issued in part to commemorate the fortieth anniversary of the former.[2] *Quadragesimo Anno* stressed, among other things, the dignity of the human person and the service nature of the state. Emphasis on this theme widened the official purview of the organization.

Since World War II peace issues generally and the nuclear threat particularly have been addressed by the several popes, usually within the context of the Just War Theory outlined by St. Augustine in the fourth century and later elaborated by Aquinas. Certainly one of the most important statements was Pope John XXIII's encyclical *Pacem in Terris* (Peace on Earth), which he offered in 1963. *Pacem in Terris,* unlike most of the documents that preceded it, was addressed to "all men of good will." Thus, Gremillion notes, "Millions who had never paid the least attention to popes and their jaw-breaker encyclicals suddenly sat up and listened."[3] Second, the encyclical helped to win a universal hearing for what came to be known during Vatican II and beyond as *aggiornamento*. This term refers to the efforts of the Catholic Church to bring itself up to date in the modern world; it is descriptive of the revitalization, the processes of spiritual renewal and institutional reform fostered by Pope John and his successor, Paul VI.[4] Third, *Pacem in Terris* was the first official document of the Roman Catholic Church to address in depth the interrelationships of nations in the nuclear age.

A dominant theme of *Pacem in Terris* was interdependence: "no political community is able to pursue its own interests and develop itself in isolation."[5] Moreover, the encyclical exhorted its audience to foster cooperation at all levels of international economic and political life. It supported the further development of transnational authorities (such as the United Nations) aimed at the protection of individual rights and at the preservation of a peaceful order.

In more specific terms the documents of the Second Vatican Council addressed the issue of nuclear warfare, condemning such an option as "far exceeding the bounds of legitimate defense."[6] And in perhaps the strongest statement against large-scale nuclear conflict anywhere in official Catholic teaching, Vatican II's *Gaudium et Spes* (The Pastoral Constitution on the Church in the Modern World) warned in 1965 that "any act of war aimed indiscriminately at the destruction of entire cities or of extensive areas along with their population is a crime against God and man himself. It merits unequivocal and unhesitating condemnation."[7] This statement was soon followed up by Pope Paul VI's impassioned plea before the U.N. General Assembly in 1965: "No more war, war never again!"[8]

Pope John Paul II denounced the dangerous and spiraling arms race during an address at Peace Park in Hiroshima in February of 1981. The Pope implored: "Let us promise each other that we will work tirelessly for disarmament and the abolition of all nuclear weapons." To do this, he insisted, "humanity must make a moral about-face."[9] In a message to the Second Special Session of the United Nations on Disarmament in June 1982 the Pope echoed his predecessor, Pius XII, who singled out "the might of new instruments of destruction" which "brought the problems of

49

disarmament into the centre of international discussions under completely new aspects." In the same address, which soon became a focal point in Catholic discussion of the arms race here and around the world, John Paul implicitly questioned the meaning of just war today while also maintaining that "in current conditions 'deterrence' based on balance, certainly not as an end in itself but as a step on the way toward a progressive disarmament, may still be judged morally acceptable."[10]

In giving voice to grave concerns about nuclear arms control, official Catholic teaching framed those concerns within a larger—and more secular—call for peace through justice. In statements such as John XXIII's encyclical *Mater et Magistra* (Christianity and Social Progress), 1961, and Paul VI's *Populorum Progressio* (On the Development of Peoples), 1967, the Church's social concern was reaffirmed and the linkage of peace to social justice in its many forms made clear. Nowhere was this more plain than in the title of one of the subsections of *Populorum Progressio:* "Development Is the New Name for Peace." In this way peace became understood by the Church not only as the absence of war, but also as a positive progression toward shared economic, political, and social responsibility. In addition, this broader perspective allowed for the criticism of the arms race for its disproportionate consumption of resources. As Paul VI declared in the same encyclical: "When so many people are hungry, when so many families suffer from destitution, when so many schools, hospitals and homes worthy of the name remain to be built, all public or private squandering of wealth, all expenditure prompted by motives of national or personal ostentation, every exhausting arms race, becomes an intolerable scandal."[11]

In the documents and years following Vatican II there was strong evidence of increasing politicization in the Church. Two statements in 1971 made this trend apparent: Pope Paul VI's apostolic letter *Octogesima Adveniens,* which observed the eightieth anniversary of *Rerum Novarum,* and *Justice in the World,* a proclamation of the world Synod of Bishops Second General Assembly.[12] Paul VI's letter spoke explicitly of political engagement; it recognized the risks of such endeavors and the need to take them. He wrote: "In order to counterbalance increasing technocracy, modern forms of democracy must be devised, not only making it possible for each man to become informed and express himself, but also involving him in shared responsibility." With such a linkage of the Church to politics as the foundation for his discussion, Paul urged his listeners to "take part in action and to spread . . . the energies of the Gospel." And taking up this call the Synod of Bishops stressed the need for local, national, and international action to bring about greater justice, especially for the overtly oppressed. Warning of the dangers of unequal distribution of wealth, a spiraling arms race, and widespread hunger, the bishops declared war on "the focus of division and antagonism [that] seem today to be increasing in strength."[13]

Thus in the two decades following Vatican II a number of positions became interrelated "stock issues" for the Roman Catholic Church: peace, justice, relative economic equality, shared responsibility, political action, and of course the dignity of human life. In fact, many Church documents came to use the last as a foundation for building arguments related to the other topics. So, for example, *Gaudium et Spes* grounds the dignity of the human person in the belief that "man" was created in the image of God. And this theme pervades Catholic teaching as a first principle.

Such an emphasis on social doctrine and accompanying social action put the U.S. Catholic Church in an increasingly tense position with respect to the American doctrine concerning separation of church and state. Along with other politically active religious groups across the spectrum, the NCCB began to face objections that it was attempting to use its religious-institutional authority to influence the secular discussion of arms control and other issues. In the early 1980s this same criticism was lodged against organizations as diverse as the conservative Moral Majority and the liberal National Council of Churches. These groups were seen by strict separationists as attempting to exert undue influence on American political life—a role for which they were organizationally and doctrinally unsuited. More often than not, of course, this argument was used selectively in attacking religious groups holding political positions different from those of particular critics: thus, liberals would frequently chastise conservative religious organizations for violating the boundary between church and state, while conservatives would voice the same opposition to the political activities of liberal religious groups—claims that were made widely and frequently during the 1980s. The rebuttals of all politically active religious organizations were essentially the same: they insisted on the right to speak as *citizens'* groups, commenting on the issues of the day.

This debate made indirect, corporate advocacy more attractive to the bishops, as similar challenges have made that rhetorical mode attractive to other corporate groups. A circular model of influence is entailed here: the organization addresses the voting public who will presumably influence public officials, leading to policies responsive to the influencing organization. By the early 1980s, and especially with the development of the peace pastoral, the NCCB adhered implicitly to this model of organizational persuasion. The bishops wanted to assert themselves in the nuclear debate but to avoid being labeled "political." Thus, the NCCB tried to speak with at least two distinct but interrelated voices: one for its Catholic audience, another for the public policy debate.

To be effective in the public policy debate the bishops had to make their message about peace *secularly* viable. That necessity in turn put the NCCB in a position where, if it acted toward the general public, it had to adapt to more than simply the doctrinal values of the Church. The Catholic principle—dignity of human life—met the rhetorical exigencies of the nuclear arms race of the 1980s. However, with this joining of religious principle and secular policy came a risk for the bishops—a risk that their arguments would become less like authoritative, religious ones and more like secular, humanistic ones. The bishops had to face the bind that the more social and the more political the Church became, the more secular became its rhetoric. This predicament faces all users of tradition-bound or doctrinaire rhetoric who must speak to pluralistic and secular audiences. Throughout U.S. history, beginning with Puritanism—and including such diverse movements as Progressivism and McCarthyism—arguments from doctrinaire groups have been coopted and adapted by pragmatists of the times.[14] In the first two decades of the twentieth century, for example, vocal and ardent progressivists found that their message was diluted through the practices of business and governmental leaders who employed the symbols but did not embrace all the goals of Progressivism. By the early 1980s the NCCB confronted the prospect that to have social-political influence they would need to mute or abandon their claims to authoritativeness. This prospect became very real as the bishops (at least many of them) began to view themselves not only as religious authorities but also as peace activists. Their rhetorical situation became analogous to that of populists who turn into advocates of expedience or business leaders who demand the regulation of free markets or governmental bail-outs.

CATHOLIC PEACE ACTIVISM

Against the backdrop of official Church teaching on the social order generally and on peace issues particularly, new kinds of Catholic political involvement developed in the United States, especially after the mid-1960s. Some observers trace outright pacifist doctrines back to the infancy of Christianity. The claim is made that pacifism was the norm for

Christians through the fourth century and that early church leaders condemned Christian participation in the Roman armies.[15] Modern Catholic social thinkers such as Dorothy Day, Thomas Merton, and James Douglass worked in the tradition of nonviolence. Day, who was characterized by *Time* as "the most significant, interesting, and influential person in the history of American Catholicism,"[16] espoused pacifism in the Catholic community during World War II. Through *The Catholic Worker* newspaper and otherwise she helped inspire many acts of nonviolent resistance in the 1960s. A Trappist monk, Merton began writing prolifically on issues of war and peace around 1960, holding a position he saw somewhere between the just war position and absolute pacifism.[17] Douglass, who was inspired by both Day and Merton, has written extensively on Christian nonviolent resistance and has participated in numerous public protests, including opposition to the Trident nuclear submarine in the early 1980s. Douglass's criticism of the Just War Theory was unequivocal: "The state of the just-war doctrine in contemporary Catholic thought is roughly equivalent to that of the prohibition against contraception: it had lost its cogency in terms of current theological thought and continues in use primarily as a point of reference for those who wish to go beyond it."[18] However, though these figures have been vocal and influential, they were until recently considered to be on the periphery of American Catholicism. In fact, their greatest influence was not felt doctrinally or institutionally but by individuals both inside and outside American Catholicism.

The tumultuous events of the 1960s and early '70s, especially the Vietnam War, aroused a great deal of questioning, both with respect to traditional Church teaching on war and peace and with regard to U.S. defense policies. As James Hennesey explains in *American Catholics,* "Participation in civil rights demonstrations primed some Catholics for direct action against unjust and oppressive structures in other areas of national life. . . . Growing American involvement in the Vietnam War fit the bill."[19] Demonstrations, draft-card burnings, and raids on Selective Service offices became familiar images on the television screens of the late 1960s. At the same time the names of Catholic activists such as Daniel and Philip Berrigan became public symbols; indeed, such figures became persuasive and provocative for wider, secular audiences. Although the U.S. hierarchy was divided on the issue of the war during much of this period, the consciences of many of them were deeply imprinted by it.[20] The peace activism of the Berrigans and others became in a sense a model for many of the bishops on how they could influence the nuclear arms debate; the bishops began to reach a wider audience through statements on, and in some cases direct protests against, U.S. defense policy.

More and more, questions about "authorization" for such statements were being discussed, and they affected the reception of political pronouncements by religious figures, Catholics and others. "For whom and by what authority do you speak?" became a viable line of questioning.

THE U.S. CATHOLIC BISHOPS ON PEACE

What changed in the years since the Vietnam War ended was that peace advocacy, and occasionally pacifism, were adopted by many members of the U.S. Catholic hierarchy. Positions critical of U.S. defense policies were simply not expressed by the bishops nor by most other religious leaders during most of our nation's history; Catholic leaders, like those of other mainstream religious groups, usually praised God and passed the ammunition. For a number of reasons the bond between nationalism and Catholicism was often seen as unbreakable.[21] From their late-coming vocal protest of the Vietnam War onward, however, the U.S. Catholic bishops, as religious spokesmen, showed a willingness to criticize and to identify themselves (individually, if not always collectively) with the peace movement. This trend culminated in the 1983 peace pastoral.

The Challenge of Peace was not the first attempt on the part of the U.S. bishops to address forcefully issues of war and peace. Previously, however, they had usually done so in support of national policy. In 1919, for example, just after the great war had ended, the U.S. hierarchy (then in the form of the National Catholic Welfare Council) issued a lengthy document commenting on the costs of the war and the just involvement of the United States. They wrote: "A great nation, conscious of power yet wholly given to peace and unskilled in the making of war, gathered its might and put forth its strength in behalf of freedom and right as the inalienable endowment of all mankind."[22]

In the latter half of this century spokespersons for the U.S. Catholic Church began to be critical of American foreign policy—first on theological and then on more secular grounds. The bishops issued a series of pastoral letters and other statements in the late 1960s and through the mid-1970s. These celebrated the virtues of peace and the right of individuals to refuse military service. In their collective statement "Peace and Vietnam" in 1966, the bishops expressed grave concern over the burgeoning conflict in Southeast Asia, and they urged Americans to consider simultaneously their patriotic duty and "the welfare of the whole human family."[23] In a follow-up statement the next year, "Resolution on Peace," the bishops responded to the gathering antiwar movement. Calling war protesters "responsible segments of our society," the bishops urged the government "to continue with even greater determination and action in the cause of negotiation."[24]

Next came the important pastoral letter by the U.S. hierarchy, *Human Life in Our Day*, in 1968. Addressing both "the Christian family" and "the family of nations," the bishops echoed Vatican II's call to evaluate war with an "entirely new attitude." *Human Life in Our Day* marked the first time that the American bishops addressed the issue of nuclear arms in any detail. While affirming the just war framework and the right of an individual nation to self-defense, the bishops also approved selective conscientious objection and questioned "whether the present policy of maintaining nuclear superiority is meaningful for security."[25]

In the seven years that followed, the bishops issued several statements on war and peace and other life-related issues. In their "Resolution on Southeast Asia" in 1971 the bishops demanded that Washington "bring the war to an end with no further delay."[26] In that same year the National Conference of Catholic Bishops declared that "in the light of the Gospel and from an analysis of the Church's teaching on conscience, it is clear that a Catholic can be a conscientious objector to war in general or to a particular war."[27] In 1974 the bishops took a more specifically political position and proclaimed their opposition to capital punishment, citing their "commitment to the value and dignity of human life."[28] In 1975 they advanced their "Pastoral Plan for Pro-Life Activities," focusing on "the pervasive threat to human life arising from the present situation of permissive abortion."[29] And in that year the bishops widened their scope of examination to include the "human dimensions" of economic life.[30] All of these statements evidenced the bishops' growing willingness to criticize popular American views, thus distancing the bishops from some elements of the "American identity."

1976 was an important year for the U.S. hierarchy for two reasons. First, they sponsored what became known as "Liberty and Justice for All," a program on Catholic social action designed to coincide with the nation's bicentennial celebration. This three-stage program was deliberately linked to Pope Paul VI's 1971 "A Call to Action" (*Octogesima Adveniens*), and it derived from a Detroit meeting in October 1976 where input from all levels of the U.S. Church was assembled, discussed, and synthesized. The primary significance of this program, which technically ended in 1983, was that it helped to institutionalize a liberal political agenda in the U.S.

Catholic Church. It helped to solidify what Joseph Varacalli calls "The New Catholic Knowledge Class," a mixture of Church leaders, intellectuals, and activists whom most observers would describe as leftward-leaning. The mid-term response to the program was not clear. The "Call to Action" was more of a secular call than had previously been issued, yet its full political potential was not realized. "In many respects, the Bishops responded to the Bicentennial Program in much the same way they responded to Vatican II. Both responses can be characterized as 'structured ambiguity.' Such an ambiguity allows the Church hierarchy to retain a privileged place in the overall Church schema while at the same time allowing for a controlled dispersion of authority" and a controlled process of change. In this way the hierarchy "attempts to keep an increasing number of disparate, at one time, peripheral, groups under one roof."[31] Ambiguity can be exploited in this way to manage an array of identities or interest groups. U.S. presidential campaigns provide vivid illustrations of how this can be done.

While the liberal cause was gaining energy, the bishops issued their pastoral letter *To Live in Christ Jesus* (1976). This statement is a lengthy comment on moral life, treating life first in the most abstract terms and then applying principles to the family, the nation, and "the community of nations." Beginning the last section by insisting that "our allegiance must extend beyond the family and the nation to the entire human family," the bishops isolated two goals for the community of nations: "the development of peoples and peace on earth." Noting the "savagery" of modern warfare in both its technology and its execution, the bishops "ask whether war as it is actually waged today can be morally justified." And in what today appears to be a prelude to their 1980s activism, the bishops declared:

> With respect to nuclear weapons, at least those with massive destructive capability, the first imperative is to prevent their use. As possessors of a vast nuclear arsenal, we must also be aware that not only is it wrong to attack civilian populations but it is also wrong to threaten to attack them as part of a strategy of deterrence. We urge the continued development and implementation of policies which seek to bring these weapons more securely under control, progressively reduce their presence in the world, and ultimately remove them entirely.[32]

With such a firm position the bishops tested the political waters of arms control to a greater depth than they had done previously. This statement prepared them to treat the arms race as one of their central concerns.

Following up on this statement, the bishops declared in 1978 that "the church must be a prophetic voice for peace."[33] Even more important was

John Cardinal Krol of Philadelphia in his 1979 testimony before the Senate Foreign Relations Committee in which he voiced the collective support of the bishops for the Salt II treaty. His statement made three interrelated judgments: first, that there is a moral imperative to prevent the use of nuclear weapons under any circumstances; second, that the strategy of deterrence cannot be justified in principle, but can be tolerated when it is used to advance toward arms limitations and reductions; and third, that the superpowers must move toward *real* disarmament. With respect to the second and most controversial imperative Krol explained: "The moral judgment of this statement is that not only the *use* of strategic weapons, but also the *declared intent* to use them involved in our deterrence policy is wrong." But he added, "As long as there is hope of [negotiations proceeding toward the meaningful and continuing reduction of nuclear stockpiles], Catholic moral teaching is willing, while negotiations proceed, to tolerate the possession of nuclear weapons for deterrence as the lesser of two evils."[34] In a sense Krol's judgments were not "morally" parallel. He claimed that the second judgment—toleration of deterrence—was a moral one, but the reason it was controversial was that the justification seemed to bend to expediency. In such instances the claim to moral authority becomes debatable, as is the case of a manager of a socially responsible investment firm who justifies some investments in *apartheid*-based South Africa as being in the long-term best interests of blacks.

Also in 1979 the NCCB issued a call for "political responsibility." This was intended to highlight the relationship of the Church to the political order and the duties of individual Catholics to participate fully and reflectively in the political process. Disavowing any intention to form a "religious voting bloc," the bishops called on all "to become informed, active, and responsible participants in the political process." Further, the Conference outlined its views on an array of issues, including abortion, arms control, the economy, Central American policy, and human rights. On the subject of arms control the NCCB cited both *To Live in Christ Jesus* and their 1978 statement, *The Gospel of Peace and the Danger of War*.[35] Their statement on political responsibility was later revised for the 1984 elections, and excerpts of it were widely disseminated in Catholic dioceses across the nation.[36]

Of course, when moral leaders pronounce on what is and is not "responsible," they open themselves to questions about where pragmatics enter into "responsibility." So, when the bishops pronounced on what is responsible in arms control and a number of other issues, they legitimated the question: "Who are you to decide the pragmatics as well as the morality of these affairs?" This was a serious challenge to the bishops' identity management. An analogous challenge faces an organization which attempts to move rhetorically from the level of morality or values or "mission" to the specifics of individual and collective choice.

At the same time that the bishops were urging and demonstrating greater political activism, they stressed the enlargement of the laity's role in the Church. This was particularly evident in their 1980 statement, "Called and Gifted: The American Catholic Laity." Designed to commemorate Vatican II's *Decree on the Apostolate of the Laity,* the statement by the American hierarchy emphasized shared responsibility and community. It described the Church as "a sign of God's kingdom in the world." And it explained that "the authenticity of that sign depends on all the people: laity, religious, deacons, priests, and bishops."[37] Coupled with their numerous prior and contemporaneous statements on the sociopolitical order, "Called and Gifted" gave further voice to the move toward dispersion of authority and responsibility in carrying out the Church's mission in the world. It marked yet another step along a path which eventually brought forth the remarkable document, *The Challenge of Peace,* and plunged the Church, as organization, into political conflict.

These developments posed (and continue to pose) problems that are rhetorical, organizational, and identity-related. As the bishops collectively moved toward positions more critical of U.S. foreign and defense policies, they simultaneously moved closer to the arguments being advanced by other religious groups and by secular critics. This shift granted the bishops a new kind of *ethos* or credibility as speakers in the wider peacemaking community and culminated in the bishops' acceptance of a leadership role during the nuclear freeze movement of the early 1980s. At the same time, however, the bishops risked a loss of institutional authority for their lay Catholic audiences because of the NCCB's adoption (and adaptation) of a corporate-advocate, interest-group role. In the process of developing a position of peace advocacy, the bishops began to appear more and more as just another political interest group, struggling to define itself and its positions vis-à-vis other interest groups, secular as well as religious.

This bind for the bishops was exacerbated by their particular rhetorical and organizational constraints. The structure and doctrines of the Roman Catholic Church limit bishops to collective pronouncements whose authority and force are largely *intra*organizational. The bishops speak with greatest authority to their faithful through individual or collective pastoral letters, particularly when they do so in concert with the pope.

Moreover, bishops cannot, in general, step outside of their hierarchical roles to speak as citizens on the socio-political issues of the day. This constraint was made explicit in the 1980s by Pope John Paul II in his attacks on prominent liberation theologians in Latin America and by his demands that the clergy and members of religious communities not be allowed to serve as elected or appointed public officials in the United States. The seriousness of this call was demonstrated when the Jesuit priest and Massachusetts congressman Robert Drinan reluctantly resigned his elected post in 1981.[38]

As would be the case for spokespersons in any highly structured and/or doctrinally based organization, the bishops were forced into risky rhetorical options. Their intraorganizational authority, their identity as Catholic spokespersons, and their identity and persuasiveness with external audiences were all placed at risk the more secular and political the bishops' pronouncements became. In developing and disseminating the peace pastoral, the bishops made their rhetorical problems more acute. They sought to speak as Catholic bishops to the widest Catholic audiences, but they simultaneously tried to reach other religious organizations, the Reagan Administration, and the general, non-Catholic public. Before each such audience their identity as "reliable" rhetors was different.

A similar rhetorical balancing act must be performed by other groups and organizations that speak with special authority. Centralized, highly structured bodies that hold to an explicit doctrine or a publicly known set of principles must simultaneously persuade insiders and outsiders in order to be influential. To persuade insiders requires reliance on arguments from principle, based on the commonly and traditionally held doctrine. To persuade outsiders requires use of more broadly held premises—say, freedom or justice or responsibility. To speak at once with two or more voices, with each in a different key, is challenging indeed. Yet this is precisely the challenge that faces many religious organizations, along with Communist parties, labor movements, social actions groups (of the right and the left), etc. The maintenance of internal cohesion and institutional authority necessitates perceivable adherence to doctrine and tradition; the engagement of the wider citizenry requires more embracing, more inclusive argumentative strategies. This dilemma is one reason that many doctrinally based organizations retreat from engagement, isolating themselves from the larger society and accepting the status of a sect or a cult. But to opt for direct engagement, as the NCCB did in the early 1980s, makes the organization conscious (even self-conscious) of a rhetorical dilemma that can only be managed, never resolved.

THE CHALLENGE OF PEACE: A SELECTIVE CHRONOLOGY

With the weight of Church teaching behind them and with their own growing momentum toward trying to influence public policy, the bishops needed only a catalyst to motivate their controversial peace letter. That came in the forms of increasing concern, even alarm, over the U.S. and Soviet defense build-ups, the breakdown in negotiations between the superpowers, and the explicitly confrontational posture assumed toward the Soviet Union in the first Reagan Administration. As former Governor of Ohio and Notre Dame law professor John J. Gilligan told me in an interview: "The signals being given off by the Reagan Administration made the nuclear question one of imminent danger, and the bishops recognized this."[39] Together with a variety of other groups and organizations the National Conference of Catholic Bishops became increasingly politicized by the perceived threat of nuclear war in the early 1980s. Bishops who urged nuclear arms control and reduction made speeches, offered congressional testimony, participated in rallies, established a peace center, gave counsel to employees of weapons producers, issued tax protests, and joined the largely pacifist organization Pax Christi USA.[40] Many observers linked the unprecedented political activity of the bishops during the first Reagan Administration with the nuclear arms freeze movement. As *Time* reported in a cover story in November 1982: "Many people both inside and outside the church are wondering how it is that bishops who only a few years ago praised the Lord and passed the ammunition are now backing what some see as a pacifist-tinged cause."[41]

When the nuclear freeze plan to halt the arms race was first published in April of 1980 by Randall Forsberg (a former editor for the Stockholm International Peace Institute and then a student of military policy at M.I.T.), it attracted little attention. It was after the November 1980 election, when voters in three state-senate districts of Massachusetts approved a freeze resolution, that the proposal began to draw substantial support. Further, most observers credit the shelving of the SALT II (Strategic Arms Limitation Talks) treaty in 1980 and the subsequent arms increases by the two superpowers for crystallizing electoral support for the freeze in many states.[42] The proposal also received the active support of Senators Edward Kennedy and Mark Hatfield, who in April 1982 published *Freeze!* a book dedicated to the advancement of the antinuclear movement.[43] In June 1982 a bilateral freeze proposal was affirmed by the House Foreign Affairs Committee in a nonbinding resolution. This action came on the heels of a massive antinuclear demonstration in New York, orchestrated to coincide with the United Nations Second Special Session on Disarmament. Estimates of attendance averaged around 700,000, making the event the single largest political demonstration in U.S. history.[44]

For the present inquiry it is particularly noteworthy that the freeze movement and larger antinuclear concerns were supported by a wide variety of groups, organizations, and institutions. Their concerns, however, were not exclusively moral concerns; nonetheless, the rather amorphous, loosely organized, antinuclear movement provided a chorus in which religious voices were exceedingly prominent.

Among these advocates appeared a number of large religious organizations, along with the secular ones mentioned previously. The powerful National Council of Churches, representing 40 million Protestants, openly endorsed a bilateral nuclear freeze in 1981. In the same year the 1.6 million–member American Baptist Churches announced that "the presence of nuclear weapons and the willingness to use them is a direct affront to our Christian beliefs and commitments."[45] The Lutheran Peace Fellowship issued in January 1982 a "statement committing members to tax resistance as a moral stand against the nuclear arms race." In March 1982 more than 125 Protestant, Catholic, and Jewish leaders voiced support for the Kennedy–Hatfield bilateral freeze proposal. In May 1982 an estimated 5,000 Catholic nuns, organized by the Leadership Conference of Women Religious, participated in an antinuclear march in Washington. And in the same year the liberal evangelical magazine *Sojourners* promoted its "New Abolitionist Covenant," a call for the immediate end to the arms race.[46] By spring 1983, when the final draft of the U.S. Catholic bishops' peace pastoral was issued, the religious groups voicing opposition to the nuclear arms race included the African Methodist Episcopal Church, American Baptist Churches in the U.S.A., American Jewish Congress, Christian Church (Disciples of Christ), Church of the Brethren, Church Women United, Episcopal Peace Fellowship, Evangelicals for Social Action, Lutheran Council in the U.S.A., National Conference of Catholic Bishops, National Council of Churches, Presbyterian Church in the U.S., Progressive National Baptist Convention, Reformed Church in America, Southern Baptist Convention, Union of American Hebrew Congregations, Unitarian-Universalist Association, United Church of Christ, United Methodist Church, and United Presbyterian Church in the U.S.A. In spring of 1983 eighteen national Christian and Jewish groups, in a collective statement released at the Capitol, denounced the Reagan Administration's defense build-up and charged that the 1984 budget "equates peace-keeping with firepower and thereby increases our insecurity as more and more destabilizing weapons systems are added to an already bloated arsenal".[47]

But, as sociologist James Wood noted at the time, "These views, while broadly representative of America's mainline denominations, are not shared by the New Religious Right, which soundly denounces such views as rooted in political liberalism and moral weakness." Moreover, the "virtually unqualified support" given by the New Religious Right for the military build-up reinforced incompatibility between that segment and mainline churches on how best to achieve peace.[48]

By the mid-1980s some of the enthusiasm (or at least the publicity) for antinuclear advocacy seemed to have subsided. There was talk of the freeze both "melting" and becoming "frozen."[49] And these descriptions suggested problems with the metaphor itself in that the notion of a *freeze* is hardly indicative of dramatic socio-political change. Rather, the term brings to mind such images as solidification of a position and the abrupt halt of movement that might occur when one is challenged by another person holding a handgun. These were not the most strategically or rhetorically appropriate images for a campaign to change substantially the status of relations between nations. Further, the Reagan Administration's arms control talk around election time 1984 and the plans for a Strategic Defense Initiative (or "Star Wars") antimissile defense system seemed to steal (perhaps quite intentionally) some of the antinuclear movement's thunder.[50]

Nevertheless, the U.S. Catholic bishops emerged in the early 1980s as a strong and sustained voice in the antinuclear chorus, and at times they even managed a solo. In reacting to the second draft of the peace pastoral by the NCCB in November 1982, a writer for the liberal *National Catholic Reporter* proclaimed:

> The U.S. bishops of the Roman Catholic Church are throwing down a gauntlet, to the current and future political powers, that any administration and any Congress that do not make nuclear disarmament a prime and continuing priority are about to contend with a new phenomenon on the U.S. political scene: a solid bloc of Catholic episcopal opposition rallying the Christian community to a political cause firmly based on Christian moral conviction.[51]

Of course, reactions to the peace pastoral were diverse, as is indicated by a comparison of the quotation above with the following commentary in the conservative Catholic weekly *The Wanderer:* "By a surprisingly lopsided vote of 238 to 9 the U.S. Catholic Bishops approved a Pastoral Letter on war and peace which appears to neuter the nation's moral right to use nuclear weapons to defend itself."[52] It is worth noting that this conservative Catholic response raised pragmatic, political considerations rather than moral ones, a response to which religious advocacy was inevitably vulnerable. The array of responses to the NCCB's advocacy is treated in chapters 4 and 5; for now I wish to consider some of the specific events leading directly to the vote on the final draft of the peace pastoral, 2–3 May 1983. This event was called by James Wood "the single most important development in the involvement of the churches in the nuclear arms race."[53]

The U.S. Catholic bishops benefited from an extraordinary coincidence of opportunities while the peace pastoral was being formulated. Among these were rising fears about nuclear war, the push for a nuclear freeze, proliferation of antinuclear organizations, and spreading uneasiness about Reagan's defense build-up. Moreover, the highly publicized second draft of *The Challenge of Peace* appeared in November 1982, when many states were voting on freeze referenda. At about the same time Yuri Andropov rose to assume the position of Soviet Communist Party chief following Leonid Brezhnev's death, and Reagan announced his support for the controversial MX missile.

I have pointed out elsewhere that the bishops' activity represented an *institutional challenge* by an organization traditionally supportive of the established order. The bishops were now acting as a "politically aware organization independently engaged in the application of moral principles to public policy."[54] But they could not avoid the fact that their challenge represented an assumption of secular as well as moral authority. Just how they came to assume such a position—and such an identity—can be seen from the historical narrative that follows.[55]

In August 1980, when the presidential campaigns of Jimmy Carter and Ronald Reagan were in full swing, then NCCB General Secretary Thomas Kelly sent letters to all bishops asking for new business (or *varia*) for their November annual meeting. In response, Auxiliary Bishop P. Francis Murphy of Baltimore called for a concise summary of the Church's teaching on war and peace and a strong educational effort. Between Kelly's acceptance of Murphy's *varium* and the mid-November meeting, Ronald Reagan was elected President of the United States, partly on a platform opposing SALT II and favoring "getting tough" with the Soviets. The significance of this election for national defense and world peace was very much on the minds of the bishops, according to Auxiliary Bishop of Detroit Thomas

Gumbleton (President of the Catholic peace organization Pax Christi, USA). "We were alerted," he said in an interview for this study.

By the time of their November meeting a number of bishops had caucused with Murphy about his upcoming presentation. Near the close of the meeting Murphy presented his statement, followed by two others on the same general subject. Murphy asked: "Do we need to speak more specifically about the nature and numbers of nuclear armaments, about the morality of their development and use, and especially about the morality of diverting massive human and material resources to their creation?"[56] The answer to this difficult, practical, and rhetorical question was a consensual "yes," both in the discussion at that meeting and in the months that followed. At the November 1980 meeting the then NCCB President, Archbishop John Quinn of San Francisco, chaired the discussion and allowed for expression of a variety of viewpoints. A sense of urgency seemed to rule. Said Bishop Gumbleton: "If we need any convincing of it, a very quick review of what has happened in our country in the past thirty-five years since we entered the atomic era will help us realize that there is an urgency today that means, in fact, that time is very short before the nuclear holocaust could indeed happen."[57]

Murphy's question reflected the rhetorical quandary facing the bishops as they began to address the issue of nuclear disarmament. In order to speak "specifically about the nature and numbers of nuclear armaments," the bishops would have to step out of the ring of churchly authority and into the secular circle of defense policy. This problem would have been similarly troublesome if the bishops were not the bishops but were, say, the American Bar Association. In the latter case the group would risk its own authority by stepping outside the realm of *legal* argumentation. Thus, Murphy's question highlights the rhetorical problem of any group when it speaks outside its recognized arena of expertise. For bishops that arena is moral theology, and they can step outside of it only with significant rhetorical risk.

In January of 1981 the new conference president, Archbishop John Roach of St. Paul–Minneapolis, announced the creation of an ad hoc committee on war and peace. It was to develop a statement for debate at the bishops' November 1982 annual meeting. Roach selected "perhaps the most respected member of the American hierarchy," Archbishop Joseph Bernardin of Cincinnati (later Cardinal and Archbishop of Chicago), to chair the committee.[58] As Archbishop Roach explained to me, "We needed a chairperson of some stature, and a man who had no clearly identifiable position on arms control. Bernardin, as a master of forging

consensus, fit the bill nicely." The other members of the ad hoc committee, selected for the exclusive purpose of drafting the war and peace
statement, were Gumbleton; Auxiliary Bishop John O'Connor (of the
Military Ordinariate, later Cardinal and Archbishop of New York);
Bishop Daniel Reilly of Norwich, Connecticut; and the Auxiliary Bishop
of Columbus, Ohio, George Fulcher (later bishop of Lafayette, Indiana).
Together Roach and Bernardin selected the other four members in an
effort "to strike a political balance," as Roach told me. As President of Pax
Christi, Gumbleton was well known as a pacifist. O'Connor, having years
of experience with the military, was viewed as a conservative on defense
matters. His 1981 book, *In Defense of Life,* for example, provided a
strong reaffirmation of the Just War Theory and argued that the Church
perhaps might be able to justify the use of " 'tactical' nuclear weapons or
other nuclear weapons if understood not as weapons of massive destruction."[59] With regard to the selection of the other two members, Cardinal
Bernardin explained to me that "the other two people I chose were not
identified with any particular constituency, but rather they were people
who held rather middle-of-the-road positions and knew what was going
on—not to suggest, of course that the others weren't middle-of-the-road."
Reinforcing the idea that the bishops, from the very outset of the process,
were conscious of multiple interest groups and loyalties, Bernardin added:
"I was very eager to see to it that all views were represented."

Importantly, Bernardin and Roach sought more of a political balance
than a theological one in selecting members for the ad hoc committee.
The diversity of the members chosen suggests that there was indeed no
clear *organizational* stand on the political matter of arms control. Further,
the commitment to achieving a political balance recognized that the
problem the bishops faced was in large part more political than moral-
theological. The manner in which the bishops organized their special
committee reflected the fact that they were altering the definition of the
problem they sought to address. They were tacitly granting that issues of
foreign policy involved considerations about which distinguished Catholics could differ. Even bishops were not expected to see these public issues
in exactly the same way. Here and elsewhere, then, there were tacit
admissions that some salient issues involved judgments not traditionally
nor doctrinally provided. Readjustment of episcopal and theological out-
looks was at issue, as subsequent events and statements showed.

The committee began its formal work in July of 1981, though there was
much informal talk between January and July. As explained in the appendix to the second draft of the letter (issued November 1982), the commit-

tee was charged "to take into consideration what the NCCB/USCC had done on the question of modern war, the arms race, conscientious objection and related issues, and . . . to use papal, conciliar, and other theological resources." Moreover, the stated aim was "to develop a new policy statement designed to respond particularly but not exclusively to the challenge of war and the need for a theology of peace in the nuclear age."[60] The committee drew extensively on the contributions of several others. Sister Juliana Casey, representing the Leadership Conference of Women Religious, and Fr. Richard Warner, representing the Conference of Major Superiors of Men, were two additional members of the drafting committee. The two staff members and the principal consultant were Fr. J. Bryan Hehir, USCC Associate Secretary for International Justice and Peace and frequent spokesman for the NCCB-USCC; Edward Doherty, a retired Foreign Service officer working in the USCC Office of International Justice and Peace; and Professor Bruce Russett, a Yale political scientist. These three were appointed for their specific expertise on defense and peace issues.

In his detailed descriptive account of the peace pastoral's development Jim Castelli describes much of 1981 as a period of "crescendo."[61] On 25 February Pope John Paul II made his now famous address at Peace Memorial Park in Hiroshima. Among other things he warned that "now . . . the whole planet has come under threat."[62]

In March, Pax Christi sent a letter to Bernardin asking that his committee study questions such as: "Is it right . . . for our country to possess nuclear weapons?" and "Is it realistic to expect that nuclear war can be fought on a limited basis?" The letter went on to suggest that "we must explore carefully the possibility of advocating unilateral initiatives as a way of breaking the current deadlock."[63] In effect Pax Christi echoed and intensified the primary rhetorical problem of the bishops. By asking "Is it right?" the interest group called on the bishops to make a *moral* judgment. But by asking "Is it realistic?" they challenged the bishops to speak in purely *pragmatic* terms. To do both things simultaneously would prove enormously difficult for the NCCB as part of a "universal" church.

One of the most dramatic gestures by an individual member of the American hierarchy came when Archbishop Raymond Hunthausen of Seattle sharply criticized the Trident submarine and any first-strike intentions on the part of the United States, urging unilateral disarmament as one way "to take up the cross." Inspired in part by Jesuit Richard McSorley's 1976 article, "It's a Sin to Build a Nuclear Weapon,"[64] Hunthausen in June 1981 asked members of his archdiocese to consider withholding half of their federal income taxes to protest the amount of revenue spent on nuclear arms. Then in January 1982 he became the first U.S. Catholic bishop publicly to resist paying federal income taxes because of Washington's defense policies. In his pastoral letter of January 1982 he explained the reasons for his actions: "I believe that as Christians imbued with the spirit of peacemaking expressed by the Lord in the Sermon on the Mount, we must find ways to make known our objections to the present concentration on further nuclear arms urging buildup." And he continued: "Accordingly, after much prayer, thought, and personal struggle, I have decided to withhold 50 percent of my income taxes as a means of protesting our nation's continuing involvement in the race for nuclear arms supremacy."[65] Hunthausen's protest was a sincerely moral response to a political situation. Clearly he did not expect his action to lead to a change in policy, or even to a significant change in attitude, in Washington or elsewhere. Thus, Hunthausen did not encounter (or at least did not accept) the same rhetorical entanglements as the NCCB as a whole, which to a degree sought to address the political and the pragmatic aspects of arms control in technical-political terms.

While dramatic, Hunthausen's action was not typical. Most bishops who spoke out did not go as far as to suggest unilateral disarmament; neither did they make overt personal protests such as withholding taxes. Nevertheless, many attracted attention within their own dioceses and beyond during 1981 and 1982. In August of 1981, for example, a bishop from the relatively small Catholic Diocese of Amarillo, Texas, Leroy Matthiesen, denounced the Reagan Administration's plan to deploy the neutron bomb, a weapon designed to kill living things but to leave buildings standing. Matthiesen's statement caused a furor locally because of the presence of a Pantex Corporation plant, a final assembly point for U.S. nuclear weapons, including the neutron bomb. Matthiesen implored: "Let us stop this madness. . . . We beg our administration to stop accelerating the arms race."[66] In an interview for this study Bishop Matthiesen commented on his political activity this way: "After the Reagan Administration gave its go-ahead on the neutron bomb, I urged defense workers in our diocese to reflect on their work. Not surprisingly, this statement was picked up by the *New York Times* and all three major [television] networks." As the controversy continued, the other twelve Catholic bishops of Texas issued a statement in September supporting Matthiesen. In this way, Matthiesen told me, "the Texas bishops made a general call to halt the arms race already in 1981." In sum, Matthiesen's moral statement led him into a political debate, but one which he defined chiefly in moral terms.

Also, on the thirty-sixth anniversary of the bombing of Hiroshima, Bishop Anthony Pilla of Cleveland issued a pastoral letter urging the Church to oppose modern war "as strongly as we oppose abortion, racism and poverty." Further, Pilla stressed that it was legitimate for the Church to criticize Washington and intervene in shaping public policy. He wrote: "Patriotism neither presupposes nor requires acquiescence to [our leaders'] every decision. Our nation's democratic traditions support, indeed are hinged upon, the right and responsibility of the governed to question and scrutinize the decisions of public officials."[67]

Overall, in 1981 more than forty U.S. Catholic bishops were "party to statements in one way or another soundly critical of U.S. nuclear policy."[68] These antinuclear voices brought criticism from a few Church leaders such as Terence Cardinal Cooke of New York. The Cardinal, as U.S. Military Vicar, argued in his own pastoral letter on 17 December 1982 that it is "legitimate to develop and maintain weapon systems to try and prevent war by 'deterring' another nation from attacking," and that "a strategy of nuclear deterrence is morally tolerable; not satisfactory, but tolerable." Throughout his letter Cooke spoke in similarly political terms.[69] This letter was given front-page coverage in the *New York Times,* as was another letter, dated 19 December, signed by more than one hundred priests and nuns, which attacked Cooke's position. Thus, it became clear that a great deal of discussion was needed if the bishops were to achieve unanimity within their own organization. Even more importantly, from the perspective of this study, bishops of both liberal and conservative persuasions revealed that they were ready to treat arms control in secular and pragmatic terms. In adopting this stance they complicated the rhetorical problems of managing their own organizational identity.

At the NCCB's November 1981 meeting Archbishop Bernardin presented an interim report on the progress of the drafting committee, and discussion followed. Significantly, one effect of the meeting was to broaden the concerns of the bishops to include non-nuclear weapons and linkages to the issues of poverty and abortion. Specifically, Bernardin argued to the bishops that "our experience with the moral turmoil provoked by Vietnam highlights the need for an assessment of non-nuclear uses of force."[70] And in his keynote address to the Conference Archbishop Roach insisted that "a consistent moral vision rooted in

Catholic social thought would link opposition to the arms race with opposition to abortion and support for the rights of the poor."[71] It was just a few months later that numerous articles began to appear in the Catholic press making similar connections among these issues. One lay Catholic group, for example, calling itself Prolifers for Survival, received some media attention. And the long-standing pacifist newspaper *The Catholic Worker* stepped up its criticism of the arms race for its indirect deprivation of the poor, linking both issues to "a basic denial of life."[72]

By linking a variety of life-related issues the bishops and their supporters could argue more broadly from a *moral* basis. After they took an embracing moral position, the movement from arms control to poverty to abortion became relatively simple. However, the bishops could not avoid the pragmatic and political aspects of each moral problem. They could not, for example, argue about arms control without being thrust against choices between unilateral disarmament and exclusive reliance on negotiation.

The ad hoc war and peace committee had been meeting since July 1981. Most of its hearings with witnesses (meetings which numbered fourteen) were held between then and July 1982. "The witnesses were selected to provide the committee with a spectrum of views and diverse forms of professional and pastoral experience."[73] These witnesses included two former secretaries of defense; several former and current arms negotiators; numerous theologians and ethicists; scriptural scholars; heads of Catholic peace organizations; conflict resolution specialists; a physician; retired military officers; and several officials of the Reagan Administration, among them Secretary of Defense Caspar Weinberger. Having in effect altered the problem to make it more moral-political than moral-theological, the bishops acknowledged the need to rely on outside expertise. They sought the input and assistance of those who did not argue from moral bases; the bishops simply could not avoid dealing with pragmatic, political *topoi* (i.e., widely understood bases for argument).

The first draft of the peace pastoral went out to the entire membership of the NCCB in June 1982 for their comments. It was not released to the general public at that time, although individual bishops were allowed to release parts or all of the document to others (such as moral theologians) for criticism as they saw fit. In July 1982 the committee met to consider the responses to the first draft and to revise the document in light of them. Because of the volume of responses (over 700 pages) the vote on the final draft, planned for the November meeting, was postponed. Instead, a second draft was prepared for general discussion, and a vote on the final draft was scheduled for May 1983. Referring to the entire process of the peace pastoral's development, Cardinal Bernardin estimated the time that the committee members spent together was the equivalent of sixty-nine days. And he reflected: "That's a long time; that's almost two and a half months!" Bishop Fulcher, a member of the drafting committee and later selected to head the follow-up program, stressed to me that most of the meetings of the committee were held as "opportunities for us to listen and learn." To support this description, Fulcher noted that "not one word [of the document] was written before March of 1982, and that was months after we had initiated the process of discussion."

The bishops achieved an amazing degree of solidarity as they formulated *The Challenge of Peace.* One reason for this was the unprecedented retreat held by the bishops at the religious center at Collegeville, Minnesota, 12–23 June 1982. This retreat was described as a chance for the bishops collectively to pray, reflect, and chat—all on a very informal basis. Most importantly, the meeting was designed for the bishops to explore and experience "collegiality."[74] As defined in one Catholic catechism, collegiality "functions to give internal cohesion within the hierarchy and, through it, to the faithful."[75] "Collegiality" became a salient symbol for the bishops as they discussed the designated themes for the meeting: *cohesiveness,* pertaining to the bishops in particular and to the Church in the United States; *identity,* concerning the Church's proper role in bringing Christ into secular affairs; *relevance,* relating the need to touch on issues of importance to lay Catholics and to communicate positions on such issues adequately; *continuity,* concerning linkages between and among various levels and groups within the Church; and *engagement,* asking the question "How best to carry all this out?"[76] The implications of these themes for the central concerns of this study are clear: the bishops were highly sensitive to the matters of identity, organization, and rhetoric.

"Renewed and refreshed" following their meeting, the bishops spoke of a "spirit of fraternity," a new feeling of "unity," movement toward a "more collegial body," and a new sense of the social "mission" of the Church.[77] In an interview Bishop Fulcher framed the Collegeville meeting for me in this way: "Many have said that the bishops will never be the same again as a result of the Collegeville experience." And Auxiliary Bishop of Milwaukee Richard J. Sklba told me that "the meeting was a major one in the way it broke down divisions among the bishops. It gave us the ability to speak more freely, even in disagreement with one another." In these words the bishops spoke of the *process* of identification.

Because of the way in which the Collegeville meeting engaged the bishops in active consideration of their roles together and individually,

Archbishop Thomas Kelly of Louisville said it "had an enormous impact on the development of the peace pastoral." At the conclusion of the meeting Bishop Maurice Dingman of Des Moines characterized the retreat's relevance to the pastoral thus:

> What we are doing is setting up attitudes. We will be more intense than ever on the war and peace document and on the greatest debate of our times—nuclear disarmament. We are learning how to dialogue at this meeting. We are learning how to share responsibility. We are learning how important it is to involve the total church, meaning all our people.[78]

All of the bishops I interviewed described this meeting in extraordinary terms; they saw the retreat as an event that gave them a true group or organizational identity, a sense of shared interests. Having defined more clearly "who they were," the bishops were more confident in addressing their multiple audiences on so difficult—and political—a question as nuclear arms control. By the end of the meeting in Collegeville, where the first draft of the peace pastoral was distributed but not formally discussed, the bishops had reached a "turning point." Bishop Matthiesen explained that they were ready to confront what they took to be the most relevant and pressing issue of the time. And they were ready to engage that issue in both religious and secular terms. In being prepared to deal in both secular and religious terms, the bishops had in effect formally changed their identities as bishops and to some extent the Church's identity as an entirely moral, doctrinal agency.

Just before the June retreat the ad hoc committee issued the first draft; in July they met again to consider the huge volume of responses. During this time literally hundreds of articles on the peace pastoral appeared in the secular and religious presses. Reactions were mixed; however, I see a common theme running through many of them. It was a view of the bishops as vacillating and being unnecessarily vague. Many of the reactions, particularly those from persons of moderate to liberal political leanings, are summarized by the title of an article by Fr. Richard McSorley, a peace activist: "First Draft Says 'Yo' to Nuclear Weapons." McSorley wrote: "They have gone ahead and done just what Bishop Michael Kenny of Juneau, Alaska, asked them not to do at last November's bishops' conference. He said, 'If we are going to say something in the name of God, let us say it clearly and without fear. After we have said it, let's not take it back in a later paragraph.'"[79] The focus of this criticism was the bishops' qualified "no" on use and seeming "yes" on possession of nuclear arms. In the first draft they wrote: "If nuclear weapons may be used at all, they may be used only after they have been used against our own country or our allies, and, even then, only in an extremely limited, discriminating manner against nuclear targets."[80] Equivocal passages such as this caused Sr. Casey, a representative to the drafting committee, to describe the draft to me as "weak." But she added, "It was a necessary first step; we had to begin with *some* position and then work to modify it and refine it."

Toward the more conservative end of the political spectrum reactions to the first draft (1) criticized the bishops for addressing defense policies, an area presumed to be outside their expertise, or (2) expressed grave concern about the more pacifist bishops and those inclined toward unilateral disarmament. In a widely cited interview Navy Secretary John Lehman (a Catholic layman) expressed the first of these criticisms baldly: "It's an abuse of [a bishop's] power to use his office, as Bishop, as spiritual leader, to interpret national defense policy—particularly when he doesn't take the time to learn what he's talking about."[81] Clearly, Lehman was questioning the *identities* of the Church as an institution and the bishops as spokespersons for the organization. He wanted to delimit the bishops' authority and rhetorical legitimacy by "pushing" them back toward their past, exclusively moral-theological domain. He and others also voiced alarm about the potential for influence within the NCCB by liberals such as Hunthausen, Matthiesen, and Bishop Walter Sullivan of Richmond, Virginia.[82] The grounds for these criticisms, again, concerned who the bishops were, as bishops, and the legitimacy of their identifying themselves as authoritative spokespersons on pragmatic issues of public affairs.

In the period before and after the first draft became public, some observers began expressing concern about the possibility of divisiveness in the Church. Michael Novak, resident scholar at the American Enterprise Institute and a Catholic layman, argued that the pastoral letter opened prospects for a twin schism within the U.S. Catholic Church—one between laity and hierarchy and the other between the Church and the secular society. With respect to these fears Novak wrote in a *Commentary* article of March 1982 that "insofar as they claim to speak not solely for themselves but for all Catholics, [the bishops'] political views need to be questioned and their appeals to 'faith' exposed for the wishfulness that they are." He went on to say that "insofar as they seek a role as citizens, [the bishops'] words carry no special moral or spiritual weight, but need to be tested against the plainly expressed will of the American people, who have chosen to preserve their institutions through deterring both nuclear war and totalitarian night."[83] Thus, Novak argued that the bishops represented neither the whole Church nor the whole of the

American people; he tried to deny the NCCB authority to speak with both moral and political authority as they addressed the issue of nuclear arms control. The two questions raised by Novak—"Do you speak for *all* of us?" and "Do you speak in your prescribed *organizational role* or not?"—are those which always face a formally organized group when it attempts to address outsiders.

Some commentators seized a special moral-theological theme: it was that the Church spoke with "prophetic" authority. Describing the bishops' discussions following the issue of the first draft as "prophetic," Jesuit Francis Winters seemed to welcome (albeit with a note of caution) the possibility of conflict within U.S. Catholicism. He posed the question: "Will there be division in the American Church after the promised letter later this year? Lamentably, one can only hope so. For in meeting their responsibility to help the people choose among the risks that encircle us, the bishops will spark choice, the irreducibly personal act that separates one from the crowd."[84]

These passages offer a representative and illustrative sampling of commentary and criticism on the first draft of the bishops' peace pastoral, issued in June of 1982. They show that months before the delayed final draft of *The Challenge of Peace* was published in May 1983, questions were surfacing about "who the bishops were" and "for whom they spoke" in their relationships to the other hierarchical levels of the Church, the U.S. government, and the larger society. These questions followed the bishops throughout the development of the peace pastoral, as former Indiana Catholic Conference President Raymond Rufo explained in an interview. He stressed that "identity became an issue for the bishops not just in terms of their own roles but also in terms of the roles of the laity and the Church as a whole." What the bishops were struggling to say about themselves necessarily suggested something about other hierarchical levels of the Roman Catholic Church. Awareness of this implication made the bishops' rhetorical and organizational "challenge of peace" enormously complex.

The fact that the bishops were beginning to take greater responsibility for the document as they moved to a second draft was indicated by the change in title from *God's Hope in a Time of Fear* to *The Challenge of Peace: God's Promise and Our Response*. The bishops moved toward a less equivocal stance. As Castelli noted, the tentative tone of the first draft can be explained in two ways. "First, much of it was written by Russett, who took pains to offer a 'centrist' position and not to unduly influence the committee. Second, the committee itself didn't want to be too far in front of the rest of the conference."[85] Clearly there were serious concerns about representation and representativeness. As Cardinal Bernardin explained to me, it was crucial that a consensus, "a true consensus," be allowed to evolve among the members of the committee and among the bishops as a whole. This is what gradually occurred through the progress from draft to draft, he added. Father Richard Warner, representative to the ad hoc committee, put it another way: "Through the drafting process, the peace pastoral came to be *owned* by the bishops." Through a thoroughly participatory decision-making process rather foreign to the Catholic hierarchy, the bishops tried to sustain their rhetorical authority as religious spokespersons by evolving a statement behind which they hoped the entire corporate body could stand. But if their emerging authority as concerned citizens were also to be taken seriously, their positions would have to be pragmatically plausible and feasible to those outside the flock.

The NCCB's meeting of 15–18 November 1982 contributed greatly to the bishops' sense of ownership of the letter, in part because of the tremendous publicity accorded it. In effect, the bishops identified with the letter as it became more strongly identified—by title and increasingly in the public mind—with them. In a very dramatic way the November meeting seemed to mark the bishops' full-scale entrance into the nuclear debate. Over three hundred reporters, including television and radio crews from West Germany and France, were present to observe and broadcast part of the six hours of deliberations devoted to the peace pastoral. The meeting and the subsequent release of the second draft made popular such phrases as "the bishops and the bomb." On the cover of *Time* (29 November) committee chair Bernardin was depicted in prayer between images of a missile and a dove of peace. Such images in popular coverage represented the bishops as both clerics and political advocates.

The second draft of the peace pastoral was both more specific and firmer than its predecessor. Having wrestled with the basic question, "Is there anything in our Catholic faith that rules out the use of nuclear weapons under any circumstances?" and concluded "no," the committee assumed an explicitly political position, opposing first-strike nuclear action. They expressed what Fr. Hehir called "profound skepticism" about the possibility of limited nuclear war, and they incorporated the Pope's observation that deterrence might be "morally acceptable" by specifying limited conditions under which that might be true.[86] Further, in making specific policy recommendations the bishops adopted language from the secular nuclear freeze resolution: "support for immediate, bilateral, verifiable agreements to halt the testing, production and deployment of new strategic systems."[87] It was probably for this reason that the bishops so quickly provoked public criticism from the Reagan Administration in the form of a letter from National Security Advisor William Clark published in the *New York Times*.[88] The bishops had identified themselves with the larger secular freeze movement.

The significance of the November 1982 issuance of the second draft of the peace pastoral is captured well by Castelli: "The American Catholic bishops as a body clearly emerged as the major moral critic of American—and, for that matter, Soviet—nuclear policy."[89] It is for this reason that Goldzwig and Cheney, in their analysis of the bishops as "corporate" advocates, treated November 1982 as a turning point for the NCCB.[90] With the benefit of a greater passage of time, I would like to nominate the same point as the *climax* in the development of the pastoral.

Much of what happened afterward was motivated by the dramatic and highly publicized events of November 1982. There seemed to be a sense among some bishops and other participants in the drama that the NCCB was committed to a new course. Bishop Dingman reacted to the November meeting this way: "We have gone from being a fortress church to a lighthouse church."[91] As John Tracy Ellis explained to me, this moment was "a sign that Catholics had arrived in the mainstream of American life." The writer of the *Time* cover story, Richard Ostling, observed that "[even] if the bishops cannot persuade skeptical Catholics to join their stand against nuclear arms, both the White House and the nuclear-freeze advocates believe they can become a potent force in shaping and influencing what is likely to become an increasingly important political issue in the months ahead."[92]

The bishops' practice illustrated several general problems of managing identities when speaking for corporate bodies. They chose to speak in multiple roles to multiple audiences. They sought to speak collectively yet individually: as a conference of bishops, as individual bishops, as an interest group, and as individual citizens. By justifying their positions with reference to moral-theological reasoning, they sought to sustain their special moral authority and thereby seem persuasive to the Catholic faithful. But of rhetorical necessity they had to resort to highly political and pragmatic arguments to justify their positions to such of the faithful as were represented by Novak, and to secular audiences such as the Reagan Administration, the American public, and the world. By following these strategies they risked violating the traditional American doctrine of separation of church and state and seeming to pronounce on political matters for which they lacked expertise. Their chosen positions required especially adept handling of multiple identities—adeptness almost impossible in a pluralistic society and yet demanded of political leaders.

Given these difficulties, it is not surprising that identity became a theme early in the bishops' own discussions and in press commentary. Their Collegeville retreat had led the bishops to address directly the question of who they were. They chose to portray themselves as spokespersons for a "lighthouse church." In so doing they sacrificed some of the rhetorical *ethos* or credibility associated with visions of the Church as a stable "fortress church." However, they wished to maintain religious authority for the faithful while simultaneously establishing some degree of secular *ethos*. Inevitably, however, by assuming the roles of secular advocates, they argued from premises from which their followers were unaccustomed to hear them argue, and just as inevitably they left themselves open to charges that they were overstepping the bounds of both their knowledge and their authority. The more the bishops began to sound like Physicians for Social Responsibility, a prominent secular freeze advocate, the more they were in danger of damaging their institutional authority. They might be granted the moral authority they and their institution claimed, but they had to *build* secular standing if their persuasion was to succeed beyond the confines of their own institution.

These identity problems persevered after release of the second draft of the peace pastoral in November 1982. The bishops had clearly entered the debates on foreign and, especially, defense policies. For this reason, in the months preceding release of the final document in May of 1983, there were important exchanges between the bishops and officials of the Reagan Administration, between the NCCB and Western European bishops, between the NCCB and the Vatican, between the bishops and numerous interest groups within the U.S. Church, and between the bishops and other U.S. religious communities.

The bishops' rhetorical difficulties were not, in principle, unique. Any element of any corporate body encounters comparable problems in managing rhetorical identities if it tries to modulate the customary corporate voice in theme or tone. Familiar questions arise: To what extent does the entity thereby subvert "corporate" tradition? To what extent does it speak with an institutional or with a dissident voice? Does it address and sustain the true constituency of the corporate body? A corporate agency is expected to speak as and with the personal and univocal voice our laws and mores assign to corporate bodies. If the multiple identities of the parent agency cannot be managed in a unifying way, then the emending voices and the agency itself become suspect, at least in the eyes of some. The bishops' ideational and rhetorical travails illustrate this general and complex principle of organizational communication.

NOTES

1. See, e.g., Oliver F. Williams, "The Making of a Pastoral Letter," in *Catholic Social Teaching and the United States Economy: Working Papers for a Bishops' Pastoral,* ed. John W. Houck and Oliver F. Williams (Washington: University Press of America, 1984), 4–5. A pastoral letter is an official communique from either an individual bishop or a conference of bishops to the faithful.

2. Joseph Gremillion, ed., *The Gospel of Peace and Justice: Catholic Social Teaching Since Pope John* (Maryknoll, NY: Orbis Books, 1976), 139.

3. Gremillion, *Gospel of Peace,* 68.

4. See, e.g., Felician A. Foy and Rose M. Avato, eds., *1985 Catholic Almanac* (Huntington, IN: Our Sunday Visitor, 1984), 308.

5. *Pacem in Terris,* rpt. in Gremillion, *Gospel of Peace,* 228.

6. *Gaudium et Spes,* rpt. in *The Documents of Vatican II,* ed. Walter M. Abbott, trans. Joseph Gallagher (New York: Guild Press, America Press, Association Press, 1966), 293.

7. *Documents of Vatican II,* 294.

8. Pope Paul VI, "Address to the General Assembly of the United Nations, October 4, 1965," excerpts rpt. in *Nuclear Disarmament: Key Statements of Popes, Bishops, Councils, and Churches,* ed. Robert Heyer (New York: Paulist Press, 1982), 23.

9. "Since Hiroshima, Popes Have Spoken Out on the Arms Race," *Our Sunday Visitor,* 29 Nov. 1981: 3.

10. In *Peace and Disarmament: Documents of the World Council of Churches and the Roman Catholic Church* (Vatican City: Pontifical Commission on Justice and Peace, 1982), 5–7.

11. *Populorum Progressio,* rpt. in Gremillion, 410, 403.

12. Both documents are rpt. in *Gospel of Peace,* 485–529.

13. Synod of Bishops' Second General Assembly, *Justice in the World,* rpt. in Gremillion, *Gospel of Peace,* 515.

14. Craig R. Smith, *Freedom of Expression and Partisan Politics* (Columbia: University of South Carolina, 1989).

15. Richard McSorley, *New Testament Basis of Peacemaking* (Washington: Georgetown Center for Peace Studies, 1979); Knut Willem Ruyter, "Pacificism and Military Service in the Early Church," *Cross Currents,* Spring 1982: 54–69.

16. "Street Saint," *Time,* 15 Dec. 1980: 74. See also Dorothy Day, *The Long Loneliness* (New York: Curtis, 1952).

17. See, e.g., Thomas Merton, "Nuclear War and Christian Responsibility," *Commonweal,* 9 Feb. 1962: 509.

18. James W. Douglass, *The Non-Violent Cross: A Theology of Revolution and Peace* (London: Macmillan, 1966), 155. See also Charles E. Curran, *American Catholic Social Ethics: Twentieth-Century Approaches* (Notre Dame, IN: University of Notre Dame Press, 1982).

19. James Hennesey, *American Catholics: A History of the Roman Catholic Community in the United States* (New York: Oxford University Press, 1981), 318.

20. See, e.g., Mary T. Hanna, *Catholics and American Politics* (Cambridge, MA: Harvard University Press, 1979).

21. Dorothy Dohen, *Nationalism and American Catholicism* (New York: Sheed and Ward, 1967).

22. "Lessons of War," rpt. in *In the Name of Peace: Collective Statements of the United States Catholic Bishops on War and Peace, 1919–1980* (Washington: NCCB–USCC, 1982), 3.

23. "Peace and Vietnam," rpt. in *In the Name of Peace,* 26.

24. "Resolution on Peace" rpt. in *In the Name of Peace,* 31.

25. *Human Life in Our Day* (Washington: USCC, 1968), 35.

26. "Resolution on Southeast Asia," rpt. in *In the Name of Peace,* 59–62.

27. "Declaration on Conscientious Objection and Selective Conscientious Objection," rpt. in *In the Name of Peace,* 56.

28. "Declaration on Opposition to Capital Punishment," *U.S. Bishops' Statements on Capital Punishment* (Washington: USCC, 1980), 1.

29. *Pastoral Plan for Pro-Life Activities* (Washington: USCC, 1975), 2.

30. *The Economy: Human Dimensions* (Washington: USCC, 1975).

31. Joseph A. Varacalli, *Toward the Establishment of Liberal Catholicism in America* (Lanham, MD.: University Press of America, 1983), xi, 73–74.

32. *To Live in Christ Jesus* (Washington: USCC, 1976), 30, 33, 34.

33. Administrative Board, USCC, *The Gospel of Peace and the Danger of War* (Washington: USCC, 1978), n.p.

34. John Cardinal Krol, "SALT II: A Statement of Support," in *In the Name of Peace,* 77.

35. Administrative Board, USCC, *Political Responsibility: Choices for the 1980's* (Washington: USCC, 1979), 3–15.

36. *Political Responsibility: Choices for the 1980s,* rev. ed. (Washington: USCC, 1984).

37. *Called and Gifted: The American Catholic Laity* (Washington: USCC, 1980), 7.

38. Drinan, however, continued to be outspoken on the arms control issue. See, e.g., Robert F. Drinan, "1983 Target Turning Point for Arms Race," *National Catholic Reporter,* 26 Nov. 1982: 15.

39. For information about this and other interviews see Appendix A. In the remainder of this book interviews are not footnoted; the reader is asked to consult Appendix A for the record of interviews and Appendix B for the composite schedule of interview questions.

40. See, e.g., "Archbishop Calls for Arms Freeze," *National Catholic Reporter,* 11 June 1982: 24; "Converting to Peace," *Sojourners,* Jan. 1982: 10–14; "War Warnings," *National Catholic Register,* 29 Aug. 1982: 2; Tom Roberts, "Cardinal Krol Turns Diocesan Machinery against Arms Race," *National Catholic Reporter,* 2 Apr. 1982: 1; Rita Jensen, "Center Created to Wage Peace," *National Catholic Reporter,* 12 Feb. 1982: 3; Terri Goodman, "Pantex Worker Quits," *National Catholic Reporter,* 21 May 1982: 2; "The Bishops as Peacemakers," editorial, *Commonweal,* 18 Dec. 1981: 707–08; E. Michael Jones, "Archbishop Hunthausen Will Withhold Taxes," *The Wanderer,* 11 Feb. 1982; 1, 6.

41. Richard N. Ostling, "Bishops and the Bomb," *Time,* 29 Nov. 1982: 70.

42. James Kelly, "Thinking about the Unthinkable: Rising Fears about the Dangers of Nuclear War," *Time,* 29 Mar. 1982: 10–14.
See also Jonathan Schell, *The Fate of the Earth* (New York: Avon, 1982), an impassioned warning about the possibility of nuclear war which was influential for the bishops.

43. Edward M. Kennedy and Mark O. Hatfield, *Freeze! How You Can Help Prevent Nuclear War* (New York: Bantam Books, 1982).

44. Fox Butterfield, "Anatomy of the Nuclear Protest," *New York Times Magazine,* 11 July 1982: 17.

45. As quoted in Kelly, "Thinking about the Unthinkable," 13–14.

46. "Lutherans to Resist Taxes," *National Catholic Reporter,* 22 Jan. 1982: 8; "Nuke Freeze Plan Wins Support," *National Catholic Reporter,* 26 Mar. 1982: 2; Tom Choman, "Pentecost Peace March Draws 5,000 Nuns," *National Catholic Reporter,* 11 June 1982: 3; "The New Abolitionist Covenant," *Sojourners,* Aug. 1981: 18–19.

47. James E. Wood, Jr., "The Nuclear Arms Race and the Churches," *Journal of Church and State* 25 (Spring 1983): 226–27.

48. Wood, "Nuclear Arms Race," 227.

49. See, e.g., James Wallace, "Nuclear Freeze Crusade: Gaining or Waning?" *U.S. News and World Report,* 25 Apr. 1983: 18–21; Robert J. McClory, "Peace Pastoral Headed for Graveyard?" *National Catholic Reporter,* 28 Dec. 1984: 1, 15.

50. See, e.g., *Time,* election special edition, 19 Nov. 1984.

51. Arthur Jones, "Bishops Issue a Second Draft," *National Catholic Reporter,* 29 Oct. 1982: 20. Jones's words suggest the complexity of holding to a *political* position that is associated with a *moral* stance.

52. Paul A. Fisher, "Bishops Hot for a Freeze," *The Wanderer,* 12 May 1983: 1.

53. Wood, "Nuclear Arms Race," 227.

54. Steve Goldzwig and George Cheney, "The U.S. Catholic Bishops on Nu-

clear Arms: Corporate Advocacy, Role Redefinition, and Rhetorical Adaptation," *Central States Speech Journal* 35 (1984): 11, emphasis deleted.

55. Much of this account is drawn from Jim Castelli, *The Bishops and the Bomb: Waging Peace in a Nuclear Age* (Garden City, NY: Doubleday, 1983). Several of the bishops interviewed identified this book as the most thorough published history of the process of the letter's development available at that time.

56. Murphy, as quoted in Castelli, *Bishops and the Bomb*, 15.

57. Gumbleton, as quoted in Castelli, *Bishops and the Bomb*, 17–18.

58. Castelli, *Bishops and the Bomb*, 19.

59. John J. O'Connor, *In Defense of Life* (Boston: St. Paul Editions, 1981), 98.

60. *The Challenge of Peace: God's Promise and Our Response*, 2nd draft, rpt. in *National Catholic Reporter*, 5 Nov. 1982, Appendix, 19 (hereafter cited as "Second Draft").

61. Castelli, *Bishops and the Bomb*, 26–39.

62. As quoted in Castelli, *Bishops and the Bomb*, 26.

63. As quoted in Castelli, *Bishops and the Bomb*, 26.

64. Richard T. McSorley, "It's a Sin to Build a Nuclear Weapon," *U.S. Catholic*, Oct. 1976: 12–13.

65. Raymond Hunthausen, "Obligation of Conscience," rpt. in *Sojourners*, Mar. 1982: 7.

66. As quoted in Castelli, *Bishops and the Bomb*, 28.

67. As quoted in Castelli, *Bishops and the Bomb*, 31–32.

68. "The Bishops as Peacemakers," editorial, *Commonweal*, 18 Dec. 1981: 707–08.

69. Terence Cardinal Cooke, as quoted in Richard Cowden, "Cooke Statement Sparks Protest," *National Catholic Register*, 10 Jan. 1982: 1.

70. As quoted in Castelli, *Bishops and the Bomb*, 42.

71. As quoted in Castelli, *Bishops and the Bomb*, 41.

72. See, e.g., Charles A. Wood, "Loesch Seeks Prolife, Anti-Nuke Alliance," *National Catholic Register*, 25 Apr. 1982: 1, 10; Peggy Scherer, "Poverty and the Arms Race," *The Catholic Worker*, June–July 1982: 1, 2, 4.

73. "Second Draft," Appendix, 19.

74. Edward K. Braxton, "American Bishops Meet: A Theological Agenda," *America*, 22 May 1982: 393.

75. John A. Hardon, *The Catholic Catechism* (Garden City, NY: Doubleday, 1975), 223.

76. These themes were read to me by Bishop Fulcher from an unpublished internal survey of the bishops (interview of 21 July 1983).

77. David K. Byers, "The American Bishops at Collegeville," *America*, 28 Aug. 1982: 87–90; Willmar Thorkelson, "U.S. Hierarchy in First-Ever Session,

Hobnob, Examine Roles in Church, Nation," *National Catholic Reporter*, 2 July 1982: 24.

78. As quoted in Thorkelson, "U.S. Hierarchy," 24. Curiously, however, the implications of the concept of collegiality for real *dis*agreement within the Church were not addressed in the reports of the retreat.

79. Richard McSorley, "First Draft Says 'Yo' to Nuclear Weapons," *National Catholic Reporter*, 27 Aug. 1982: 17.

80. *The Challenge of Peace*, 1st draft, reprinted in *National Catholic Reporter*, 2 July 1982: 12.

81. Paul A. Fisher, "Interview with Secretary of the Navy John Lehman," *The Wanderer*, 7 June 1982: 5.

82. See, e.g., Fisher, "Church Cause for Concern in Anti-Nuke Campaign," *The Wanderer*, 20 May 1982: 5; Terry Hall, "Nuclear Deterrence," *National Catholic Register*, 4 July 1982: 4.

83. Michael Novak, "Arms and the Church," *Commentary*, Mar. 1982: 40.

84. Francis X. Winters, "Catholic Debate and Division on Deterrence," *America*, 18 Sept. 1982: 129.

85. Castelli, *Bishops and the Bomb*, 99.

86. Castelli, *Bishops and the Bomb*, 99–107.

87. "Second Draft," 15.

88. "Text of Administration's Letter to U.S. Catholic Bishops on Nuclear Policies," *New York Times*, 17 Nov. 1982: 11.

89. Castelli, *Bishops and the Bomb,* 106–07.

90. Goldzwig and Cheney, "U.S. Catholic Bishops on Nuclear Arms," 14.

91. As quoted in Richard H. Ostling, "Bishops and the Bomb," 71.

92. Ostling, "Bishops and the Bomb," 77.

4

MANAGING IDENTITIES WHILE ADDRESSING ISSUES

I see that the bishops are caught because they've got three hats on. They're trying to deal with the [nuclear arms control] issue as theologians, as pastors and as public figures.

Sr. Mary Evelyn Jegen, National Coordinator of Pax Christi USA, as quoted in Richard N. Ostling, "Bishops and the Bomb," *Time,* November 1982

As the process developed it became clear that the Committee on War and Peace was trying to steer a course between what might be called a "prophetic" approach and an "accommodationist" approach. Bishops and others who adopt the "prophetic" approach were inclined to move directly from biblical injunctions against use of the sword to either pacifism or at least a kind of nuclear pacifism that allowed for no compromises in matters of policy. The "accommodationist" approach was inclined to limit episcopal teaching to general statements about the work for peace and to leave to the political or military experts judgments about details in weapons policy. The former approach placed emphasis on the universal family of humanity while the latter emphasized the moral prudence of western democracy over Soviet Communism. The committee and ultimately the pastoral diligently tried to avoid the fundamentalism of the former and the chauvinism of the latter.

Philip J. Murnion, Introduction, *Catholics and Nuclear War: A Commentary on* The Challenge of Peace, *the U.S. Catholic Bishops' Pastoral Letter on War and Peace*

The whole process surrounding the [peace] pastoral represents a revolution of positive ambiguity. . . . While the pastoral has been rightly called "prophetic," it's still amazing how mainstream its policy recommendations are; they would appear far more moderate in a different political climate.

Jim Castelli, *The Bishops and the Bomb:*
Waging Peace in a Nuclear Age

THE LEVELS OF MANAGEMENT

The quotations above suggest the range of identities that spokespersons for corporate bodies must shape. The bishops struggled with complex issues at the intersection of religion and politics. They did not have a specific political identity on which they could draw. In comparable cases corporate spokespersons struggle with issues at the intersections of commercial marketing and democratic politics, of educational goals and fiscal management, of public relations and "truth in advertising," of profitability and social responsibility. Like the bishops, spokespersons for corporate groups try to be publicly influential, but they must do so while responding to the many diverse voices that claim to share in such judgments.

To analyze what the bishops did in these circumstances, I shall, in this and the following chapter, explore their management of multiple identities under the broad headings listed below. In this chapter I shall address these four questions:

1. *How did the bishops "manage" the relationship of the Roman Catholic Church to the world?* In their deliberations and in their document the NCCB had to balance the spiritual and earthly concerns of the Church.
2. *How did the bishops manage the relationship of the United States to the world?* For the bishops, as for the Roman Catholic Church as a whole, the United States represented just one part of their larger audience, the world.
3. *How did the bishops manage the relationship of the Roman Catholic Church to the United States?* The U.S. context is one of many national contexts for a "universal" Church, a transnational organization.
4. *How did the bishops manage the relationship of themselves (that is, the NCCB) to the universal Catholic Church?* The bishops struggled with their own identity as a national conference, the NCCB.

Three additional issues to be managed by the bishops concerned problems that required them to create or redefine constructs and terms in ways that would conserve traditional teachings of the Church but at the same time introduce degrees of reconceptualization that would be consistent with their "political" objectives for the Church and the society at large. The questions that forced these rhetorical moves were:

5. *How did the bishops manage the relationship of the individual Catholic, especially the layperson, to the Church as a whole and specifically to the hierarchy?* The bishops were conscious of what they were saying, explicitly and implicitly, about the role of individual Church members.
6. *How did the bishops manage the relationship of peace/nuclear arms control/defense issues to other issues of Church concern?* The NCCB sought to relate their stance on nuclear arms to their positions on other life-related matters.
7. *How did the bishops manage the interrelationships of various interests and interest groups, particularly inside the Church?* The bishops invited dialogue and debate with an amazing array of groups from across the political spectrum.

These last three issues shall be developed in chapter 5.

Each of the questions above identifies a problem of identity, organization, and associated rhetoric likely to arise in corporate rhetoric. Altered to suit specific cases, each is pertinent to understanding any corporate rhetoric. There are often problems of relating institutional voices to the world, to larger and affiliated agencies and institutions, to the hierarchy of command or control within the institution, to interest groups within the institution, to external special interests, to external public policies, and to the individuals who comprise the institution for which the "voice" presumably speaks. Some or all of these identities or roles are always at issue when organizations attempt to speak with corporate and authoritative voices. The case of the bishops is an instance in which the "corporate voice" attempted to speak as a spiritual, universal agency and also as a national and political agency.

THE CATHOLIC CHURCH AND THE WORLD: WHAT KIND OF RELATIONSHIP?

The query, How did the bishops manage the relationship of the Roman Catholic Church to the world? is a useful place to start, because it engaged the bishops with the fundamental issue of the Catholic Church's (or any transnational group's) role in the world order. Of course, this question was particularly relevant to Catholicism; "Catholic," after all, is derived from the Latin *catholicus* or *universalis,* "referring to or directed toward the whole, general."[1] In addition, as Peter Nichols notes, "It would be difficult, I think impossible, to find another 18 percent of the world's population with the same sort of strong loyalty in common and with equal influence."[2] Thus, the way in which the Church's "place" in the world is expressed—by Catholics and non-Catholics, but especially by the hierarchy—is essential to understanding what the world's largest religious organization (and the world's oldest formal organization) was, is, and will be.

The Church's understanding of itself includes a basic element which transcends the world, as is the case with most religious groups. Religion and religious organizations exploit the full power and "magic" of language by using ultimate, transcendent terms that point to what is beyond the natural world.[3] Avery Dulles explains, for example, that the most ancient model of the Church was a mystical-organic one which saw the members as parts of the body of Christ, with Christ as the head.[4] Says Dulles:

> The term "Church" may be understood either as organization or as community. In the former sense, it is an institution distinct from other "worldly" institutions; it is a sacramental sign and agent of that saving unity of mankind which God intends to establish in Christ. In the second aspect, the Church is that portion of mankind which is visibly gathered in the Body of Christ and which lives by his spirit. It stands where God wills the whole world to stand.[5]

The last sentence of this passage brings us directly to the relationship of the Church and/in/of the world. I use "and/in/of" deliberately because it grants terminological recognition to the blurred line between the Church and the world with which it is only partly equated. In its argument for universality the Church presents itself with a tough rhetorical problem: how to be both of this world and beyond it.

It is probably correct to say that the Second Vatican Council centered on the idea of what it means to be Church, the Church's theological and organizational identity. "Both John and Paul stated that the first purpose of Vatican II was the examination of the intimate nature of the Church, *her awareness of herself.* This resulted in *Lumen Gentium* (Dogmatic Constitution on the Church) and in *Gaudium et Spes* (Pastoral Constitution on the Church in the Modern World)."[6] *Lumen Gentium* (meaning literally "the light of all nations") reinforced the mystery of the Church ("which cannot be fully captured by human thought or language") while striking biblical and democratic chords in calling "all men . . . to belong to the new People of God." The document began with a notion of Church as people to whom God communicates his love, and it treated authority in terms of service rather than domination. This was in marked contrast to the tendency of Vatican I (1870) to stress hierarchy and structure, the government of the Church.[7]

The Pastoral Constitution on the Church in the Modern World (*Gaudium et Spes*) is largely a synthesis of Catholic teaching on social issues from the late nineteenth century through Paul VI, though there are "significant new emphases and occasional advances in thought or attitude."[8] The document treats at length the Church's role in the contemporary world, stressing the *service* or *servant* nature of the Church with respect to mankind. Importantly, the Constitution aims "to speak to all men in order to shed light on the mystery of man and to cooperate in finding the solution to the outstanding problems of our time." And the opening line of the document proclaims: "The joys and hopes, the griefs and the anxieties of men of this age, especially those who are poor or in any way afflicted, these too are the joys and hopes, the griefs and anxieties of the followers of Christ." A few paragraphs later the Constitution reads: "To carry out such a task, the Church has always had the duty of scrutinizing the signs of the times and of interpreting the light of the gospel."[9]

In this way, before it proceeds to the analysis of specific social issues, *Gaudium et Spes* clearly identifies the Church with the world and lays the rhetorical groundwork for an emphasis on social action. Such groundwork is important for any doctrinally based organization. The Pastoral Constitution constitutes a rhetorical touchstone, like any charter or constitution, from which the members of an organization can (in fact, must) be seen to argue consistently, even while effecting change. As a "constitution," *Gaudium et Spes* tells us something important about how the Church as organization is constituted.[10]

However, while acknowledging the "close links between earthly affairs and those aspects of man's condition which transcend this world," the Council insisted that "the role and competence of the Church being what it is, she must in no way be confused with the political community, nor bound to any political system."[11] These two positions, while not incompatible, are difficult to hold simultaneously. How to be *of* the world, *in* the world, and yet something *added to* the world all at the same time is a key difficulty for the Church, one that has to be "managed" through the transcendental power of language. The problem was confronted rather directly by the U.S. Catholic bishops in drafting their peace pastoral.

Significantly, *The Challenge of Peace* opens with a quotation from the Pastoral Constitution, and it makes generous references to that constitutional statement in the pages following. The bishops used *Gaudium et Spes* in three separate ways: (1) to support a view that the Church should address "the most urgent issues of the day," (2) to explain their allowances for disagreement among the faithful on matters of specific moral application ("prudential judgments"), and (3) to justify dismissal of nuclear war as "far exceeding the bounds of legitimate defense."[12] The first point is the most relevant here.

Cardinal Bernardin explained in a personal interview that "*Gaudium et Spes* is kind of a model for the peace pastoral; it is a justification for our getting into the whole question of arms control." The grounding for the bishops' involvement, Bernardin continued, was the Pastoral Constitution's determination "that the Church cannot be separate from the world because it is incarnated in the world." Once again the premise of consistency with and reliance on tradition was reinforced.

Similar points have been made by Fr. J. Bryan Hehir, of the USCC's Office of International Justice and Peace and a staff member of the ad hoc committee who wrote much of the second draft. In a published essay Hehir was very specific in advancing his case for the linkage of the two documents. There he stated clearly that "the distinctive contribution of the conciliar text [*Gaudium et Spes*] is that it provides a theological rationale for the entire social ministry of the Church."[13] Moreover, explained Hehir, the linkage between "the moral vision of Catholic social teaching and its ecclesiological significance" is made in two steps. First, the Church is seen as being at once "a sign and a safeguard of the transcendence of the human person."[14] Second, "the deeper issue [is] how the Church influences the social order without itself becoming politicized." The Church both transcends and "compenetrates" the world. In "dialogue with the world" the Church must learn and teach, all the while engaging the political order in an *indirect* manner.[15]

These claims bring to mind the idea of corporate advocacy because the Church is seen as exerting its socio-political influence by defending human dignity and promoting human rights, but without becoming too closely identified with any particular governments, parties, or movements.[16] Thus, the bishops, like many other religious and non-religious interest groups, tried to *be* political without being labeled as such. An attendant issue was how best to preserve the Church's spiritual identity while making a contribution to social change in the world. The balance here is a precarious one to maintain both conceptually and linguistically.

The problem was recognized by Hehir: "To choose to speak to *both* the Church and the world is to lose some of the 'prophetic edge' of the scriptures. To attempt to shape public policy leads inevitably to consensus positions which are not a clear witness against the evil threatened by nuclear war."[17] Such trade-offs are, of course, inevitable, and they have a direct bearing on the question of identity, or how one's institution is represented. A parallel problem is faced by other mainstream Christian denominations which have sought to be increasingly influential in public policy. Their spiritual, transcendent identity becomes threatened in the process of their direct engagement with politics.

Hehir used the term "identity" in his discussion and astutely explained it in terms of dialogues—between church and state, between religion and science, between church and academia, and within the Catholic community. He said: "The questions of identity arise from the dialogue to which the church is called by Vatican II. As the pastoral letter was being prepared and the successive drafts were published for public scrutiny, [the] four different forms of dialogue became evident."[18]

I found indirect support for Hehir's analyses in the thoughts of some of the other persons whom I interviewed. Father Theodore Hesburgh, then President of the University of Notre Dame, explained that the peace pastoral "very deliberately echoes *Gaudium et Spes* so that it can tackle a question which touches all disciplines and all humanity. . . . And the pastoral makes necessary applications to public policy, seeing these as a calling of the Church." Along the same lines Fr. Richard Warner, a representative to the ad hoc peace committee, saw the pastoral as symbolizing "the engagement of the Church in social issues and concerns in a very public way" and thereby fulfilling part of the plan of *Gaudium et Spes*. Finally, the pivotal Collegeville retreat of June 1982, as explained to me by John Cardinal Krol, "took as a basis the Vatican documents, particularly the Pastoral Constitution." This orientation was adopted at Krol's suggestion, and it led the bishops to consider directly their "role within the Church and beyond the Church."

Diverse parties with varying roles in the peace pastoral's development saw adherence to precedent as critically important. And the constraints of tradition are powerful indeed for an organization in which history, doctrine, and institutionalized authority are so central.[19] In fact, any hierarchical organization must take comparable pains to show that it is being true to its mission when it attempts something new, or else the authority of the change agents can be undermined or destroyed.

"Managing" the relationship of the Church to the modern world posed an interesting challenge for the bishops in their effort to treat the Church as something distinct from, yet having a place and a presence in, the world. Rather than treating the Church as "either or," they treated it as "both and." In taking a position that was "constitutional," the bishops aligned themselves with recent and official Church teaching. At the same time, however, they sought to adopt a specific stand on how the Church relates to the world *in their view*. This rhetorical strategy enabled the bishops to be both traditional and groundbreaking—both priestly and prophetic—but it opened them to charges of being too political. The bishops' increased political awareness and their public advocacy put them on a course of more organized "engagement" (one of the Collegeville retreat themes) and contributed to a new or at least a more focused way of representing the Church's social mission. From the bishops' perspective the Church was "a people on the march toward the realization of the Kingdom of God . . . but [who] share for good or ill in everyday human problems."[20] For the NCCB, as for a leadership group in any other hierarchical organization, the practical test of authority (and, for that matter, identity) resides in the level of confidence members have in their leaders. The bishops' authoritative standing would rise or fall depending on whether U.S. Catholics found the NCCB's extensions into social action pragmatically wise or unwise.

THE UNITED STATES AND THE WORLD: A BIG "WE," OR "US" AND "THEM"?

In a 1981 article boldly titled "Steps toward a New Planetary Identity," political scientist Louis Beres offered his suggestions "on how to eliminate the threat of nuclear war." Beres offered three suggestions for reversing the slide toward nuclear devastation: (1) "General publics throughout the world must experience an aroused consciousness of the threat"; (2) "a far-reaching and feasible agenda for world order reform must be created"; and (3) "we require the implementation of promising plans for world order reform."[21] These proposals touch a common ground of realism. That is, division in the world tends to breed hostility, and hostility makes warfare almost inevitable. Only through perceiving and acting on common interests—by promoting broader identifications—are divisions transcended.

The bishops seemed well aware of the dimensions of this problem as they considered the relationship of the United States to the world. From the outset they were responsive to their "special responsibility" as bishops of one of the two nuclear superpowers. Bishop James Malone of Youngstown, Ohio (Vice-President of the NCCB during the peace pastoral's development and later President), told me in an interview, "We were convened as Catholic bishops addressing a question that related to our country as the first possessor of nuclear power and the first user of it. And we were aware of the international tension between the U.S.A. and the U.S.S.R. We were also aware of the military build-up of the Reagan Administration." His words indicate a consciousness of the global nature of the problem, while recognizing the unique positions of both the United States and the Soviet Union within the global context.

Analyzing the problem on an abstract level, the bishops reached an easy consensus that world peace was their goal. Archbishop John O'Connor (now of New York) explained to me how the drafting committee members stood on this principle: "We started with a basic principle. All five of us kept asking, 'How can we help move the whole world closer to peace?' Or, 'If the world has to have war, how can we reduce the horrors?' This was our passion." And O'Connor added emphatically: "There wasn't a moment at which any one bishop questioned another's commitment to this principle." Discussion at this abstract level, of course, would probably produce agreement within almost any group we might assemble.

As the bishops moved from world peace to more specific concerns, disagreement inevitably arose. Thus, while the peoples of the United States and the Soviet Union are often seen as sharing a common humanity and a common interest in avoiding nuclear war, these same peoples had been consistently portrayed as being divergent or alienated in nearly every other respect. Former U.S. ambassador to the Soviet Union George Kennan outlined clearly two major areas of this divergence.

> The old factor was what might be called the substructure of tensions, misunderstandings, irritations, and minor conflicts flowing from the great disparity between the two political systems, not only in ideology but, even more important, in traditions, habits, customs, and methodology. . . . It must be regarded as a permanent burden on the relationship, probably never to be wholly overcome, certainly not to be importantly mitigated in any short space of time.
>
> The new factor was the military and geopolitical situation arising from the circumstances of the war and its aftermath: a situation destined, as it turned out, to overshadow all other aspects of the relationship in intensity, in endurance, and in gravity—gravity for the two countries and for the world at large.[22]

Not surprisingly, some of the criticism of the bishops during the development of the peace pastoral centered on what was perceived as their failure to address adequately "the Soviet threat." Headlines such as this one in *The Wanderer* were not uncommon: "Hunthausen Admits Adoption of His Stance Could Lead to Red Takeover."[23] Reacting to the bishops generally and responding to the peace pastoral's second draft, conservative activist Phyllis Schlafly said that "the pastoral we wish the bishops had written" would declare that "the nuclear weapon *in the hands of the United States* is the most powerful material vehicle for peace the world has ever known." Moreover, she suggested that the bishops' letter led Catholics toward "pacifism . . . and disarmament and loving the Russians."[24] Philosopher Sidney Hook called the second draft "uninformed, unrealistic and morally irresponsible" for ignoring "the guiding dogmas of Communist theory and practice" and "the history of Soviet aggression."[25] And in commenting on the same version of the letter, Michael Novak noted "the profound anti-Americanism of the document."[26]

Throughout the development of the letter Archbishop Philip Hannan of New Orleans opposed its political positions on similar grounds. In a published interview in *U.S. News and World Report* in 1982 Hannan stated that "this letter belittles the enormous problem of resisting Communist enslavement." And he justified his claim with the following words: "The Holy Father said, and I agree, that the violation of conscience by the Communists is the most painful blow that can be inflicted on human dignity. In a sense it is worse than inflicting physical death."[27]

Historian Edward Cuddy examined this debate up to the point just before the final draft of the peace pastoral was issued in May 1983. After surveying some of the criticisms and reviewing U.S.–Soviet relations over the previous twenty-five years, Cuddy insisted that "the bishops have not glossed over the Russian perversions that have threatened world peace. Yet, their theology of peace is embellished with a bundle of premises that collide with our cold war mentality." And he concluded: "To season the final document with a stronger dose of anti-Soviet rhetoric, in response to hawkish critics, might be good politics but it would be bad history and questionable strategy."[28]

Regardless of the appropriateness of Cuddy's judgment, such "seasoning" did occur. In the final draft, to the greater satisfaction of some observers, there appeared a more developed treatment of "the Soviet threat." In reference to this change Michael Novak told me: "One just has to look at whom we're trying to deter—the Communist bloc. The bishops seemed to recognize this a bit more in offering a more defined view of the Soviets in the third draft." Edward Doherty, staff member for the war and peace committee, explained this change, saying: "At first [the bishops] didn't deal much with the Soviet threat; they were focusing more on means than ends. Later, this position eroded. In the third draft there emerged a section on comparative justice written by [Bishop] O'Connor which stressed the need to take into account the nature of the enemy and its possible or probable actions." Then, he said, "we needed a section on the relations between the superpowers; I wrote the first draft of that." Finally, Doherty added that "neither [new] section has been used to distort the thrust of the letter."

The resulting final draft of the peace pastoral included a larger section on "Shaping a Peaceful World." It embraced the subsections entitled "World Order in Catholic Teaching," "The Superpowers in a Disordered World," and "Interdependence: From Fact to Policy." As might be guessed from these simple headings, the bishops stressed "the unity of the human family," relying on Church documents such as John XXIII's *Pacem in Terris* and Paul VI's *Populorum Progressio*. Moreover, they addressed the need for a "concerted effort of the whole world community" to solve worldwide problems. Then in fairly specific terms they spoke of the "fragile" nature of the relationship between two superpowers "divided by philosophy, ideology and competing ambitions." They acknowledged "the fact of a Soviet threat, as well as the existence of a Soviet imperial drive for hegemony" but cautioned that "our own system is not without flaws." They highlighted interdependence between the superpowers and among nations generally, yet they noted that "there is a difference" between NATO and the Warsaw Pact in that the former is a "freely chosen" association. Finally, in one of their summarizing statements in this section, the bishops wrote: "Sensible and successful diplomacy, however, will demand that we avoid the trap of a form of anti-Sovietism which fails to grasp the central danger of a superpower rivalry in which both the U.S. and the U.S.S.R. are the players, and fails to recognize the common interest both states have in never using nuclear weapons."[29]

An important influence on the bishops in this regard was an article published in the spring 1982 issue of *Foreign Affairs* by former government officials McGeorge Bundy, George Kennan, Robert McNamara, and Gerard Smith. The four explained how they separately came to hold "new views" on the relation between nuclear weapons and peace and freedom. Then they argued: "The one clearly definable firebreak against worldwide disaster of general nuclear war is the one that stands between all other kinds of conflict and any use whatsoever of nuclear weapons. To keep that firebreak wide and strong is in the deepest interest of all mankind." They concluded: "So it seems timely to consider the possibilities, the requirements, the difficulties, and the advantages of a policy of no-first-use."[30] This statement, which tied defense policy to the threat of global disaster, was employed by the bishops both in condemning first use of nuclear weapons and in expressing their "profound skepticism" about the possibility of a *limited* nuclear exchange.[31]

In the final analysis the bishops adopted a view of the United States in the world that stressed its necessary interconnections with other nations, particularly the Soviet Union, but which at the same time accorded some legitimacy to fear of a Soviet threat. A peaceful world order was still the overarching symbol for the bishops here, bolstered by "solid realism which recognizes that everyone will lose in a nuclear exchange." However, they suggested that "there are political philosophies with understandings so radically different from ours, that even negotiations proceed from different premises, although identical terminology may be used by both sides."[32] This complex position is well characterized by the phrase "yes but." The spectre of disaster was presented as sufficient reason for the superpowers to undertake mutual efforts toward peace and disarmament, but in the bishops' view the superpowers did not take the threat seriously enough to put aside their political, moral, and cultural differences in pursuit of peace. The bishops implied that this perception was dangerously mistaken, even though they granted that the differences were substantial.

As the bishops moved down from the abstract level of a commitment to peace to specific policy recommendations, the political and national differences between the United States and the Soviet Union became debatable, and the identities and resources of moral theology and Church doctrine could contribute little to discussion. At this point the peace pastoral *had* to be based on political choices, but neither the bishops nor the Church possessed identities that automatically qualified them to make such choices. Nonetheless, the bishops claimed the right to make general judgments. Similar constraints arise for any organization where a public statement on behalf of all of the organization's members transcends the commonly credited authoritative qualifications of the group per se. Beyond the organization's interests and preferences, outsiders' specific beliefs, knowledge, and attitudes must now be accommodated. Sometimes accommodation is very difficult—logically and/or morally. To make matters more difficult, the authoritative, moral positions of the Roman Catholic Church make accommodation to worldly circumstances almost sinful. By definition, moral truths are neither accommodating nor qualifiable. This position has broad implications for persuasive communication. Any person or group or nation that takes an explicitly *moral* stand on any matter vastly reduces the range of its available rhetorical resources for discussion of that position. For example, consider the intransigence of competing moral positions relative to abortion. Controversialists sometimes refuse even to consider qualifying what they see as first principles: right to life versus freedom of reproductive choice.

The bishops' rhetorical difficulties arose because of their self-defined moral authority. Even though they acceded to the existence of a "Soviet threat," they *had* to make a "peaceful world order" the keystone of their pronouncement. Only so could their moral authority withstand pragmatic, political challenges. One may generalize: "yes but" is the only unassailable position for spiritually based pronouncements on worldly questions. People and organizations who argue from sacred texts or authorities inevitably face tensions between sacred doctrine and mundane facts or pragmatic judgments. The case of the bishops illustrates powerfully that those tensions must be somehow managed if the organization is to maintain authority with its internal audiences and exercise influence with outsiders. Spokespersons must be seen as loyal and true to the organization even when venturing rhetorically "outside" of it. This is the case for labor unions, businesses, social-action groups, and other sources of organizational rhetoric.

A few more things about the positive vision of global interdependence in the pastoral should be noted. Chapter 3 of the document was entitled "The Promotion of Peace: Proposals and Policies." It was a positive statement on ways to create a more peaceful world. Father Theodore Hesburgh explained to me the importance of this section: "It is a step toward developing a systematic theology of peace." He elaborated: "We've had a well developed theology of *war* since Augustine, but we need a strict and intellectually sound theology of *peace*. The bishops have made a move in this direction." In late 1984 Fr. Richard Warner told me that "the whole section on peacemaking is one of the strongest statements on peace you'll find anywhere." But, he complained that "it has yet to be discovered, really. People tend to focus on the specific recommendations regarding arms control." The widespread discussion of "the bishops and the bomb," of course, supported Warner's analysis.

The third chapter of the peace pastoral occupied 22 pages of the final draft, and it included sections on promoting negotiations, minimizing the use of war, developing nonviolent means of conflict resolution, the role of conscience, and the three subsections mentioned earlier—on world order, the superpowers, and interdependence. Viewed as a whole the chapter could be seen as another part of "an overall program for 'constructing

94

peace' which embraces the economic, social, cultural, and political spheres."[33] The bishops placed the two superpowers in a large frame:

> While the nuclear arms race focuses attention on the U.S.—Soviet relationship, it is neither politically wise nor morally justifiable to ignore the broader international context in which that relationship exists. Public attention, riveted on the big powers, often misses the plight of scores of countries and millions of people simply trying to survive. The interdependence of the world means a set of interrelated human questions. Important as keeping the peace in the nuclear age is, it does not dissolve the other major problems of the day.[34]

Putting things in broad contexts was the basic strategy in the bishops' treatment of the United States in the world. They coordinated their position as religious leaders in a superpower, the acknowledged threat of the Soviet Union, and the nations' mutuality of interests in ways that emphasized the threat to the *world*. And the world was threatened not just by nuclear destruction, but also by gross economic, social, and political inequalities. By these processes of association, argumentation was shifted from focusing on superpowers as individual nations to a focus on the entire world with its full range of problems. The bishops thereby defined a network of identities and roles in the global community.

Rhetorically the bishops tried to draw out some specific policy implications from their moral vision and to do so in ways that would jeopardize neither their authority as religious leaders nor their credibility as vocal U.S. citizens. For the peace pastoral to be coherent *and* pragmatic, the bishops had to speak with more than one identity while keeping the voices somehow in harmony. The NCCB had the rhetorical benefit of the Church's moral authority; however, as I have shown, that authority also functioned as a constraint. This is a rhetorical and organizational predicament of any group that attempts to persuade different audiences that operate from different argumentative premises. To be effective the spokespersons must retain their organizational authority for their internal audience while establishing "political" authority for outsiders. The goal is that the two types of authority will reinforce rather than undermine each other.

THE CHURCH IN THE UNITED STATES: AMERICAN–CATHOLIC OR CATHOLIC–AMERICAN?

The Roman Catholic Church in the United States has a long history of struggle over its proper relationship to the broader society. The hierarchy

95

has had to define and redefine its stance with respect to the government in a society which officially—though not always in practice—celebrates pluralism and relatively unbridled religious expression. Catholics in this country have had to face occasional, and sometimes violent, challenges to their patriotism and to the legitimacy of their religious commitment to Rome. This history makes the question, How did the bishops manage the relationship of the Roman Catholic Church to the United States? an important one.

The peace pastoral, along with the attendant debate and publicity, quickly became an important marker on the Church's path of development in the United States. The preeminent Church historian John Tracy Ellis described it for me as "a sign that Catholics have arrived in the mainstream of American society." His reasoning was that a group could not comfortably take a critical posture toward the government unless it was fully accepted as "American." Bishop Daniel Reilly of Norwich, Connecticut, one of the five who served on the drafting committee, agreed with Ellis's analysis, but he also said to me: "The election of JFK in 1960 was a sign that Catholics had entered the mainstream; the peace pastoral is proof." In another interview Bishop Gumbleton said: "We today have a kind of maturity that enables us to be secure about our place in American society. And we have a right and responsibility to engage in public policy debates and to persuade others of the merit of our positions." Referring to this right and responsibility, Archbishop John O'Connor said to me: "I now feel no need to apologize for addressing the body politic. I derive this consciousness in large part from working on the [war and peace] committee." Finally, in response to the same question, Fr. Warner described the situation as "the coming of age of a post–Vatican II Church. In the United States, the Church is more than ever a force to be reckoned with."

At least two things are important to notice about these statements. (1) They all implied that the "proper" relation of church and state had been achieved in the pastoral letter. This was, however, entirely an *insiders'* view. Each of the commentators quoted above presupposed that Catholicism *ought* to have political influence. Each felt that their document established that "right" *from the point of view of the organization.* (2) None of the statements I have quoted directly considered how the claims to political "rights" would be viewed by other Christians, by non-Christian religious groups, or by people with entirely secular orientations. Critical responses were not long in coming, however.

The language of articles in the secular and religious presses during the development of the peace pastoral stressed the idea of tension between the bishops and Washington. Headlines included such provocative words as: "Why the Pastoral Is Shocking," "Bishops Plan Pastoral Letter at Odds with Defense Policies," "The Bishops Speak Out," and "America's Roman Catholic Bishops Take on the Pentagon."[35] In rather dramatic form a *New Yorker* editorial described the relationship of the NCCB to Washington:

> In the Catholic bishops' pastoral letter on war and peace . . . two orthodoxies collide. One is the teaching of the Catholic Church, which extends back almost two thousand years, and the other is the more recent but hardly less obdurately ingrained teaching of the nuclear-deterrence theorists, who now sit at the elbows of the powerful, giving them guidance in the deployment and possible use of their nuclear arsenals.[36]

It was common to portray the bishops as opposed to or at least as alienated from the federal government. The bishops had moved squarely into the public policy arena, and that fact invited observers either to align them with the government or to place them in the role of antagonists.

The bishops were aware of the symbolic importance of the step they were taking. Their view was not, however, the same as that of the commentators I have just cited. Committee staff member J. Bryan Hehir explained to me the bishops' understanding of church and state. They saw the two entities as two actors capable of influencing that society, not by usurping one another's roles but by acting on the general public. Several bishops I interviewed affirmed this view of indirect engagement; however, as I have pointed out, this was a difficult position to define and to hold in practice.

At no time was the difficulty more plain than in the 1984 presidential election. There were charges of candidates' being "un-Christian," "not devout," and as "misrepresenting" the teaching of the Catholic Church. And an exchange on abortion between Democratic vice-presidential candidate Geraldine Ferraro (a Roman Catholic) and New York Archbishop O'Connor was a public embarrassment.[37] Meanwhile media attention to the religion-and-politics issue increased. In a *Newsweek* cover story of September 17, for example, "religion" was termed "a code word symbolizing serious divisions in American society."[38] Contributing to the controversy were the vocal political efforts of "televangelists" such as Jerry Falwell of Moral Majority, Inc. In an interview former Indiana Catholic conference Director Raymond Rufo put the matter in slightly different terms: "No longer are we dealing just with religious issues in the campaign. Religion *itself*, religion as a *category*, has become an issue." The controversy brought the bishops' collective identity into the bright lights of the public arena.

The bishops, of course, had to contend with this growing religio-political controversy in the fall of 1984, a time when they were working to implement the over-one-year-old peace pastoral and to formulate the first draft of their pastoral letter on the U.S. economy. They released the latter just after the November elections. The situation became so tense that the USCC Executive Committee authorized two statements by the Conference President, Bishop James Malone—one in August and another in October. Both statements were attempts to de-politicize the public image of the bishops. In the first Malone maintained: "As an agency of the Catholic bishops of the United States, the U.S. Catholic Conference speaks on public policy issues, but it does not take positions for or against political candidates. This point needs emphasizing lest, in the present political context, even what we say about issues can be perceived as an expression of political partisanship."[39] In his second statement Malone was more emphatic: "We do not seek the formation of a voting bloc nor do we preempt the right and duty of individuals to decide conscientiously whom they will support for public office. Rather, having stated our positions, we encourage members of our own Church and all citizens to examine the positions of candidates on issues and decide who will best contribute to the common good of society."[40]

While it was certainly a complex of events and factors that contributed to the church–state debate in the fall of 1984, the peace pastoral was one of the prime factors. During the drafting of the peace pastoral the bishops had numerous exchanges with the Reagan Administration—both publicly and privately. Moreover, the Administration consistently made its views on the progress of the letter known in the news media. All the while the bishops tried to distance themselves from both the Administration and the freeze advocates. Understandably, this was difficult to do.

Several officials of the Reagan Administration were heard by the NCCB's war and peace committee during their consultations. These included Secretary of Defense Caspar Weinberger; Lawrence Eagleberger, Undersecretary of State for Political Affairs; Eugene Rostow, Director of the Arms Control and Disarmament Agency; and Ambassador Edward Rowny. Interestingly, this was the last group to testify before the committee during their consultations in 1981 and 1982. Archbishop John Roach, then NCCB President, described these exchanges as "open discussion." There was, he said to me, "no attempt to close down dialogue. They recognized the legitimacy of our concern and our position. We listened carefully to them." However, Roach added: "Ultimately, the bishops told [the Reagan Administration], 'Thank you very much, but you are trying to bring us into a technical-political arena, and that is not our place. We are operating in a moral-political one.' " In an afterthought Roach acknowledged that this distinction was a tough one for the NCCB to maintain in light of the bishops' fragile and newly emergent collective identity as political advocates.

Roach's words epitomize the serious rhetorical problem the bishops faced. They also point up a problem that is common for organizational rhetors in general. If an organization defines a position in in-group terms (e.g., "moral-political"), that position may or may not translate effectively for outsiders. This problem is powerfully evident in the long-standing abortion controversy. Pro-life groups talk of "killing babies," and pro-choice groups talk of "the right to choose." In the public debate not only do the two sides talk past one another but they also confuse many persons who are somewhat in the middle on the issue. Roach's statement expresses just such an impasse between spokespersons for different organizations with different, self-defined scopes of authority. In the case of the bishops many critics—especially some in the Reagan Administration—argued that to make a distinction between "technical-political" and "moral-political" domains of argument was equivalent to ignoring the facts of the case.

An important exchange between the bishops and the Reagan Administration occurred in the fall of 1982, before and after the November release of the provocative second draft of the pastoral letter. In a letter to Archbishop Bernardin, Defense Secretary Weinberger criticized the bishops' handling of deterrence: "I find most troubling the [first] draft letter's implication that the policy of deterrence itself should be forsaken if complete nuclear disarmament is not imminent. The truth is that the continued safety and security of all nations requires that we maintain a stable military balance even as we negotiate reductions."[41] A later communication, this time from National Security Adviser William Clark (a Catholic layman), went one step further in seeking "to persuade the nation's Roman Catholic bishops that the administration's policies on nuclear arms were guided by compelling moral considerations."[42] Clark was trying to steal some of the bishops' rhetorical force by moving the Administration somewhat into the realm of moral argument. Clark's letter was printed in the *New York Times* just two weeks after the release of the second draft. It detailed Washington's efforts to effect arms reduction and to initiate "confidence-building measures." It also accused the bishops of putting forth a draft that "continues to reflect fundamental misreadings of American policies, and continues essentially to ignore American proposals that are currently being negotiated with the Soviet Union."[43] With these words the Administration sought to boost its own moral-political identity and at the same time undermine the bishops' technical-political authority. As might be expected, the letter fueled the fires of controversy even more; Professor Bruce Russett, principal consultant to the bishops' committee, described it to me as "unfortunate and clumsy activity on behalf of the Administration."

In January of 1983 the ad hoc committee was invited to the State Department, ostensibly to "learn more of U.S. nuclear policy." The bishops and the others met with Robert McFarlane, deputy assistant to the President for national security affairs, Joseph Lehman of the Arms Control and Disarmament Agency, Ronald Lehman of the Defense Department, and Elliot Abrams, head of the Human Rights Office. As reported by Castelli, Archbishop Bernardin was direct in asking: "What was the 'fundamental misreading' of American policy Clark had described?" The reply was that the bishops seemed to think that U.S. policy *targeted* civilian populations, but the policy was not of that order. But Russett noted, and the officials acknowledged, that there were over sixty military targets in the city of Moscow alone.[44] Because of this, Hesburgh explained to me, "the Administration was telling the truth to the bishops but also telling one of the biggest lies around."

Of course, one of the most difficult issues in all of the bishops' discussions and challenges was deterrence. Interestingly, discussion of deterrence is found precisely at the textual center of the peace pastoral.[45] It is one matter to rule out a first-strike policy on moral grounds and to express radical skepticism about the possibility of a limited nuclear exchange, which the bishops did. It is quite another thing to condemn *possession* of nuclear arms, which the bishops did not do but had considered.

Doherty told me that "deterrence was undoubtedly our most difficult problem." Nor did the bishops completely resolve it. In fact, the treatment of deterrence in the pastoral letter has come under much criticism, and it continues to be debated by the NCCB and their staff.

The deterrence dilemma stayed with the bishops throughout the peace pastoral's development. Private correspondence reveals the mixture of organizational constraints, personal judgments, and forecasts of responses from audiences that were influencing the bishops as they hammered out their ultimate public pronouncement. In a memo from Edward Doherty to Fr. Hehir in January 1983 the tensions thus created were clearly spelled out. With respect to the policy of deterrence, Doherty asked urgently, "What are we to do?" He pointed to the difficult linguistic problems, identity problems, problems of authority, and to the logical complexities involved:

> There are two main answers. The treatment of deterrence in the first draft, employing the argument of the Krol testimony (1979), was immediately criticized by theologians for proposing to tolerate an evil in order to achieve a good, i.e., reversing the nuclear arms race and making nuclear war less likely. While the Committee was wrestling with this challenge, Pope John Paul II in his address to the U.N. Special Session on Disarmament delivered his opinion that deterrence is "morally acceptable." Although the statement was ambiguous, and not supported by argument, the Committee gladly embraced it, not as an intellectual solution but as a tactical one: Who would dispute the Pope's judgment?
>
> As it should have, the tactical solution did not come off. The theologians who were dissatisfied with the Krol formulation saw the change as semantic; how could the deterrent become "morally acceptable as a means to the progressive reduction of armaments" without begging the question of the intrinsic moral quality of the conditional intention which is of the essence of deterrence?
>
> The second answer to the question, why the issue of deterrence is so controversial, lies in the unwillingness to deal with the consequences of a clearly adverse moral judgment on deterrence. At the minimum, such a judgment would require the bishops to say, although without censure, this policy is wrong, correct it. At either the first or second meeting of the Committee . . . the members decided that they wanted to avoid becoming advocates of "unilateral disarmament," apparently in the belief that this would divide the bishops and polarize the Catholic community.
>
> So, to condemn nuclear deterrence as a moral evil would contradict Pope John Paul II and it would seem to require the bishops to advocate some kind of unilateral disarmament. To do either would require intellectual (and moral) courage of the first order; to do either would require that all of the implications had been thought through and that the conclusions would be presented logically and persuasively.[46]

I have quoted Doherty's memo at length because of its clear expression of the serious tensions faced by the bishops in managing who they were and where they stood on the deterrence problem. To move toward any kind of outright endorsement of U.S. (and Soviet) deterrence policies would have put in jeopardy the bishops' almost complete condemnation of the *use* of nuclear weapons. And to move toward a thoroughgoing proscription of the *possession* of nuclear weapons would have pointed the bishops to the conclusion of unilateral disarmament. Because of the various interests the bishops struggled to balance, particularly those related to the U.S. government, neither stance was acceptable.

Thus, as Bishop Reilly acknowledged to me, the bishops found "an out" in the Pope's rather equivocal proclamation that deterrence may be "morally acceptable" when used as "a step on the way toward progressive disarmament."[47] The Pope's words served as an all-important resource of ambiguity for the bishops. Nevertheless, in their final draft the bishops added: "The possession of nuclear weapons, the continuing quantitative growth of the arms race, and the danger of nuclear proliferation all point to the grave danger of basing 'peace of a sort' on deterrence."[48] Again the questions arose: Where *did* they stand? And, For what Catholics and others did they speak?

The bishops were in a rhetorical bind because they had made a *moral* judgment on the arms race. Nuclear arms were almost defined as evil *in themselves*. Not to oppose deterrence would greatly weaken this moral stance. On the other hand, to condemn U.S. deterrence policy explicitly would put the bishops on an unalterable collision course with the Reagan Administration and with many other Americans, and it would commit them to policy positions that could not be altered easily.

Ultimately the language the bishops adopted on deterrence yielded three things: (1) a measure of ambiguity that left the bishops room to maneuver with respect to criticism of U.S. defense policy; (2) an invitation for criticism from both left and right for not standing more firmly in a posture of condemnation or legitimation; and (3) a moral imperative to reexamine U.S. deterrence strategy sometime in the future. The first point is, by now, clear. The second requires a more extended discussion. So I turn first to the final point.

In several of my interviews during the latter half of 1984 it was explained to me that the bishops, while not wanting to become monitors of U.S. defense policies, were taking steps at least to reassess the potential for eventual disarmament. The best example of this, Cardinal Krol noted, was testimony by Archbishops Bernardin and O'Connor before the House Foreign Relations Committee on 26 June 1984. They introduced their statement with these words: "Our purpose in appearing today before this committee is not so much to address specific issues as to invite attention to the growing concern of leaders of the Catholic community in the United States about the dangers of nuclear war and to their view that the means employed either to fight nuclear wars or to deter them are subject to rather definite moral limitations."[49] At the same time, however, the bishops *did* address specific issues. For example, they commented on the deployment of new missiles in Western Europe and the controversial MX missile. This is especially noteworthy because, presumably under pressure from the more conservative men among them, the bishops had dropped a passage criticizing the MX. In their second draft the bishops had explained their opposition to "the addition of weapons which are likely to invite attack and therefore give credence to the concept that the U.S. seeks a first-strike, 'hard target kill' capability; the MX missile might fit into this category."[50] The final draft included a much less provocative statement in a footnote: "Several experts in strategic theory would place both the MX missile and Pershing II missiles in [the first-strike] category."[51] In their statement Bernardin and O'Connor called for "intense political and moral assessment" of the MX, citing its vulnerability, its first-strike implications, and its high cost. And the bishops argued: "With the deployment of U.S. Pershing II and cruise missiles in Europe, any escalation from the use of tactical weapons almost certainly risks escalation to the strategic, intercontinental level."[52] Just as they had in the pastoral letter, the bishops, as represented by Bernardin and O'Connor, severely questioned specific policies. They did this under the rubric of "prudential moral judgments" linked to "binding moral principles." Clearly this critique was an attempt by the bishops to give substance to their somewhat ambiguous position.

An article by Richard Miller in *The Bulletin of the Atomic Scientists* wrestled with the bishops' logic. Miller wrote:

> The issues of use and deterrence comprise the fundamental aspects of the letter, but the relationship between the morality of use and the morality of deterrence is most puzzling. On the one hand, both use and deterrence could be logically linked. Thus, if all use is unacceptable, so are the corresponding threats which deter use. But if some legitimate use of nuclear weapons is possible, then some aspects of deterrence might be acceptable. On the other hand, it might be argued that use and threat could be separated so that the former is proscribed while the latter is reluctantly condoned.

Miller expressed beautifully the choices involved in managing the deterrence issue: How and to what degree should one associate or link it with the issues of use and intention? He claimed that the bishops opted for the first line of reasoning, though they qualified it with the severe limitations on the use or threat to use nuclear weapons. Miller concluded by questioning how the bishops could call the situation, with their proscriptions, "deterrence." Said Miller: "Deterrence would not be effective if the threat that it must carry were unrealizable due to moral restraints. Toleration of deterrence must therefore include *toleration of use*. Yet even the slightest acceptance of the use of nuclear weapons is undesirable. The logic of the bishops' discussion, however, leads in that direction."[53]

Clearly the bishops were in a position of qualified, although strong, opposition to the deterrence policy, which they called a "moral and political paradox."[54] Yet they assumed some of the paradoxical aspects of that policy themselves in finding their niche in the debate. Some of the ambiguity in the bishops' position seemed to mirror the ambiguity in U.S. deterrence policy, though the reflection was not perfect. Philosopher Michael Walzer posed the problem this way: "The real ambiguity of nuclear deterrence lies in the fact that no one, including ourselves, can be sure we will ever carry out the threats we make."[55] The bishops, like so many others, were willing to accept some kind of deterrent with the fervent hope that it would never be transformed into the actual launching of missiles (either through intention or by accident). As Bruce Russett explained, "The bishops' position in the final letter is not so ambiguous as it is frankly torn between desirable ends." For, he admitted, "there is *no* perfect practical solution to the problem of nuclear deterrence."[56]

In the end, the bishops had to engage in a bit of casuistry. Casuistry is the pattern of moral reasoning, developed by the Church in the Middle Ages, in which moral principles are applied to cases or specific instances where the circumstances of the case alter the way in which the principles are applied. Accordingly, the biblical injunction "Thou shalt not kill" may be modified by specific circumstances where it clashes with one or more additional moral principles. The method of casuistry, well known to moral theologians and moral philosophers, is especially valuable in cases where duties conflict (such as in the controversy over abortion) and where different authorities and different identities must be weighed to determine an appropriate course of action.[57] For the bishops, as for anyone, to alter a moral position is to suggest compromise or error in a previous position. However, casuistic argument is well established in the Catholic tradition and the method grants that circumstances may justify only partial or qualified application of a principle to a given case. This is how the bishops reasoned in the peace pastoral. They affirmed their broad moral stance, but they granted that the stance might not be wholly appropriate to certain technical-political specifics.

In a similarly equivocal, but nonetheless rhetorically astute manner the bishops managed their position with respect to the nuclear freeze movement. I have shown how the freeze movement of the early to mid-1980s served as a catalyst for the bishops' own activism. Ironically, however, freeze advocates also posed a threat to the bishops because they were partisan, secular, transitory, and single-issue oriented. The bishops felt comfortable with the arguments of the "freezers," but not with their interest-group identity. Hence, the final draft of the peace pastoral echoed the freeze proposal: "*We recommend* . . . support for immediate, bilateral, verifiable agreements to halt the testing, production, and deployment of new nuclear weapons systems." At the same time (and on the same page) the bishops cautioned: We do not want "either to be identified with one specific political initiative or to have our words used against specific political measures."[58] The bishops differed among themselves about explicit identification with the freeze movement. As Bishop Malone explained to me, "I did not feel as sensitive on that issue as some others articulated. My awareness is, of course, that 'nuclear freeze' was a phrase used to cover a variety of concepts [nuclear arms limitation, reduction, etc.]. So I was comfortable with the notion that we would seize the nomenclature and that we would affirm the concept that—Hey, we have to call a *halt* to this mindless building of nuclear stockpiles!"

The word "halt," however, became a focus of controversy in the bishops' identity management when the third draft was set forth by the ad hoc committee in early April 1983. According to Bishop Fulcher, the committee voted 4–1 to change "halt" to the softer "curb," thereby departing from "freeze" language. This move was partly at Archbishop O'Connor's urging. He stressed the flexibility of the term "curb" and the fact of its usage in certain Vatican documents. The press, however, interpreted this change as a "watering down" of the bishops' position. Even more important, Bishop Fulcher told me, was the response of the Reagan Administration.

As reported on the front page of the *New York Times* for two successive days (6, 7 April 1983), the Administration took the third draft as an opportunity to identify the bishops with U.S. defense policy. As reporter Kenneth Briggs wrote on 6 April: "Cardinal Bernardin, at a news conference, said some of the earlier emphases of the document had been altered after consultation with the Reagan Administration and Church officials here and in Europe." Included in the same article was the subheading "Nuclear 'Halt' Softened."[59] The following day the *Times* ran this story: "Administration Hails New Draft of Letter: Says Bishops 'Improved' the Nuclear Statement." Specifically, the article quoted a State Department announcement that "we are pleased that the letter explicitly endorses many of the far-reaching objectives which the Administration seeks—notably, negotiated agreements for substantial, equitable and verifiable reductions in nuclear arsenals."[60] Clearly the Administration was trying to claim the bishops as allies.[61]

The flurry of media attention to the term "curb" and other changes in the third draft led to a "general impression . . . of a retreat from the freeze"[62] and to a disclaimer by the bishops issued on 8 April 1983. Archbishops Roach and Bernardin said plainly: "We could not accept any suggestion that there are relatively few and insignificant differences between U.S. policy and the policies advocated in the pastoral." Further, the two bishops stressed the need to avoid "premature and risky" judgments before the pastoral was finalized and adopted by the entire NCCB.[63]

When the whole body met the following month, they restored the term "halt" in passing one of over five hundred amendments that were considered. Malone spoke on behalf of the amendment, noting that "the content and symbolism of 'halt' sets the tone for the rest of the document." Bernardin explained the committee's support for the amendment in a premeeting speech, saying that in view of the widespread public support for the freeze, the bishops could use "halt" while preserving *their own identity* and the distinctiveness of their moral-theological positions. O'Connor spoke against the amendment, arguing that the bishops should avoid specific political identifications. Archbishop Edmund Szoka of Detroit offered the term "cease" as a compromise which would not suggest a specific political leaning by the bishops. At the end of discussion, though, the vote was overwhelmingly in support of restoring "halt." Castelli explained: "The size of the vote surprised everyone, but the Reagan Administration, which had alternately frightened, angered, and insulted the bishops, could claim a great deal of the credit; its blessing of the third draft and 'curb' made it clear that, for the Administration, anything other than support for the freeze would be interpreted as a blanket endorsement of Reagan policies."[64]

Here one sees another aspect of identity management in institutional rhetoric. It can be asked whether or not official spokespersons are succumbing to outside pressures in framing messages. In choosing a single word the bishops chose to emphasize that their identity was significantly independent of the stance of official secular entities. One finds similar issues of identity arising when there are questions about whether a board of directors is more or less loyal to the interests of stockholders vis-à-vis the interests of other groups of stakeholders; when it is asked whether a socialist government is too responsive or not responsive enough to market-side pressures; when it is asked whether university professors are speaking for their disciplines, their departments, "the administration," funding sources, or for the wider community. Individuals in many types of organizational situations must manage identities and interests, though they may not be fully aware of which ones they privilege.

In discussing a number of other amendments some of the bishops further distanced themselves from the Administration and from U.S. defense policies. Many of the proposed changes were offered by Archbishop John Quinn of San Francisco. He told me that he was "particularly vocal on the rejection of all uses of nuclear weapons." Perhaps the most significant of Quinn's offerings was Amendment 68, which stated: "Nevertheless, there must be no misunderstanding of our opposition on moral grounds to any use of nuclear weapons." Bernardin, representing the collective judgment of the committee, opposed it, arguing that it would upset the delicate reasoning of the document. The amendment passed easily. However, in subsequent discussion and at Bernardin's urging, the amendment was rescinded. Collectively, the bishops were not prepared to endorse such a strong stand.

An actual change regarding the document's quoted material was particularly interesting. The bishops discussed what material ought to be quoted in the text and what should be relegated to a less prominent position in footnotes. Previously they had included within the text quotations from Weinberger and Clark explaining U.S. nuclear targeting policy. In advancing an amendment to move these statements to footnotes, Bishop Roger Mahony of Stockton, California, stressed an issue of identification when he observed that the only other sources quoted within the text were popes, Vatican II, and other Church documents. "He also said, that, given the history of 'curb–halt,' keeping the quotes in so lofty a position might create the wrong impression." In accord with Mahony's request, Weinberger's and Clark's words were moved to a footnote.[65]

Ultimately, then, the bishops adopted another position that put them at odds with Reagan Administration policy—but not in complete opposition to it. Their jockeying on policy issues during the letter's development reflected a growing sense of the need to distinguish themselves as moral-political critics by not getting too close to either the Administration or the nuclear-freeze advocates. In the event, their rhetorical strategy had only limited success. The bishops were widely seen as disapproving existing defense policy. For example, a *New York Times* editorial of 6 May 1983 said: "In supporting a nuclear weapons freeze the bishops seem unmindful of the risk that such negotiations, if successful, could end up freezing the existing nuclear instabilities and actually add to the risk of war."[66] As I have already indicated, others also interpreted the final letter as an anti-Administration document.

In managing the issues I have discussed, the bishops were managing the relationship of the Roman Catholic Church to the United States as represented by the federal government. For many observers the bishops' problem could be reduced to which identification was more important: as Catholic or as American? Professor Russett told me that the letter made a clear distinction between the two labels and came down on the side of a religious commitment over and above national allegiance. "The intent of the bishops," he said, "was to soft-pedal the nationalism a bit." In a similar manner Msgr. Daniel Hoye, NCCB–USCC General Secretary, told me: "Before, the 'my-country-right-or-wrong' position was used especially by Catholics because of their doubt about their own position. Now the Church is free to challenge policies and trends in society."

The tension between allegiances could be kept on a level of specifics or moved to a much broader one. Archbishop John Quinn told me that he saw the "main conflict" as being with "the present Administration." "Previous administrations," he added, "displayed a greater commitment to arms reduction and to reducing the risks of war." In this connection Bishop Sklba told me that the Reagan Administration was "outstandingly absent" in the list of audiences at the end of the pastoral. "Yet it was in effect at the top of the list." Toward the other end of the spectrum was Bishop Gumbleton. He was especially firm in saying to me: "In the fourth part of the letter it stresses that our first allegiance is to the community of the disciples of Jesus. We're saying that you'd better expect that you're going to come into conflict with secular society, with commonly accepted axioms of our culture." Somewhere in the middle on this continuum of opinion was Archbishop Kelly, who said, "For me the biggest problem is the national-security thinking. . . . The symbol of national security prevents people from seeing the implications of their religious beliefs for world peace."

Cardinal Bernardin took a characteristically diplomatic position, but he still recognized the pervasive issue of how far it was possible for true Roman Catholics to identify primarily with their nations in political affairs. He explained to me, "We're working out of an age-old Catholic tradition to say certain things are morally permissible and certain things are not. . . . And we're working out of the context of devotion to our country—that we have the right and obligation to defend our country against unjust aggressors." He concluded: "So I don't see any inherent dichotomy or conflict between being a good American and at the same time taking part in this public debate." Yet Bernardin was acknowledging that the dual allegiances may often cause tension for individual Catholics.

There were those, including some bishops (e.g., Hannan of New Orleans), who saw the NCCB as too clearly disregarding national interests.

Michael Novak told me: "Those who believe that the United States is in a period of great danger, that the power of the Soviet Union is not adequately recognized, that the clergy is not as pro-American as they used to be, will probably never forget the sense of betrayal they felt when they read the bishops' words, particularly in the second draft."

The institutional and long-term consequences of the bishops' rhetorical attempt to manage Catholic identities remain to be worked out through time. What their record shows is that organizational messages have frequently to deal with how organizational identity and transorganizational identities are to be associated. The bishops' peace pastoral did not fully resolve this for the U.S. Church, and whether or when a member of the flock was to identify himself or herself as an American–Catholic or a Catholic–American remained sharply at issue after release of the peace pastoral. As William McCready of the National Opinion Research Center insisted to me, "American Catholics haven't seriously reflected on their hyphenated status since nativism reared its ugly head in the 1880s. I think that the bishops' peace pastoral will cause many of them to think carefully about their hyphenation—whether they are in fact American–Catholics or Catholic–Americans." While the outcome of this pattern of reflection is uncertain as of this writing, what *is* clear is that the bishops brought an enduring problem to the surface.

Such conflicts of identities are common to the experience of many ethnic and religious groups in U.S. society and elsewhere. To give allegiance simultaneously to one's nation and to an "outside" group can be managed by an individual, but the problem nearly always raises the question for some: Which loyalty is the more important? Immigrants are asked this. So are persons who attempt to maintain a distinct subculture or group identity within a larger context. So are new organizational members who transfer from another organization. So are religious converts.

A parallel problem arises for some individuals in organizations that demand great loyalty. For a scientist in a corporation loyalty to the profession and to general research goals often exceeds organizational loyalty.[67] Predictably, this leads to tensions with management. For organizational whistle-blowers the tensions are acute and the risk great. The management of multiple identities becomes an issue at any point at which identities conflict or when a loyalty is called into question. The U.S. Catholic Church has faced this problem repeatedly, though its "management styles" have changed. In the 1980s the bishops felt moderately comfortable in questioning their American identity. The Catholic faithful, however, did not all share this feeling. In fact, many were, and many may continue to be, more likely to embrace nationalism while questioning Church authority.

THE NATIONAL CONFERENCE OF CATHOLIC BISHOPS: AN ORGANIZATION WITHIN AN ORGANIZATION

The bishops' authority, role, and identity as a national, episcopal conference within the universal Church left further identity problems for the NCCB. Problems of how an entity like the Conference "fits" within the larger ecclesiastical organization were not new. Bishop Fulcher explained to me that the authority of sub-agencies within the Church became an issue in 1919 when the U.S. episcopacy wanted to call itself the National Catholic Welfare Council. The Vatican and some U.S. bishops were disturbed by the implication that the bishops would be implicitly placed on a par with a Vatican Council. Subsequently, in 1922 the bishops opted for the less institutional title National Catholic Welfare Conference.[68] Said Fulcher, "The Church has always been concerned about granting too much authority to a national or regional conference of bishops."

As an organization within an organization the NCCB sought to establish its identity and domain of authority without violating or threatening its relationship to the higher organizational authority, the Vatican. The NCCB is in a "reporting" relationship to the Vatican, comparable to the situation of departments in corporations, congressional committees, or regional offices of national organizations.

The possibility that a local identification can supersede a broader one always exists. This is why Simon's theory of organization holds that ultimate decision-making responsibility should be accorded to a position in the hierarchy of an organization where decisions will be viewed and made with the interests of the entire organization in mind. A department head, for example, will be likely to try to maximize the benefits to his or her department, but a chief executive officer (CEO) will be likely to consider more seriously the interests of the whole organization.[69] For the Roman Catholic Church, allegiance to the universal Church is paramount. Therefore, whenever an episcopal or bishops' conference (in the Netherlands, or Brazil, or the United States) asserts itself, the "catholic" quality of the Church organization may be seen as becoming subordinate to local interests.

This issue touches on matters that are enormously complex in their theological and ecclesiological entailments. I will sketch the problem

110

briefly before considering how it surfaced during the development of the peace pastoral. My discussion aims to answer the question: How did the bishops manage the relationship of themselves (i.e., as the NCCB) to the universal Catholic Church?

Apostolic authority in the Roman Catholic Church has two forms: the power of the priesthood and the power to rule. The sacred priesthood has its major function in the administration of sacraments and is termed the "power of orders." The second form, the power to rule, is called the "power of jurisdiction." While the power of orders refers to all priests and deacons (i.e., to those ordinarily permitted to administer sacraments), apostolic succession of jurisdiction has reference only to the episcopacy (i.e., the bishops as a whole). In this sense apostolic succession is considered to be collegial: "a group succeeds a group and not a person another person."[70] Therefore, the collective identity is placed in a role superior to that of the individual.

The jurisdiction of the Roman Catholic Church is organized in such a way that everyone is subject to the authority of an individual bishop. The "ordinary" bishop's territory is called a diocese, a term borrowed from the reorganization of the Roman Empire under Diocletian. Bishops without territorial jurisdiction are called "titular"; they are assigned the title of an ancient "see" that no longer exists and they sometimes reside in Rome. In larger dioceses and in most archdioceses (regional or provincial centers) "auxiliary" or associate bishops assist the ordinary, or principal, bishop in his work.

The appointment of bishops is technically done by the pope through the Congregation for the Bishops, an executive office of the Roman Curia. Bishops in turn have the power to communicate Holy Orders—that is, to confer the priesthood. "A bishop is a bishop" in the sense that "no ordinary is any more or less of a bishop of his diocese than any other ordinary."[71] The pope as the Bishop of Rome is the "first among equals" and is a member of the "communion" of the episcopacy. To further explain this complex and somewhat equivocal arrangement, I quote from Vatican II's *Lumen Gentium* (Dogmatic Constitution on the Church):

> Just as, by the Lord's will, St. Peter and the other apostles constituted one apostolic college, so in a similar way the Roman Pontiff as the successor of Peter, and the bishops as successors of the apostles are joined together. The collegial nature and meaning of the episcopal order found expression in the very ancient practice by which bishops appointed the world over were linked with one another and with the Bishop of Rome by the bonds of unity, charity, and peace. . . . One is constituted a member of the episcopal body

by virtue of sacramental consecration and by hierarchical communion with the head and members of the body.

But the college or body of bishops has no authority unless it is simultaneously conceived of in terms of its head, the Roman Pontiff, Peter's successor, and without any lessening of his power of primacy overall. . . .

The order of bishops is the successor to the college of the apostles in teaching authority and pastoral rule; or, rather, in the episcopal order the apostolic body continues without a break. Together with its head, the Roman Pontiff, and never without this head, the episcopal order is the subject of supreme and full power over the universal Church.[72]

With these words the Second Vatican Council described the complex (and seemingly paradoxical) principle of "hierarchical communion." Claude Dagens interprets the principle's relevance to the Church this way: "The hierarchy is only *for* communion in the Church. Communion in the Church comes about only through the hierarchy."[73] This tautological statement may justify the principle of hierarchical communion, but it does not satisfactorily explain how it works in practice. The principle suggests the difficulty involved in the practice of maintaining a "first among equals." Because of its embrace of two seemingly conflicting ideals, hierarchical communion offers both advantages and disadvantages in organizational and rhetorical practice.

Pope John Paul II reinforced the words of *Lumen Gentium* in repeated statements on the role of bishops before, during, and after the issuance of *The Challenge of Peace*. In 1982 he addressed the bishops of Nicaragua, describing the bishop as a "principle of unity." And such unity, he maintained "can be applied in due measure to the ecclesial communities at all levels."[74] In 1983, in an address to a group of U.S. bishops, the Pope echoed this theme: "The bishop is . . . called to be *a sign of Catholic solidarity* in the local church, which is the miniature reflection of the one, holy, catholic and apostolic Church, which really and truly does subsist in the local church."[75] In 1984 John Paul spoke to the Swiss bishops on the scope of collegiality, again stressing universal unity in the Church. He said: "Collegiality in the strict sense is more than your collaboration among yourselves. It unites all the bishops with each other around the successor of Peter to teach the doctrine of the faith, to put a common discipline into practice and to meet the needs and provide for the progress of the universal church."[76]

It is against this backdrop of hierarchical communion that the identity and authority of a bishops' conference must be viewed. Vatican II explicitly articulated the principle of hierarchical communion, but it also established the foundation for national bishops' conferences. For this reason the Council has been called by some "the council of the bishops," to contrast it with Vatican I's focus on the papacy.[77] In the Vatican II document *Decree on the Bishops' Pastoral Office in the Church* the Council fathers explained the relationship of bishops to the universal Church, the governing role of individual bishops in their dioceses, and "the cooperation of bishops for the common good of many churches." In the chapter addressing the third of these concerns the Council "considers it supremely opportune everywhere that bishops belonging to the same nation or region form an association and meet together at fixed times." And in the brief but important discussion that follows it was written: "An episcopal conference is a kind of council in which the bishops of a given nation or territory jointly exercise their pastoral office by way of promoting that greater good which the Church offers mankind, especially through forms and programs of the apostolate which are fittingly adapted to the circumstances of the age." Also:

> Decisions of the episcopal conference, provided they have been made lawfully and by the choice of at least two-thirds of the prelates who have a deliberative vote in the conference, and have been reviewed by the Apostolic See, are to have juridically binding force in those cases and in those only which are prescribed by common law or determined by special mandate of the Apostolic See, given spontaneously or in response to a petition from the conference itself.[78]

Although far from unambiguous, these words were justification for the reorganization of the National Catholic Welfare Conference. The NCWC was transformed in 1966 into the National Conference of Catholic Bishops, with a standing secretariat, the United States Catholic Conference. A special kind of rhetorical challenge now faced the NCCB (as it would any other group in a similar position): how to (1) preserve its national identity, (2) while allowing for a comparable teaching authority by bishops of other nations who might disagree on certain concrete issues, (3) but keep the position of the Vatican uppermost in mind.[79] As Gerald Fogarty observes in his exhaustive study of relations between the Vatican and the U.S. episcopate: "Only gradually in the years after the council . . . did the American bishops begin to see what their nineteenth-century predecessors had seen: that true loyalty to the Holy See might mean a respectful representation based on pastoral experience."[80]

Fogarty's words capture remarkably well a challenge to the U.S. bishops in developing the *Challenge of Peace:* how "respectfully to represent" the position of the universal Church as centered in the Vatican and yet offer something derived from unique "pastoral experience."

113

Addressing this problem and keeping in mind their multiple audiences, the bishops between drafts two and three identified *a hierarchy of moral authority* to frame their statement. This strategy was sensitive, nuanced, and explicit; with it the bishops sought to deal directly with the problems of multiple identities, multiple audiences. In the final draft of the peace pastoral the bishops said:

> [Here] we address many concrete questions concerning the arms race, contemporary warfare, weapons systems, and negotiating strategies. We do not intend that our treatment of each of these issues carry the same moral authority as our statement of universal moral principles and formal Church teaching. Indeed, we stress here at the beginning that not every statement in this letter has the same moral authority. At times we reassert universally binding moral principles (e.g., non-combatant immunity and proportionality). At still other times we reaffirm statements of recent popes and the teaching of Vatican II. Again, at other times, we apply moral principles to specific cases.[81]

Part of the inspiration for this framework came from a meeting between representatives of the NCCB, Western European bishops, and several officials of the Curia, held at the Vatican 18–19 January 1983. As explained to me by Cardinal Bernardin, this meeting was held at the initiation of the ad hoc war and peace committee, although it was organized by the Vatican. He said: "The meeting was very important; but to put it in perspective, you must keep in mind that *we* were the ones who set the stage for that meeting. Every time we completed a draft, we sent it not only to the bishops [in the U.S.] but also to all those who had come to the hearings, to other experts, to many episcopal conferences in other countries, and to the Holy See [the Vatican]." And Bishop Malone commented: "I know that Bernardin, Roach, and Hehir went to that meeting with the secure conviction that they were going as the writers of a letter from the American Conference. . . . They did not feel that they had to negotiate a position, for example, with the Holy See that would allow them to write the letter, because the letter was being written with the full awareness of the authority of the Holy See."

Both the meeting and the articulation of the moral hierarchy touched directly on the question of *what it means to be a national conference* of bishops. The U.S. bishops, in particular the committee and the conference president, struggled to balance their own distinctiveness as bishops in the United States with their commitment to the official teaching authority of the Church, the Magisterium. The tension here was understood by Archbishop Roach, who told me: "We were expressing ourselves as the Catholic Church of the United States . . . [and] we realized that we had to be more careful in expressing a distinction between absolute moral principles and their application." In his interview Bishop Reilly voiced a similar position and added that "the meeting was misconstrued in the press as the U.S. bishops' being called on the carpet. People began asking, 'Why were the American bishops summoned to Rome?' " Reilly added: "It was a very positive thing to have members of different national conferences meet. The Western Europeans and the Vatican essentially told us: 'Carry on what you're doing.' "

The American bishops' situation was complicated by disagreement among different conferences of bishops on how best to pursue arms control. An article in the *National Catholic Reporter* in 1983 declared that "bishop to bishop, nation to nation," there was "little consensus" on "nuclear morality."[82] As several bishops explained to me, there was concern on the part of the French and the West German bishops about the NCCB's no-first-use posture and its grave questioning of deterrence as a policy. Bishop Fulcher described this situation as a "difference in perspective" because of "the French and German position on the NATO defense line." The difference was articulated on several occasions. In responding to the first draft in August 1982, both German and French episcopal representatives cautioned the American bishops. Joseph Cardinal Höffner, Archbishop of Cologne and President of the German Bishops' Conference, observed: "In studying your draft . . . I felt the struggle of the authors for solving the tense relation between the moral norms and the application of these norms in a given case." Then, in more specific terms, Höffner discussed "conceivable cases where a first nuclear attack might be justified."[83] In another letter, of the following month, Gerard Defois, General Secretary of the French Bishops' Conference, quoted the Pope's qualified judgment on deterrence and then stated: "The efficacy of a [nuclear] deterrent as a means of containing the violence of the adversary is only real if it is credible. . . . So one must consider deterrence as a lesser evil [compared to war] and a provisional safeguard."[84] These views continued to be expressed by the Western European bishops and made their way into pastoral letters of the French and West German bishops, also published in 1983.[85]

But the Western European conferences faced the same problem as the U.S. bishops. "None of [their] analyses . . . can claim to be definitive. Nor, in Catholic practice, can any particular hierarchy or combination of hierarchies by themselves do more than present their views. They must allow dissenting opinions within their own membership and permit the views of other hierarchies to be heard and considered openly by their own people."[86] This was, by most accounts, the central issue discussed at the Vatican meeting of January 1983.

In attendance at the Rome meeting was Vatican Secretary of State Agostino Cardinal Casaroli, who participated in most of the discussions. The chairman was Josef Cardinal Ratzinger of West Germany. Casaroli relayed the Pope's concern that all hierarchies of the Church be uniform in their teaching so that no one disavows another.[87] The meeting resulted in a joint communique which reaffirmed the necessity "for the episcopal conferences to act in concert in order to be informed about the realities experienced in different countries."[88] Ratzinger argued that national episcopal conferences do not have a *mandatum docendi,* a mandate to teach. That authority was said to reside with individual bishops in their respective dioceses or with the whole episcopacy acting in concert with the pope. This position attended to Vatican fears that "various bishops' conferences, involving themselves in controversial issues of an international character, might issue mutually conflicting statements, thus dividing the Catholic community . . . [and calling] attention to one another's shortcomings and imbalances."[89]

To distinguish their own views from those of the Vatican and other national conferences, the U.S. bishops fortified their arguments and stressed their unique responsibility. Bishop Gumbleton described the Vatican meeting this way: "It helped to highlight and clarify certain issues. But all of these issues had been raised *within* our own Conference." Moreover, in traveling through Western Europe to represent the NCCB after the May 1983 publication of *The Challenge of Peace,* Gumbleton said: "It's our responsibility to be the moral leaders of the U.S. Catholic community. . . . [And] we take full responsibility for [the letter's] contents."[90] In a similar way Bishop Fulcher expressed to me that the peace pastoral "represents the collective wisdom of the bishops of the United States."

There was understandable but significant disagreement among observers as to just whom or what the U.S. bishops represented in advancing their peace pastoral. The question of the authority of a national bishops' conference remained after *The Challenge of Peace* was issued. In acknowledging this tension Avery Dulles reviewed official Church teaching on the subject, which, I have shown, left considerable room for interpretation. Dulles concluded: "In the final analysis the authority of the letter . . . will depend on the way it is received. If the discussion it engenders leads to greater wisdom than is to be found in the text itself, the bishops will, I assume, be more than satisfied."[91] Edward Vacek expressed a comparable view, arguing that the bishops were to some degree putting authority in the hands of the U.S. Catholic community.[92] The true test of the bishops' authority, then, seems to have been placed in the pragmatic results of their action.

Of course, there were those who held that the bishops had already lost authority. Michael Novak in his interview argued forcefully that the bishops undermined their own authority by trying to go beyond it. Part of the reason for this, he said, was that "the staff they chose was too ideologically narrow." Further, in his *Moral Clarity in the Nuclear Age* Novak quoted a Vatican memo from the January 1983 meeting and explained how the bishops eventually came around to Rome's view, a "far wiser" one than "the itchings and urgings of the most extremist American bishops."[93] James Hitchcock, in an article on what he called the "new class" in U.S. Catholicism, interpreted the drive toward the peace pastoral as representing the interests of a liberal USCC staff and some of the more "left-wing" bishops. This, and moves on other socio-political fronts, had caused "a tension between positions which some in the national Catholic bureaucracy espouse and the official teachings of the Church itself."[94] Arguing on a more general level, George A. Kelly criticized liberal members of the hierarchy and their staffs, saying: "[Those] seeking radical change in Catholic doctrine are content with the present Catholic drift or have become convinced that the U.S. bishops, not the Pope, represent the wave of the Church's future."[95]

The point of special importance for the study of "corporate" rhetoric is that the "true" role, the identity, of national councils of bishops was not fully clarified by the NCCB's asserting a hierarchy of authoritativeness for its pronouncements. By including specifically political and pragmatic considerations in their letter, the bishops went in directions that even they had to admit could not be dealt with in doctrinally authoritative ways. Nonetheless, because those political claims (though avowedly not doctrinal) were incorporated in a pronouncement by a body that purported to speak authoritatively on moral-political issues, just where the NCCB did stand and with what corporate authority it spoke on pragmatic matters remained understandably confusing to fellow Catholics and to others.

The position of the U.S. bishops with respect to the universal Church was important for the NCCB and for all of its observers. This is indicated by headlines such as the one that appeared in the *Washington Post* in April 1983: "The Bishops May Have Deferred More to Rome Than to

Reagan."[96] The question of *what the bishops represented—and to what degrees*—was bound to stick with them, especially since, as Archbishop John Quinn said to me, "The peace pastoral serves as a kind of paradigm for bishops' teaching today." But the rhetoric of the peace pastoral struck to the heart of Church identity. Because of the ambiguities one observer could depict teaching on nuclear morality across episcopal conferences as "kaleidoscopic," but definitely "not catholic."[97]

Many of the bishops' identity and authority problems exist for subsidiary units of organizations that do not have the Catholic Church's quasi-legal distribution of authority nor its claim to moral universality. Even among religious denominations with congregational structures that stress local control (e.g., congregational churches, the Friends, and Baptists), the issue of *who speaks for whom* surfaces periodically. In fact, it is precisely that issue which has led to many religious schisms and organizational splits. A similar problem faces the national divisions of international agencies and multinational corporations. Some multinationals explicitly recognize the problem by allowing division heads to speak with some autonomy and independence while emphasizing the shared values of all of the organization's constituent parts. In this way local and global identities are allowed to co-exist in the organization, although the broader one clearly takes precedence in matters where the two come into conflict. And, of course, the degree of centralization in the organization determines how seriously the "global" identity is to be taken.

The stakes in managing such tensions are especially high for the Roman Catholic Church because of (1) its universal or global reach, (2) its transcendence across time, and (3) its espousal of central "moral truths." To give too much authoritative or institutional leeway to any subsidiary unit—such as the National Conference of Catholic Bishops—can undermine one or all of these organizational claims. To be universal yet specific is the dialectical challenge facing all organizations that span time and space (religions, governments, corporations, unions, etc.), but the "moral character" of Catholicism intensifies that challenge for all of its spokespersons.

NOTES

1. Hans Küng, *The Church* (Garden City, NY: Doubleday, 1976), 283.

2. Peter Nichols, *The Pope's Divisions: The Roman Catholic Church Today* (Harmondsworth, England: Penguin Books, 1981), 21.

3. See Kenneth Burke, *The Rhetoric of Religion: Studies in Logology* (Berkeley: University of California Press, 1961).

4. Avery Dulles, *Church Membership as a Catholic and Ecumenical Problem* (Milwaukee: Marquette University Press, 1974).

5. Avery Dulles, *The Dimensions of the Church: A Postconciliar Reflection* (New York: Newman Press, 1967), 73.

6. Joseph Gremillion, ed., *The Gospel of Peace and Justice: Catholic Social Teaching since Pope John* (Maryknoll, NY: Orbis Books, 1976), 10.

7. *Lumen Gentium,* rpt. in *The Documents of Vatican II,* ed. Walter M. Abbott, trans. Joseph Gallagher (New York: Guild Press, America Press, Association Press, 1966), 14, 30.

8. Donald R. Campion, Introduction to *Gaudium et Spes, Documents,* 183.

9. *Gaudium et Spes, Documents* 209, 199–200, 201–02.

10. Kenneth Burke, *A Grammar of Motives* (1945; rpt., Berkeley: University of California Press, 1969), xviii–xix.

11. *Gaudium et Spes, Documents,* 287–88.

12. *The Challenge of Peace: God's Promise and Our Response* (Washington: USCC, 1983), 1–9; *Gaudium et Spes, Documents,* 293.

13. J. Bryan Hehir, "From the Pastoral Constitution of Vatican II to *The Challenge of Peace,*" in *Catholics and Nuclear War: A Commentary on The Challenge of Peace, the U.S. Catholic Bishops' Pastoral Letter on War and Peace,* ed. Philip J. Murnion (New York: Crossroad, 1983), 72.

14. *Gaudium et Spes, Documents,* 288.

15. Hehir, "From the Pastoral Constitution," 74.

16. See, e.g., Steve Goldzwig and George Cheney; "The U.S. Catholic Bishops on Nuclear Arms: Corporate Advocacy, Role Redefinition and Rhetorical Adaptation," *Central States Speech Journal* 35 (1984): 8–23.

17. Hehir, "From the Pastoral Constitution," 81.

18. Hehir, "From the Pastoral Constitution," 85–86.

19. See, e.g., Carol J. Jablonski, "Promoting Radical Change in the Roman Catholic Church: Rhetorical Requirements, Problems, and Strategies of the American Bishops," *Central States Speech Journal* 31 (1980): 282–89; and Kathleen Hall Jamieson, "Antecedent Genre as Rhetorical Constraint," *Quarterly Journal of Speech* 61 (1975): 406–15. See also Lloyd F. Bitzer, "The Rhetorical Situation," *Philosophy and Rhetoric* 1 (1968): 1–14, where he explains how a constraint can function both as an impediment to and a catalyst for change.

20. Peter Hebblethwaite, "The Popes and Politics: Shifting Patterns in 'Catholic Social Doctrine,' " in *Religion and America: Spirituality in a Secular Age,* ed. Mary Douglas and Steven Tipton (Boston: Beacon Press, 1983), 195.

21. Louis Rene Beres, "Steps toward a New Planetary Identity," *The Bulletin of the Atomic Scientists* 37 (Feb. 1981): 43–47.

22. George F. Kennan, "America's Unstable Soviet Policy," in Murnion, *Catholics and Nuclear War*, 191.

23. Frank Morris, "Hunthausen Admits Adoption of His Stance Could Lead to Red Takeover," *The Wanderer*, 1 Apr. 1982: 3.

24. As quoted in Steve Askin, "Conservative Voices Rise up against Bishops," *National Catholic Reporter*, 3 Dec. 1982: 6.

25. As quoted in Edward Cuddy, "The American Bishops and the Soviet Threat," *America*, 16 Apr. 1983: 292.

26. As quoted in Walter Isaacson, "A Blast from the Bishops," *Time*, 8 Nov. 1982: 18.

27. Philip M. Hannan, interview, *U.S. News and World Report*, 20 Dec. 1982: 47.

28. Cuddy, "The American Bishops," 295.

29. *The Challenge of Peace*, 73–84, esp. 79.

30. McGeorge Bundy, George F. Kennan, Robert S. McNamara, and Gerard Smith, "Nuclear Weapons and the Atlantic Alliance," *Foreign Affairs* 60 (1982): 757.

31. *The Challenge of Peace*, 44–50.

32. *The Challenge of Peace*, 79, 78.

33. Gremillion, *Gospel of Peace*, 69, in commenting on the "planetary Catholic peace movement" launched by Pope John XXIII.

34. *The Challenge of Peace*, 80. See also the widely publicized article by Albert Wohlstetter, "Bishops, Statesmen, and Other Strategists on the Bombing of Innocents," *Commentary*, June 1983: 15–35, where he discusses the threat of worldwide destruction as a part of international politics.

35. Gerald P. Fogarty, "Why the Pastoral Is Shocking," *Commonweal*, 3 June 1983: 335–38; "Bishops Plan Pastoral at Odds with Defense Policies," *Indianapolis Star*, 19 Nov. 1982: 13; Michael Novak, "The Bishops Speak Out," *National Review*, 10 June 1983: 674–81; William Greider, "The Power of the Cross: America's Roman Catholic Bishops Take on the Pentagon," *Rolling Stone*, 28 April 1983: 12ff.

36. "Notes and Comment," *New Yorker*, 23 May 1983: 31.

37. See, e.g., Kurt Andersen, "For God and Country," *Time*, 10 Sept. 1984: 8–10; Jacob V. Lamar, "God and the Ballot Box," *Time*, 17 Sept. 1984: 26–29; "Religion and the Campaign," editorial, *America*, 25 Aug. 1984: 61.

38. Walter Shapiro, et al., "Politics and the Pulpit," *Newsweek*, 17 Sept. 1984: 25.

39. "Religion and the '84 Campaign: USCC Statement," *Origins*, 23 Aug. 1984: 162.

40. "Text of Bishops' Statement on Role of Church in Politics," *New York Times*, 14 Oct. 1984: 13.

41. Personal letter from Caspar W. Weinberger to Archbishop Joseph L.

Bernardin, 13 Sept. 1982 (obtained through the permission of the office of the late Bishop George Fulcher).

42. Richard Halloran, "U.S. Tells Bishops Morality Is Guide on Nuclear Policy," *New York Times,* 17 Nov. 1982: 1.

43. "Text of Administration's Letter to U.S. Catholic Bishops on Nuclear Policies," *New York Times,* 17 Nov. 1982: 11.

44. As paraphrased in Jim Castelli, *The Bishops and the Bomb: Waging Peace in a Nuclear Age* (Garden City, NY: Doubleday, 1983), 129. Castelli reported Russett's figure as forty, but Russett told me it was actually sixty.

45. George Cheney and Phillip K. Tompkins, "On the Facts of the Text as the Basis of Human Communication Research," in *Communication Yearbook 11,* ed. James A. Anderson (Newbury Park, CA: Sage, 1988), 455–81; see also George Cheney, "Speaking of Who 'We' Are: The Development of the U.S. Catholic Bishops' Pastoral Letter *The Challenge of Peace* as a Case Study in Identity, Organization, and Rhetoric," (Ph.D. diss., Purdue University, 1985), 355.

46. Edward Doherty, memo to J. Bryan Hehir, 3 Jan. 1983 (obtained through permission of the office of the late Bishop George Fulcher).

47. Pope John Paul II, "Message to the U.N. Second Special Session on Disarmament," June 1982, as quoted in *The Challenge of Peace,* 54.

48. *The Challenge of Peace,* 55.

49. Joseph Bernardin and John O'Connor, "Questions of Politics, Strategy, and Ethics," testimony before the House Foreign Relations Committee, 26 June 1984, rpt. in *Origins* 9 Aug. 1984: 154.

50. *The Challenge of Peace,* 2nd draft, rpt. in *National Catholic Reporter,* 5 Nov. 1982: 15.

51. *The Challenge of Peace,* 59, n. 84.

52. Bernardin and O'Connor, "Questions of Politics," 156, 157.

53. Richard B. Miller, "Catholic Bishops on War," *The Bulletin of the Atomic Scientists,* May 1983: 12. See also the detailed discussions of the bishops and deterrence in Mark R. Amstutz, "The Challenge of Peace: Did the Bishops Help?" *This World* 11 (Spring/Summer, 1985): 22–35; McGeorge Bundy, "The Bishops and the Bomb," *New York Review of Books,* 16 June 1983: 3ff.; Germain Grisez, "The Moral Implications of a Nuclear Deterrent," *Center Journal* 2 (1982): 9–36; Kenneth R. Himes, "Deterrence and Disarmament: Ethical Evaluation and Pastoral Advice," *Cross Currents* (Winter 1983–84): 421–31; Susan Moller Okin, "Taking the Bishops Seriously, *World Politics* 36 (July 1984): 527–54; Ronald E. Powaski, "Is Nuclear Deterrence Immoral?" *America,* 16 May 1987: 401–05; and Michael Quinlan, "The Ethics of Nuclear Deterrence: A Critical Comment on the Pastoral Letter of the U.S. Catholic Bishops," *Theological Studies* 48 (1987): 3–24.

54. *The Challenge of Peace,* 52.

55. Michael Walzer, *Just and Unjust Wars: A Moral Argument with Historical Illustrations* (New York: Basic Books, 1977), 282.

56. Bruce M. Russett, "Ethical Dilemmas of Nuclear Deterrence," *International Security* 8 (Spring 1984): 36–54, esp. 51.

57. See Albert R. Jonsen and Stephen E. Toulmin, *The Abuse of Casuistry* (Berkeley: University of California Press, 1988).

58. *The Challenge of Peace*, 60, n. 85.

59. Kenneth A. Briggs, "Bishops' Letter on Nuclear Arms Is Revised to 'More Flexible' View," *New York Times*, 6 Apr. 1983: A-1.

60. Bernard Gwertzman, "Administration Hails New Draft of Arms Letter," *New York Times*, 7 Apr. 1983: A-1.

61. Steve Askin, "Administration: 'Draft Substantially Improved': Claims Bishops 'Allies,' " *National Catholic Reporter*, 15 Apr. 1983: 5.

62. Castelli, *Bishops and the Bomb*, 149.

63. John Roach and Joseph Bernardin, "How the Proposed Pastoral Relates to U.S. Policy," statement on 8 Apr. 1983, rpt. in *Origins*, 21 Apr. 1983: 738–39.

64. Castelli, *Bishops and the Bomb*, 161–62.

65. Castelli, *Bishops and the Bomb*, 165.

66. "Bishops and the Bomb," *New York Times*, 6 May 1983: A-30.

67. See, e.g., William Kornhauser, *Scientists in Industry: Conflict and Accommodation* (Berkeley: University of California Press, 1962); Donald C. Pelz and Frank M. Andrews, *Scientists in Organizations* (Ann Arbor: University of Michigan, 1976); Herbert Kaufman, *The Forest Ranger* (Baltimore: Johns Hopkins, 1960).

68. Gerald P. Fogarty, *The Vatican and the American Hierarchy from 1870 to 1965* (Stuttgart: Anton Hiersemann, 1982), 214–28. It was in 1966, following a post–Vatican II reorganization, that the title of the secretariat changed to the U.S. Catholic Conference (USCC) and the bishops adopted the corporate label National Conference of Catholic Bishops (NCCB).

69. Herbert A. Simon, *Administrative Behavior*, 3rd ed. (New York: Free Press, 1976).

70. John L. McKenzie, *The Roman Catholic Church* (Garden City, NY: Image Books, 1971), 24.

71. McKenzie, *Roman Catholic Church*, 66.

72. *Documents*, 42–43.

73. Claude Dagens, "Hierarchy and Communion: The Bases of Authority in the Beginning of the Church," *Communio* 9 (1982): 67–78, esp. 73.

74. John Paul II, "The Bishop: Principle of Unity," address of 29 June 1982, rpt. in *The Pope Speaks* 27 (1982): 338–43.

75. John Paul II, "The Bishop: A Living Sign," address of 5 Sept. 1983, rpt. in *The Pope Speaks* 28 (1983): 337.

76. John Paul II, "Collegiality's Scope," address of 15 June 1984, rpt. in *Origins*, 12 July 1984: 126.

77. Paul J. Hallinan, Introduction to *Decree on the Bishops' Pastoral Office in the Church*, *Documents*, 389–95.

78. Documents, 424–26.

79. Goldzwig and Cheney, "U.S. Catholic Bishops," 20.

80. Fogarty, *Vatican and the American Hierarchy,* 400.

81. *The Challenge of Peace,* 4.

82. Peter Hebblethwaite, "Nuclear Morality Debate: Bishop to Bishop, Nation to Nation, Little Consensus," *National Catholic Reporter,* 28 Jan. 1983: 1, 18.

83. Joseph Cardinal Höffner, letter to archbishop John Roach, 31 Aug. 1982 (obtained with the permission of the office of the late Bishop Fulcher).

84. Gerard Defois, letter to Daniel Hoye, 24 Sept. 1982 (obtained through the permission of the office of the late Bishop George Fulcher).

85. James V. Schall, ed., *The Joint Pastoral Letters of the West German and the French Bishops* (San Francisco: St. Ignatius Press, 1984).

86. James V. Schall, "Risk, Discussion and Political Prudence," *Joint Pastoral Letters,* 9.

87. Patricia Scharber Lefevre, "Vatican Tells Bishops: 'Take Nuclear Morality Wherever It May Go,'" *National Catholic Reporter* 11 Feb. 1983: 26, 27; see also insert in Patty Edmonds, "Bishops Commit Church to Peace," *National Catholic Reporter,* 13 May 1983: 10.

88. Christopher Winer, "U.S. Bishops' Stand May Spur Europeans on Issue," *National Catholic Reporter,* 28 Jan. 1983: 4.

89. Avery Dulles, "The Teaching Authority of Bishops' Conferences," *America,* 11 June 1983: 454; see also Ladislas Orsy, "Episcopal Conferences: Their Theological Standing and Their Doctrinal Authority," *America,* 8 Nov. 1986: 282–85.

90. As quoted in Patricia Scharber Lefevre, "Gumbleton: 'Pastoral Our Full Responsibility,'" *National Catholic Reporter,* 27 May 1983: 26.

91. Dulles, "The Teaching Authority," 455. The quotation from Dulles is suggestive of Chester I. Barnard's theory of authority, in which he emphasizes the role of the *receiver* of a directive as determining its authoritativeness; see *The Functions of the Executive,* 30th anniv. ed. (Cambridge, MA: Harvard University Press, 1968).

92. Edward Vacek, "Authority and the Peace Pastoral," *America,* 22 Oct. 1983: 225–28.

93. Michael Novak, *Moral Clarity in the Nuclear Age* (Nashville: Thomas Nelson, 1983), 106–17.

94. James Hitchcock, "The Catholic Bishops, Public Policy, and the New Class," *This World* no. 9 (Fall 1984): 54–65, esp. 59.

95. George A. Kelly, *The Crisis of Authority: John Paul II and the American Bishops* (New York: Regnery Gateway, 1982), 5.

96. Mary McGrory, "The Bishops May Have Deferred More to Rome Than to Reagan," *Washington Post,* 7 Apr. 1983: A-3.

97. Francis X. Winters, "Nuclear Deterrence Morality: Atlantic Community Bishops in Tension," *Theological Studies* 43 (1982): 428–46, esp. 428.

5

CREATING CRUCIAL RHETORICAL
CONNECTIONS

For better or for worse, in the West it is mostly Catholicism which has remembered . . . moral absolutes [such as against the deliberate taking of human life] and their rational expression and built them into social identity.
James R. Kelly, "Catholicism and Modern Memory: Some Sociological Reflections on the Symbolic Foundations of the Rhetorical Force of the Pastoral Letter, *The Challenge of Peace*," *Sociological Analysis*, 1984

[The Challenge of Peace *is a*] *subtle document of consensus whose more immediate policy proposals . . . fit within the bounds of political discourse in the United States, albeit on the left-liberal side.*
Phillip Berryman, *Our Unfinished Business: The U.S. Catholic Bishops' Letters on Peace and the Economy*

In the case of nuclear war, the bishops put the problem with all its complexities in the hands of the whole Catholic community itself.
Webster T. Patterson, "Nuclear War, the Bishops, and the *Sensus Fidelium:* A New Process for Consensus?" *Chicago Studies*, 1983

The preceding chapter focused on what may be loosely thought of as maintaining identities in the face of structural-political complexities and constraints. I now turn to processes of constructing, reconstructing, defining, and redefining concepts so that they could fit within the constraints of the organization yet allow new sorts of advocacy by spokespersons for the organization. This kind of manipulation of concepts and symbols is fundamentally rhetorical because it involves invoking and sometimes reshaping received notions to fit challenging situational circumstances.

THE BISHOPS AND THE INDIVIDUAL CATHOLIC:
COLLEGIALITY, COMMUNITY, COMMUNICATION

This discussion first addresses the question of how the bishops managed the relationship of the individual Catholic to the Church as a whole and specifically to the hierarchy. "Individual Catholics" include clergy (priests) and non-clergy religious (nuns and brothers), although the emphasis here is on how the bishops treated the laity in and with respect to the peace pastoral. The three "co-" terms above—collegiality, community, communication—emerged prominently in the discourse of and about the peace pastoral and the terms identify constructs the bishops reshaped to some degree in order to evolve positions concerning the relationships of individuals to the Church and its hierarchy.

A pastoral letter is a traditional form of communication between bishops and the faithful; it is designed as moral guidance or teaching, but not as binding rule or law. Pastoral letters of the National Conference of Catholic Bishops (or any other national episcopal body) are to be taken *very seriously* by the faithful and are to play a major role in the refinement of Catholic conscience in the numerous dioceses of the nation.[1]

The NCCB has a history of issuing pastoral letters on a variety of topics. From 1980 to 1989, for example, they touched on such topics as Marxism, Central America, the Hispanic population of the United States, war and peace, the economy, and women (the last is still being debated). Usually, however, the official messages of the NCCB receive limited attention. Bishop Fulcher told me that the 1980 *Pastoral Letter on Marxist Communism* had been read by very few people—Catholic or otherwise. "Most Catholics don't even know that we issued that letter, yet we [the bishops] consider it to be a significant statement."

A number of things changed after that letter was released. One was that the bishops organized their later efforts to a significant extent on the model of Church-as-community, emphasizing the spread of collegiality with a stress on highly interactive communication with the laity. This represented a new episcopal posture toward U.S. Catholics.

Tim Unsworth, a journalist, reacted to the follow-up on the peace pastoral this way: "The bishops have now had the excitement of challenging us. In doing so, they have been challenged themselves."[2] In other words, the way the bishops handled the role of the individual Catholic necessarily said something about their own collective role as the American hierarchy and vice versa. Broadly speaking, changes in the identity of one actor must affect the identity of a co-actor, and the bishops put emphasis on "co-" with their *Challenge of Peace*.

125

The bishops were especially conscious of the term "pastoral." According to Fulcher, the bishops saw themselves as "religious and moral teachers who were willing to listen and learn." Their peace pastoral was offered as "an invitation and a challenge to Catholics in the United States" to reflect on the arms race and to influence public policy. Even more broadly, the letter called "Catholics and all members of our political community to dialogue and specific decisions about this awesome question." At the same time, the bishops maintained that "prudential judgments are involved based on specific circumstances which can change or which can be interpreted differently by people of good will."[3] In this way, Fr. Hesburgh told me, "The bishops offered the letter not as the *last* word on nuclear weapons—from them or for the U.S. Church—but as a kind of *first* word to get the discussion moving." As I have shown, however, the pastoral was not universally interpreted in this way.

The bishops interpreted "pastoral" to mean allowing for and even encouraging all Catholics to reflect on and voice their positions on issues of war and peace. "To be sure, it would have been more satisfying if the bishops had issued a catechism of do's and don't's on nuclear arms, but they did not."[4] Father Hehir said in an interview that the style of the peace pastoral was influenced by the words of the Pastoral Constitution of Vatican II: *Gaudium et Spes* "describes an attitude which the church brings to [the] dialogue with the world: the church has something to learn and something to teach." In *Gaudium et Spes* the Council committed all bishops "to a teaching style which seeks a precise understanding of contemporary problems in all their complexity prior to making moral judgments or providing religious guidance about these questions." With such a perspective as guide the NCCB conducted its numerous hearings and ultimately "put their finished product into the hands of the people of the Church."[5] This approach was first explored—although to a more limited extent—in 1980 when the U.S. bishops actively sought out lay opinions before attending the family-life synod in Rome.[6]

One way the bishops worked through their renewed interpretation of the pastoral function was by centering on the term "collegiality." This became a vibrant and compelling term for the bishops, one connected with notions of sharing responsibility, ministry, teaching, decision-making, and social action. In reacting to the Collegeville meeting, where collegiality was a key term, Bishop Malone stated: "The phrases 'role of the bishop,' 'the body of bishops,' 'I, Bishop Malone,' 'we, the bishops' call up new images, prompt new intellectual and emotional responses in the wake of the . . . assembly."[7] This "we-ness" that was so deeply felt by the bishops became associated with the term "collegiality" and was applied to the whole Church, according to Malone.

From this it was an easy step to the kind of stress on communication that also emerged from the Collegeville retreat. The five themes of post-meeting reflections were cohesiveness, identity, relevance, continuity, and engagement. Collectively these terms suggest deliberate interaction both within and beyond the Church. The importance of such two-way communication was highlighted by Detroit's John Cardinal Dearden at the retreat. Mentioning "the desire and intention" of Pope John Paul II to use the Synod of Bishops "expressly as an instrument of collegial activity," the Cardinal said:

> This suggests the importance of seeing the synod as a channel of communication in two directions. Though the synod has not the character of an ecumenical council, it offers a vehicle for fruitful exchange. This means, therefore, that the bishops' conference must be prepared to insert its thinking into the process as well as to profit from the insights and experiences of others.[8]

And this is what the bishops worked toward, according to Bishop Fulcher. He cited the growing recognition among NCCB members of a need to communicate effectively with the people, "to move closer to them through consultation and through teaching."

Many of these ideas about the pastoral role, collegiality, and communication were symbolically drawn together in the notion of the Church as community. The idea of community is based in the description of the church as a community of believers in the New Testament (Acts 4:32), and has been developed in recent years, most notably by theologian Avery Dulles. Dulles's landmark work *Models of the Church* in 1974 discussed alternative visions of the Church—institution, mystical communion, sacrament, herald, and servant—and more recently Dulles has explored the community model. Any model or metaphor for the Church, says Dulles, necessarily encounters ambiguities because of the inherent mystery of the Church: "The mysterious character of the Church . . . rules out the possibility of proceeding from clear and univocal concepts, or from definitions in the usual sense of the word."[9] Operating with this view gives a significant rhetorical advantage to the user of a term such as "community"; the term may be thought to synthesize the seemingly disparate notions of communion and hierarchy.

In *A Church to Believe In,* Dulles elaborated the community model as "a more modest conception of Church than some others" (e.g., sacrament, mystical communion, etc.). In the spirit of post–Vatican II reflection, and following the lead of John Paul II's teaching, Dulles offered the "community of disciples" as a designation for the Church "that can help to overcome the existing polarizations and serve to integrate and channel the ecclesial experience of contemporary Catholics." This model, claimed Dulles, has several advantages, including an explicitly biblical basis—the fact that Jesus actually founded a community of disciples. It also has "congruence" with "our everyday experience of Church." Moreover, this model is seen as Christ-centered, dynamic, and suggestive of shared responsibility. There is a distinctly democratic tone to the community model, although not to the extent of suppressing authority or hierarchy. As Dulles argued, "By viewing ministry as discipleship, we can avoid making too sharp a distinction between the minister and those ministered to." Finally, Dulles explained that the "community of disciples" can be used in conjunction with key elements of the other models of Church to "save what is valid" in them.[10]

The NCCB apparently agreed with this assessment, for they quoted Pope John Paul II's first encyclical to describe the Church—"It is the community of the disciples"[11]—and they framed a section of the peace pastoral, "The Church: A Community of Conscience, Prayer and Penance," around Dulles's work. Wrote the bishops: "As believers we can identify rather easily with the early Church as a company of witnesses engaged in a difficult mission." The bishops used this idea as a springboard for their final call to various groups in society to work for peace. The whole Church, they insisted, "must develop a sense of solidarity, cemented by relationships with mature and exemplary Christians who represent Christ and his way of life."[12]

Of course, there are a variety of models and understandings of "community." In general, however, if true community is engendered, there will be such qualitative features as: (1) "an orientation toward process" through which participants find a sense of community; (2) recognition that "cooperative effort is required in order to act effectively"; (3) a belief that "tangible rewards will result from cooperative effort"; and (4) a linkage of "common attitudes and aspirations of individuals with groups [generating] . . . realizable prospects of achievement through strategic use of existing . . . communicative channels."[13] The general notion of community implies such democratic aims and processes. And the bishops, as bishops, tried to apply these qualities to their own organization, especially after their Collegeville retreat. They had to do so, however, within the constraints of a larger organizational system, the hierarchy and doctrine of the Roman Catholic Church. This meant that the final feature of community listed above—involving use of available channels of communication—posed a real difficulty for the bishops. Their commitment to community was genuine, but it had to be pursued within the bounds established by institutional authority. The bishops' use of ambiguity in handling the tension between hierarchy and community could only partially resolve this paradoxical rhetorical problem.

Their particular model of community contributed to the bishops' own transformation during the development of the peace pastoral. Former Indiana Catholic Conference President Raymond Rufo said in an interview: "Coupled with the stress on the expanded role of the laity [as articulated in 'Called and Gifted,' the bishops' statement on the laity in 1980], the community of disciples became a powerful image of shared responsibility." Moreover, as a number of bishops have said, the term "community" applies equally to the local church and to the universal Church, helping to draw those two levels together symbolically.[14] From this perspective every member of the Church is seen as having special gifts. The bishops called on individual Church members to use these gifts in responding to the peace pastoral.

The community model of the Church suggested a simultaneous "unity and diversity"[15] while it imaged the Church as "a coherent whole, structured in such a way that each element is nothing unless connected to the whole."[16] According to Fr. Hehir, the community model allowed for "structured pluralism."[17] Moreover, "the whole of the Church must be present in each of her parts."[18] In this way, "the bishop is in the Church and the Church in the bishop."[19] The community model thus linked individual and collective identity in ways that were supposed to promote community *and* preserve hierarchy.

To conceive of a religious organization as a community has profound and challenging implications for practice. Among other things the notion of "community" specifically implies that organizational positions on internal and external issues involve the active participation and critical endorsement of all members of the organization. The same happens when a business organization moves toward a more democratic and participative structure by, for example, instituting quality circles and other techniques involving participative decision making. We, as members of organizations, need to notice that every elevation of community as an organizational value implies some diminution of hierarchy as an organizational value. That problem promptly arose in the minds of people who reacted to the NCCB's peace pastoral.

In an editorial on the peace pastoral several months after its publication John Hanson maintained that this kind of move toward community "overloads the communication circuit for most lay[persons]." He explained that the bishops simply did not effectively manage the inclusion of the three levels of moral authority in *The Challenge of Peace:* the "universal morally authoritative principles and formal church teaching," the reaffirmation of "statements of recent popes and the teachings of Vatican II" on war and peace, and the specific applications as "prudential moral judgments." Hanson asked whether the bishops can have both authority and equal rights at the same time." And he concluded his critique by saying, "If what we are all seeking is a *solution,* is not one opinion likely to be more 'legitimate' than others?" *The Challenge of Peace* confused this issue, Hanson, insisted, thereby making it difficult for the laity to accept "the challenge."[20]

A major critical response to the peace pastoral came in Michael Novak's *Moral Clarity in the Nuclear Age* (functionally an anti- or counter-pastoral), published three times in various forms.[21] In an interview Novak explained the rationale for his book this way: "I and a number of others saw the bishops moving into strategic and technical questions, a development with which we were not comfortable. Therefore in order to voice the legitimate role of laypersons and avoid the criticism that laypeople weren't doing anything, we decided to do what the bishops were doing—produce a document on the moral dimensions of war and peace." Novak and other members of the American Catholic Committee, who were sharply critical of the bishops' second draft, became more favorable toward the final document, in part because of the greater stress on a hierarchy of moral authority. Nevertheless, Novak reported to me that "many saw an excessive use of authority by the bishops in moving at all beyond principles to specifics. And this jarred many people into resistance." Ironically, Novak's group took up the bishops' call for debate while at the same time criticizing them for inviting debate, thus implicitly rejecting the bishops' community model of the Church. In a broader criticism of trends in the U.S. Church, Msgr. George Kelly complained that a number of Church leaders had since Vatican II distorted the intention and product of Vatican II. He argued, for example, that ambiguous notions of the Church—such as the "People of God"—were often used "to justify public criticism of and public dissent within the Church" to an inappropriate extent.[22] From my reading of Kelly I conclude that he would disapprove of recent advocacy efforts by the U.S. Catholic hierarchy.

Catholic responses to the peace pastoral have been diverse, even *within* categories that might be labeled "pro" and "con." It is clear also that the bishops anticipated this development. That is one reason why, as Archbishop John O'Connor told me, he insisted that teachers and "listeners" "consider the peace pastoral in its entirety" and "observe absolutely the three levels of the moral hierarchy." These imperatives, he added, "provide the only reasonable framework for dialogue." "Dialogue" was a key term for implementation of the letter, said Bishop Daniel Reilly in an interview. "We're talking *with* the people, not down to them." Daniel Hoye, NCCB General Secretary, offered yet another angle on this matter: "We first want to get people to know what the letter says. . . . Second, we want to get them to go through the same process as the bishops—to examine church teaching, the world situation, and then the intersection of the two." Another interviewee, Auxiliary Bishop Richard Sklba, maintained that the entire process will help "to present the bishops as listening much more carefully to the people while offering moral judgments."

In sum, the bishops incurred both advantages and risks in operating from their community model of Church. How to maintain unity and diversity, hierarchy and communion, binding principles and disparate applications, represents a profound challenge to managing any organization as complex as the Roman Catholic Church. And conveying these subtleties to the Catholic community was no elementary rhetorical task. Perhaps the recognition of this multifaceted challenge (one that implicates identity, organization, and rhetoric) led Fr. Hehir to say to me: "The bishops wanted to take seriously the ideas of collegiality, dialogue, and community. But I wouldn't push the community-of-disciples image *too* far; it does not represent a fundamental change in the Church's understanding of herself." Nevertheless, as one observer put it, "In the case of nuclear war, the bishops put the problem with all its complexities in the hands of the whole Catholic community itself."[23]

The ideal of community is a popular one in contemporary philosophy, politics, and organizational practice.[24] The fact that the bishops adopted it to some extent suggests that their ideas were part of a larger *Zeitgeist*. The values and practices associated with community—equality, dialogue, and adaptability—have been advocated for groups and organizations as diverse as corporations, the U.S. peace movement, and the Catholic Church in Latin America. Indeed, much of the desire and drive toward community may be thought of as a reaction to the types and extent of alienation found in our society.[25] But for any organization that is elaborately hierarchical, "community" is a seriously challenging notion. To encourage ongoing, critical, and widely participative dialogue is to allow for the possibility that the very authority that opened the discussion could be eliminated or reduced in importance. This is a challenge being faced in contemporary China, the Soviet Union, and Eastern Europe. Powerful hierarchical structures do not surrender authority easily; nor do they readily accept a transformed identity for their group, organization, or nation.

For the hierarchy of the Roman Catholic Church, or any part of it, to foster more open discussion within the organization means that criticism of the hierarchy itself is inevitable. The organizational metaphors of hierarchy and communion (or community) do clash; no amount of rhetorical and organizational effort can resolve *all* of their differences. Therefore, any hierarchical, bureaucratic organization will have difficulty in reconciling the two images. This is also the problem with which large universities struggle as they seek to maintain the symbol of collegiality for faculty and students while at the same time becoming more administrative and business-like.[26] In managing their own identity and the identities of their internal audiences, then, the bishops were left with the position articulated by Fr. Hehir: taking community *seriously,* but not pushing it *too far*. This ambiguity will probably confront the bishops and the Church as a whole as long as the Church itself exists.

TRYING TO FORGE CONNECTIONS ACROSS ISSUES: PEACE, JUSTICE, LIFE

The best way to capture the concerns of this section is by introducing two papal quotations included by the bishops in *The Challenge of Peace.* The first is from Pope Paul VI's 1967 encyclical *Populorum Progressio* (The Development of Peoples): "Peace cannot be limited to a mere absence of war, the result of an ever precarious balance of forces. No, peace is something built up day after day, in the pursuit of an order intended by God, which implies a more perfect form of justice among men and women."[27] The other is also from Paul, from his 1977 "World Day of Peace Message." He declared: "If you wish peace, defend life."[28] The first quotation, of course, links "a positive conception of peace" to progress toward justice in what the bishops called a summary of "classical Catholic teaching." The latter was a message the bishops called "resolutely clear": "We plead with all who would work to end the scourge of war to begin by defending life at its most defenseless, the life of the unborn."[29]

Such pronouncements from popes (especially in the form of papal encyclicals) are directives that bishops must observe if they are to speak with institutional authority. In this respect the Catholic Church is the type of organization in which the top authority can direct the general positions that other members *must* incorporate within their thoughts and statements on more specific matters. The Church thus shapes the premises of its potential spokespersons in a more direct and explicit and authoritative way than do most other organizations. However, in many matters the Vatican allows Church members (bishops and others) maneuvering room in determining specific religious and moral choices. Language—rhetorical adjustment—thus becomes extremely important. Points of ambiguity have to be explored, refined, and perhaps even stretched. Within the Church, however, ambiguity about *moral* choices could not be allowed to remain, at least in theory. Accordingly, moral choices are tied to fundamental principles, and the fundamental principle to which the bishops chose to tie their peace pastoral was the dignity of human life, a fundamental, unassailable doctrine of the Church.

By most accounts the bishops attempted to achieve two things by their embrace of a "life-oriented" perspective: (1) to present a consistent moral-ethical stance across important issues by grounding their positions in the traditional Catholic affirmation of the dignity of human life; and (2) to bridge across positions thought to be "liberal" and "conservative" and to do so with one theme, one principle. These rhetorical strategies and their implications are considered in detail in the following discussion of the question: How did the bishops manage to relate issues of peace/nuclear arms control/defense to other issues of Church concern?

Both a number of bishops and a number of groups within the Church had pushed for explicit consideration of the issues of poverty and abortion in the peace pastoral. "A consistent moral vision rooted in Catholic social thought," Archbishop Roach told the Conference in November 1981, "would link opposition to the arms race with opposition to abortion and support for the rights of the poor."[30] In fact, whatever the bishops said on any of these issues *had* to be linked somehow to the sanctity-of-life premise if the bishops were to speak with institutional consistency and authority. These connections made their way into the various drafts of the peace pastoral. In the final document the bishops declared with respect to abortion: "We must ask how long a nation willing to extend a constitutional guarantee to the 'right' to kill defenseless human beings by abortion is likely to refrain from adopting strategic warfare policies deliberately designed to kill millions of defenseless human beings."[31] The bishops thus drew a direct parallel between the widespread resort to abortion and the threat of widespread nuclear destruction: one involves

133

the *actual* killing of many innocents; the other involves a *potential* for the same. The fundamental moral premise of the Church required such a linkage.

The way the bishops handled the peace-poverty connection was slightly different. Here their argument was two-pronged. First, they called arms build-ups "a massive distortion of resources in the face of crying human need," thereby coming down on the side of butter instead of guns in the allocation of the superpowers' resources. Second, the bishops offered a positive vision of global interdependence, which I have already discussed. Their argument seemed to be not that true peace and economic justice are parallel concerns, but that the latter should be considered a foundation or a basis for the former. The bishops warned: "If the monetary and trading systems are not governed by sensitivity to mutual needs, they can be destroyed." And they continued on a more specific level: "If the protection of human rights and the promotion of human needs are left as orphans in the diplomatic arena, the stability we seek in increased armaments will eventually be threatened by rights denied and needs unmet in vast sectors of the globe."[32] Thus, the bishops called not only for the reactive step of eliminating nuclear weapons but also for the proactive step of building a peace based on justice. In this instance the bishops had more rhetorical freedom than with abortion because the Church's position on social justice was not so specifically defined.

These linkages became more explicit in two speeches by Cardinal Bernardin. Both involved the further identification of the several issues with one another, using the dignity of human life as the symbolic glue to hold them together. On 6 December 1983, in an address at Fordham University, Bernardin introduced his concerns this way:

> I do not underestimate the intrinsic intellectual difficulties of this exercise nor the delicacy of the question—ecclesially, ecumenically and politically. But I believe the Catholic moral tradition has something valuable to say in the face of multiple threats to the sacredness of human life, and I am convinced that the church is in a position to make a significant defense of life in a comprehensive and consistent manner.[33]

Explaining that "The *Challenge of Peace* provides a starting point for developing a consistent ethic of life but it does not provide a fully articulated framework," Bernardin highlighted "(1) the *need* for a consistent ethic of life; (2) the *attitude* necessary to sustain it; and (3) the *principles* needed to shape it." Defending the need, Bernardin argued that "asking [important moral] questions along the spectrum of life from womb to tomb creates the need for a consistent ethic of life. For the spectrum of life cuts across the issues of genetics, abortion, capital punishment, modern warfare and the care of the terminally ill." From there he moved to associate "right to life" and "quality of life," saying, "Those who defend the right to life of the weakest among us [i.e., the unborn] must be equally visible in support of the quality of life of the powerless among us: the old and the young, the hungry, and the homeless, the undocumented immigrant and the unemployed worker."[34] Thus, the Cardinal identified a whole range of life-related issues with one another, an association he and the media came to call the "seamless garment."

Bernardin reinforced and elaborated this position in an address at St. Louis University on 11 March 1984. There he made a careful refinement of his position, apparently responding to criticisms of the "seamless garment" as crude and simplistic. He explained:

> In response to those who fear otherwise, I contend that the systemic vision of a consistent ethic of life will not erode our crucial public opposition to the direction of the arms race; neither will it smother our persistent and necessary public opposition to abortion. The systemic vision is rooted in the conviction that our opposition to these distinct problems has a common foundation and that both Church and society are served by making it evident.

Moreover, Bernardin continued:

> A consistent ethic of life does not equate the problem of taking life (e.g., through abortion and in war) with the problems of promoting human dignity (through humane programs of nutrition, health care and housing). But a consistent ethic identifies both the protection of life and its promotion as moral questions. It argues for a continuum of life which must be sustained in the face of diverse and distinct threats.[35]

With these distinctions Bernardin acknowledged the complexity of tackling several controversial issues simultaneously and offered strategies for building "a constituency" in both "the church and the nation."[36] In his second address Bernardin admitted that while "it is possible to identify a single principle with diverse applications," it is important at a "second level" to stress "the distinction among cases rather than their similarities." This acknowledged the importance and necessity of casuistic reasoning, which allows the complexities of cases to affect how moral principles are applied. Bernardin articulated this refinement in response to the diverse constituencies in society (e.g., those against abortion, those for disarmament, those fighting poverty), noting that "no one can do everything."[37]

Bernardin's statements, taken as a whole, echo the peace pastoral's hierarchy of moral principles, allowing for some range of interpretation while insisting on the inviolability of an overarching principle. This was necessary both in the interest of consistency with the bishops' newly articulated framework for moral application and in deference to the diverse, often conflicting, constituencies Bernardin sought to unite. The use of calculated ambiguity can go a long way in defusing actual or potential criticism from several sides, and Bernardin was making use of this rhetorical fact.

The "seamless garment" idea evoked diverse responses, indicating that ambiguity could not solve all of Bernardin's rhetorical problems. Bernardin's St. Louis address was followed by one by Archbishop John O'Connor on 28 April in Harrisburg, Pennsylvania. Presumably to explain *his* understanding of the "seamless garment" concept, O'Connor defended his "obsession" with abortion as an issue. In doing so he linked abortion to the nuclear threat. Of his personal position he said, "I have an obsession about the *worth* of the human person,"[38] and he used the "worth of the human person" as the basis for opposing both abortion and nuclear armament. On the other hand, journalist Richard O'Connor complained of the kind of connection Archbishop O'Connor made. Said he: "Linking abortion with disarmament is neither logical nor wise. Saying that the rights of the innocent, unborn babies are no different from the rights of hardened, condemned criminals, or that abortion . . . demands an equal amount of concern as nuclear warfare . . . is not only illogical, but grotesque."[39] It was common for conservative, anti-abortion groups to portray the bishops as diluting the attack on abortion by blending it with concerns for other issues. Responding to such criticism, Joseph Allegretti wrote: "Ironically, those who seek to support life wherever it's threatened may be attacked by those who call themselves pro-lifers but who may, in fact, be less pro-lifers than pro-birthers."[40] And while some liberals were uncomfortable with the linkage of an anti-abortion position with a call for arms control or disarmament, a Rhode Island state senator welcomed it: "For people like me, it serves to situate the Catholic anti-abortion position within what may loosely be called a liberal or progressive framework of political thinking, and to rescue it from the conservative or right-wing ideology within which it is frequently found."[41] All of these observations show how individuals manage identities, particularly by reconciling conflicts and differences.

While it was difficult but manageable to bridge an array of positions on diverse issues with a single principle, the identification of a constituency proved an even more challenging problem. How to develop an identifiable constituency was one question posed by Cardinal Bernardin in his two "seamless garment" addresses, and it was clearly a pivotal one. Could the politically and temperamentally divergent groups who took strong positions on abortion, nuclear arms, capital punishment, aid for the poor, and so forth rethink their positions' relationships to other issues and other groups? Would they come to recognize and express *common* interests? Some of the bishops and their associates believed so. Bishop Leroy Matthiesen of Amarillo told me that "Cardinal Bernardin is right on target. The Church has got to move toward a careful examination of all issues using a consistent ethic of life." General Secretary of the NCCB-USCC Daniel Hoye argued in an interview that "the seamless garment will force single-issue people to think of other issues." Father Richard Warner of the war and peace committee maintained that people would become members of a variety of organizations—fighting abortion, capital punishment, the arms build-up, and supporting human rights in many forms. "This is," Warner said to me, "the only approach that makes sense." The then NCCB President, Bishop James Malone, was quite optimistic: "The Church in the U.S. is now more ready to link the gospel to social ills and contemporary Catholic social teaching to a range of issues. There's a consciousness raising going on which is taking us beyond privatized religion."

Of course, there were others within the Church who disagreed about the rhetorical-practical effectiveness of the consistent-ethic-of-life approach. Michael Novak contended that "there isn't really a seamless garment; it's more like a quilt. There may be appeal to a logician in the Bernardin approach, but for a tactician or a strategist to try to move on all fronts at once can be fatal." An article in October 1984, nearly one year after Bernardin's first address, seemed to support Novak's view. "The 'seamless garment,'" an *Our Sunday Visitor* editorial stated, "has been torn apart by this year's national election." And the same article continued:

> Neither side sees any linkage among these issues. The liberal political establishment sees abortion as regrettable, but an area of private morality in which the state has no right to interfere. The conservative right totally rejects any linkage. They see no relation, for example, in the execution of a convicted murderer and the legalized destruction of innocent unborn life. The vast "middle ground" between the left and right tends to pick and choose among the life issues. They lean toward the liberal position on nuclear arms and euthanasia, but toward the conservative position on abortion and capital punishment.[42]

The last comment about the middle-of-the-roaders brings to mind Andrew Greeley's description of "selective Catholicism" (derisively called "cafeteria Catholicism"), where the faithful take what they will from Church teaching and disregard other parts of it.[43] Such is the process by which Catholic identities are often appropriated in contemporary Western society. In a personal letter Greeley applied this notion to the situation of the bishops, writing: "Curiously, it seems to me that left-wing Catholics expect the ordinary laity to obey the bishops on nuclear weapons but not to obey them on sex while right-wing Catholics expect them to obey the bishops on sex but not on nuclear weapons." And he concluded: "In my experience and observation—as well as looking at the data—the typical Catholic layman doesn't take a bishop seriously as a teacher on either sex or politics—save in the unusual situation where the lay person believes the bishop knows what he's talking about."

Whatever the relative legitimacy of these different interpretations, the seamless-garment notion was a major effort by the bishops to identify the Church as holding a coherent position on a range of issues. Rhetorically it was a strategy that aimed to broaden the Church's dialogue with the secular order on issues thought to be "Catholic" and on others not typically associated with the Church. Organizationally the move posed an undeniable and formidable challenge by asking the many interest groups to take the concerns of one another into account. And, of course, the "seamless garment" imaged something significant about what the bishops believed the Church to be. The editorial quoted above concluded: "One would be foolish to expect that the Church will ever abandon the seamless garment. It cannot, because it is a fundamental understanding of the Church's teachings on the life issues!" The seamless-garment idea was a way of expressing the Church's socio-political mission writ large, though it could not—at least from the hierarchy's point of view—be allowed to be equated perfectly with the Church's religious identity. That would lead to a political reduction of the Church, a danger which, as we have already seen, must be steadfastly avoided.[44]

Internal Catholic challenges to the bishops' "seamless garment" arose from doubts about one or both of (1) whether all taking of life is of the same quality, and (2) whether the dignity-of-human-life premise could fairly be extended and applied as far as the seamless-garment idea required. These same issues are likely to be encountered in various forms by other doctrinaire or doctrinally based organizations. The key question is: How much does the doctrine (e.g., a set of moral principles) cover? This is a question for insiders primarily. If we step outside a doctrinal organization's own community (e.g., the Catholic faithful), we quickly find a different basis for criticism. Sweeping applications of doctrine or moral principles are criticized, using such *topoi* as relevance, feasibility, effectiveness, and practicality. The bishops faced each of these challenges: the first from Catholics and the second from the wider political community. Insiders questioned the reasonableness of the seamless-garment idea and outsiders questioned its pragmatic applications and consequences.

The notions of a "seamless garment" and a socio-religious "ethic of life" were virtually impossible for any entity within the Church to ignore. The ideas constituted episcopally built, symbolic bridges interconnecting a fairly complex array of doctrinal positions. Every self-identifying group or faction within the institution had to define itself in relation to the "garment" because the garment idea was presented as a relatively authoritative pronouncement, although not on every point binding. No matter how narrowly a faction within the Church defined its mission, it would deal with the "seamless garment" and "ethic of life" doctrines— either as points of departure or as positions to be discussed in institutional argumentation, especially if some aspect of those positions were to be qualified. The situation illustrates a further, general feature of organizational communication. Any organization's "constitutional" definitions (as in charters, directors' announcements, official goals, and the like) make claims and promises that must be recognized and dealt with by every element of the body that wishes in any degree to reinforce or deviate from the constitutional stance of the institution.

When more than a single constitutional concept has been promulgated, the relative status of each must also be considered. The U.S. Church's experience, with its multiple pastoral letters, illustrates this. For example, issuance of the peace pastoral was followed by development of a pastoral on economics. Auxiliary Bishop Richard Sklba pointed out to me the need to link the economic pastoral with the peace pastoral and to link both with other pastorals that had been issued. This was necessary to elaborate the consistent ethic of life claimed by the Church's official pronouncements. "Of course," said Sklba, "there is always the danger that any particular issue may get suppressed, and that is something we must guard against." The importance of consistency was also underscored in a March 1985 newsletter from the liberal Catholic social-justice lobby, Center of Concern. The Director of the Center, Peter Henriot, wrote: "The way to avoid each new pastoral letter's overshadowing of the previous ones is . . . to show the close linkage of the letters with each other."[45] Similar needs to maintain both the reality and the appearance of consistency confront any organizational rhetoricians who seek to exert influence within the framework and "constitution" of the organization.

THE PRACTICAL CHALLENGE:
MANAGING MULTIPLE INTERESTS
AND MULTIPLE GROUPS

A quotation from one of my interviewees, Sister Juliana Casey, captures the spirit and meaning of the following discussion. Casey, as provincial of the Sisters of the Immaculate Heart of Mary, represented women's religious communities on the ad hoc war and peace committee. She described participation in the process this way:

> Each of us, in a sense, brought *our people* with us. Archbishop O'Connor, with his years of experience as a military chaplain, was knowledgeable about and sensitive to the military point of view. Bishop Gumbleton was quite conscious of his role as President of Pax Christi, USA. Cardinal Bernardin, as chair, was thoughtful about the authority and position of the bishops. Father Warner worked hard to represent the Conference of Major Superiors of Men. And I tried to add the point of view of women religious. What we had all together was a wonderful convergence of a Christian community.

Casey articulated in clear terms the pragmatic implications of identifying with different interests represented within a group or organization. Through strong identifications we do—in a very real sense—carry something of the social order around with us; we hold, consciously and unconsciously, the interests of various groups to which we belong and with which we associate. All organizations experience the effects of multiple interests and multiple identities: there are likely to be different groups or factions within any organization; individual members thus may have multiple loyalties; there may be pressures from outside groups. Once again, those who would speak for an organization need to "invent" unifying, inclusive conceptions and language that will minimize members' and other listeners/readers' senses of otherness with respect to the propounding organization. In drafting their peace pastoral the bishops had to resolve just these kinds of rhetorical problems.

Earlier I offered two definitions of identification. On a broad level the process may be expressed as "the appropriation of identity."[46] In a more specific, "operationalized" way we may say that "a decision maker identifies with an organization when he or she desires to choose the alternative which best promotes the perceived interests of that organization."[47]

Casey's comments were attuned to both formulations. On the specific level Casey's words acknowledge that the representatives to the committee were just that, *representatives*. Each came to the group from a different background and even a different organizational context within the U.S. Catholic community and the more embracing universal Catholic Church. Each member displayed a somewhat different set of alignments and perspectives, though all shared "an unshakeable commitment to the Church," as Bishop Fulcher told me. Their overlapping and differing identifications took the form of expressed interests, as Casey's observations suggest. The verb "to appropriate" is certainly fitting here because of the ways in which members of the committee (like members of any group) "took" certain interests as their own even though those interests set them apart from others. In this way the very ambiguity or equivocality of the verb "to appropriate" is useful for expressing the inherently paradoxical nature of these multiple identifications and identities. What we take and express as our own interests are always fashioned to some extent from social or collective interests. Thus, the members of the bishops' committee and the members of the NCCB generally participated in the process of the peace pastoral's development using the terms of their various but interrelated interests. In the end they arrived at a sufficient consensus to produce a 238–9 supportive vote.

The need to manage multiple identities in developing any corporate position is illustrated in many ways in the account I have given of the bishops' development of their peace pastoral. They had to weave a rhetorical document, the fabric of which included a variety of public and religious issues, and they had to do so in ways that at one and the same time conformed to the interests of the universal Church, their Conference, individual Church members, their special interests, and, in lesser degree, the interests of groups outside their corporate body. To accomplish all of this the bishops chose to stress certain values, labels, symbols, and principles that aligned the various identifications being managed. For example, the bishops wanted to avoid direct identification with nuclear freeze advocates, even though they adopted much of the language of the popular political freeze proposal. What they tried to avoid were the *labels* of the movement. To have aligned themselves with such labels would have implied a kind of specialized and transitory political interest that the bishops wanted their document to transcend. Instead, they deliberately used terms that would identify them strongly with the Vatican and the interests of the universal Church. To preserve their identity and authority as spokespersons for the Church this sort of unmistakable identification was rhetorically essential, and they knew it. Reflecting their sense that they spoke as representatives of a *universal* institution, the bishops often gave sweeping, inclusive status to their observations, as when they spoke of "a world" at "a moment of supreme crisis." At other times, and equally because of the identity they wanted to maintain, they resorted to language that would separate ideas into categories. Thus, they were at pains to differentiate "binding principles" from "prudential judgments." Only so could they produce discourse that would reflect the inclusive authority they claimed and at the same time show that they respected some limits on their institutional authority.

Some of the identities the bishops had to manage were considerably more specific and "local" than those I have just alluded to. I turn, therefore, to their management of specific interests and interest groups.

I use the term "interest group" here loosely, to refer to an identifiable body of persons who advocate a position in a public arena. I received both positive and negative reactions to my use of the term during my interviews. Some respondents, including Sr. Casey, suggested that I "shy away from that label" because of its connotations of narrow, self-serving political action. Father Bryan Hehir told me he was "not at all comfortable" with applying the interest-group idea to the development of the peace pastoral. Not surprisingly, political scientist Bruce Russett, the principal consultant to the bishops' committee, felt more at home with my use of the term and commented on the document's representativeness (with respect to diversity within the U.S. Church) this way: "Overall, it's a centrist statement that does pretty well. It received a majority vote within a conference that includes many kinds of bishops. By Chicago [the site of the May 1983 vote] the bishops knew what they had to do to produce a document with wide appeal." Later in the interview Russett said, "I'd say that the pacifist wing got everything they reasonably expected. The right wing was not as happy, but was still relatively satisfied." Finally, Russett observed that most of the bishops were mildly left of center with respect to the public at large on this issue." What is most important for my purposes is that all respondents—whether comfortable with the interest-group terminology or not—spoke in terms for which I was comfortable with using such a label.

A few more examples support my point. Cardinal Krol: "The Committee itself was picked to reflect the range of doctrinal and popular attitudes toward peace. O'Connor became something of a theologian for the military man. Gumbleton was clearly the peace man." Bishop Reilly: "Because of the potential for division, we went out to groups and listened to them and allowed *their interests* to be heard." Archbishop Kelly: "We did everything possible to take into account the diversity of opinion." Bishop Malone: "It seems to me that in formulating this document we were uniquely conscious of the groups that needed to be consulted in the preparation of it, and we were also uniquely aware of the various publics we were addressing in the published letter." Archbishop O'Connor: "The question of multiple loyalties could have been more of a critical problem if the committee hadn't used the moral hierarchy. . . . [And] we would have violated our loyalties to the Magisterium, the nation, American Catholics, and the truth if everything we said had been couched in terms of official Church teaching or doctrine." Thus, the bishops' sensitivity to multiple identities, interests, and groups was a prevailing awareness. Indeed, any large organization has to be sensitive to this matter, particularly if the organization is characterized by hierarchy and divisions or departments.

In the remainder of this section I shall treat two focal points of the NCCB's management of multiple identities: (1) reliance on New as opposed to Old Testament scripture, and (2) the management of the tension between the just war tradition and the pacifist option. On these issues we can clearly observe the bishops' rhetorical responses to multiple interests and multiple interest groups.

I have already commented on the perceived limitations of the first draft of the peace pastoral, issued in June 1982. As Castelli complained, "The draft was reminiscent of the horse that was built by a committee and came out a camel. It was hard to follow, with the same point often repeated several times and two halves of a point separated by fifteen pages." One "point" that was insufficiently covered, many felt, lay in the scriptural section. The problem was that the first draft "relied heavily on a New Testament description of peace."[48] Bishop Fulcher told me that because of this one-sidedness the first draft received some strong criticism inside Church circles. The primary critics here were not bishops but rather priests, members of religious communities, and theologians. This observation was confirmed by my own survey of a collection of responses to the first draft obtained through Bishop Fulcher's office. One respondent, Fr. John O'Grady of Voorheesville, New York, maintained that scriptural texts created a "limited position" for the bishops. He felt it was better "to emphasize the existence of evil in this world" as documented in the Old Testament and how in Jeremiah and Ezekiel God offers a "new heart and a new spirit."[49] In an interview for this study, Auxiliary Bishop Richard Sklba, a biblicist by background, agreed: "When I read the first draft I instinctively felt that there were some omissions in the section on scripture. For example, the whole issue of a warrior God was not even mentioned. There was a great need to treat Hebrew literature and the holy wars theme right up through the Apocalypse. This would round out the biblical section."

Bishop Sklba was consulted by Sr. Casey in further developing the scriptural section of the peace pastoral between drafts two and three. Moreover, as President of the Catholic Biblical Association, Sklba was one of about ten people invited by the bishops to a meeting specifically on the biblical basis for peace. "There," he said, "my contribution was substantial." Sklba described the final draft of the pastoral as "enhanced" because of the changes. "It is more cognizant of a variety of scriptural bases, even as it supports a New Testament vision of peace in justice. The final draft is more balanced, more credible to biblical scholars, both Catholic and non-Catholic."

In reacting to the scriptural section of the second draft the Catholic peace organization Pax Christi USA showed a somewhat different attitude. In a letter to the ad hoc committee in December 1982 representatives of the organization urged forcefully that the bishops "truly be prophetic." They meant this in the broad sense—as a term opposed to priestly or pious (though they did not use such terms); they wanted the bishops to take "bold," challenging positions and "stand by them." They asked that the bishops both model themselves on the character of the Old Testament prophets and proclaim the peace message of the New Testament Gospels. Father William N. Matthews, who drafted the letter on behalf of Pax Christi, explained: "When I wrote the ad hoc committee after the distribution of the first draft, I asked of the bishops of the U.S. that they truly be prophetic. I again make that request, and I mean it in the sense of the Old Testament prophets. They did not make bold statements and then immediately step back from them. I ask that the U.S. bishops not do this, either." And Matthews also said: "The bishops are, first and foremost, representatives of the Gospel. Yet, whenever the Pastoral takes steps in the direction of really being Gospel–prophetic for our twentieth-century ears, it hastens to step back, as though fearful of any overly evangelical stance." Matthews went on to point out specific areas of the nuclear arms discussion where the bishops might be more prophetic by condemning possession as well as use. The Pax Christi letter suggested that the "detailed and nuanced" (the bishops' words) aspects of the second draft's wording undermined a prophetic stance.[50] Several of my interviewees indicated that similar disappointment followed even after the final draft.

Significantly, over fifty of the bishops had joined Pax Christi by the time the peace pastoral was issued. Many of them held to a prophetic or radical position so strongly as to adopt what George Weigel called "an . . . implicitly sectarian ecclesiology in which the Church is understood as a community of the saved *over against* the wider society" (emphasis added). Weigel, who was an expert witness before the committee and who was a scholar in residence at the World Without War Council of Seattle, described the emergence of a vigorous "Mennonite caucus" in the NCCB. "By 'Mennonite caucus' I mean a loosely organized grouping of bishops who are essentially sectarian in their understanding of the relationship between the church and the wider secular community." Along with such a sectarian understanding, Weigel explained further, there were also pacifist and prophetic orientations.[51]

Sister Casey told me that the prophetic-priestly tension was "one of the most fascinating things to observe during the development of the pastoral," not just in the handling of scripture but in the discussions generally. "It was curious to watch which one was going to win—the prophetic role or the teaching authority of the Church, the Magisterium. Of course, it was necessary continuously to quote tradition, but this was difficult in some cases because some traditions were being shaped at the moment. For example, we issued the first draft in June of '82 . . . and the Holy Father's U.N. statement was made two days later." Casey continued: "I kept asking, 'Would the teaching role overrule the prophetic role?' In the final analysis the bishops were not so prophetic in their wording as they were in their courage to say what they were saying. For this courage I credit the conversion which went on among many of the bishops about their proper role in the Church and in the world."

Of course, when Catholics talk about the teaching authority of the Church, they direct attention toward Rome. This is what the bishops did to some degree in revising the biblical section of the peace pastoral between drafts two and three. At the Rome meeting of January 1983 Cardinal Ratzinger asked the following question: "Has the draft pastoral clearly and faithfully presented the scriptural evidence, especially with regard to the relationship between the kingdom and temporary society?"[52] There was concern at the Vatican about the bishops' treatment of the Kingdom of God and the extent to which it can be achieved on earth. The summary of the proceedings of the Rome meeting concluded: "The text should clearly avoid mixing up two distinct levels and different realities: our faith that the Kingdom of God will come and the realization that it is not certain if and when true peace will effectively exist in the world that is ours."[53]

As James Rhodes explains, the bishops took the Vatican criticisms seriously. In the third draft "they [became] much more cautious in their efforts to pioneer new understandings of the Kingdom of God and its prophesied tranquillity."[54] That draft and the final version pointed out several meanings of the word "peace," including individual well-being, the end of armed hostilities, "a right relationship with God," social justice, and the eschatological image of God's salvation for man. Further, the bishops dropped the statement apparently most troublesome for Rome: that "Isaiah's promise of the reign of God must be achieved in history."[55] The bishops quoted the Pope's 1982 World Day of Peace message to this effect: "Experience convinces us that in this world a totally and permanently peaceful human society is unfortunately a utopia, and that ideologies that hold up that prospect as easily attainable are based on hopes that cannot be realized, whatever the reason behind them."[56] The bishops seemed not to be totally comfortable with this position, however. As Rhodes points out, they "hedged" in other passages. For example, the final draft proclaimed: "A theology of peace should ground the task of peacemaking solidly in the biblical vision of the Kingdom of God, then place it centrally in the ministry of the Church."[57] This statement of course implied a vision of empirically realizable global peace.

Much of the tension and difficulty surrounding management of the biblical tradition centered on "the relatively recently recovered sense of the centrality of scripture" in Catholicism[58] and on the uncertain status of a "theology of peace." In the final draft of the peace pastoral the bishops acknowledged that "since the scriptures speak primarily of God's intervention in history, they contain no specific treatise on war and peace."[59] Father Hesburgh, in an interview, bemoaned the lack of an explicit and developed theology of peace in Church tradition.

To fill part of this gap and extend the peace pastoral's suggestion of a "covenantal vision," Sr. Casey wrote about a biblical vision of peace based on the symbol of the *Covenant* as a means of presenting an overarching interpretation of the two Testaments. The covenant which God made with Israel "is not static," said Casey. "It is always growing and developing as the people of the covenant grow and develop and change." Moreover, she maintained, "Peace is the fruit of the *new* covenant, because the covenant is union and relationship, and it is in union and relationship that reconciliation and peace begins." The new covenant, Casey claimed, "is a covenant where God is not any longer on a high mountain, but is in their very midst. . . . Jesus Christ is the mediator and the inaugurator of the new covenant." Finally, Casey insisted that "to enflesh the covenant in our lives is to live in peace."[60] The covenantal vision was only suggested in the peace pastoral. Sister Casey's observations indicate directions along which churchly rhetoric might go in elaborating the concept. What her ideas indicate is that such rhetoric would need to emphasize "covenant" as *processually* developed, thereby grounding a theology of peace.

The implications of Casey's covenantal vision are extremely important in reference to identity, organization, and rhetoric. If the Church fully adopted the symbol of the covenant as process, it would be very difficult to continue to identify Catholicism as the universal Church. The model of Church-as-covenant would undermine a number of the authoritative justifications of what the Church *is*. In Casey's sense of the term, covenant meant continual development or change; it was thus a concept in dialectical opposition to permanence. For the Church to adopt fully this version of the covenant would be tantamount to changing its charter or constitution or identity. That would require an enormous organizational transformation.

Once more, the point illustrated is general. When a group reinterprets its history and its identity (as the Soviet Union began doing in the late 1980s), it may lose much of what it was and perhaps lose its membership. Sensitive and nuanced rhetorical strategies can help, but in the dialectic of permanence and change the Roman Catholic Church has usually sided with the former in cases of specific decisions.

The bishops' interpretations of scripture and their rhetorical uses of those interpretations opened the way for almost revolutionary definitions of what the Church *is*. A more technically theological and less radical issue also arose, again with considerable "danger" to tradition. As Fr. Hesburgh expressed it, the Church had a theology of war, but it had no theology of peace. The Augustinian-Aquinean Just War Theory was well established in the organization's tradition, but how the Church should react to universalized pacifist-nonviolent positions was unsettled. Because of its pragmatic ramifications this presented an even stickier rhetorical problem than the problem of the covenant.

Both the Just War Theory and the pacifist-nonviolent option have long traditions in the Church. Just War theology owes credit for development to Augustine and Thomas Aquinas. In *The Challenge of Peace* the bishops explained: "Historically and theologically the clearest answer to the question [of justifiable use of lethal force] is found in St. Augustine. Augustine was impressed by the fact and the consequences of sin in history—the 'not yet' dimension of the Kingdom. In his view war was both the result of sin and a tragic remedy for sin in the life of political

147

societies."[61] As a remedy, war could be justified if used to restrain or contain evil and to protect innocent people. The theory was elaborated by Aquinas particularly so as to justify a right of self-defense for states in a non-unified world. This logic has infused twentieth-century papal teaching and the documents of Vatican II. In summarizing the teaching of Pope Pius XII on war, John Courtney Murray expounded two principles: (1) that "all wars of aggression, whether just or unjust, fall under the ban of moral proscription"; and (2) "a defensive war to repress injustice is morally admissible both in principle and in fact." In this conception, of course, a war of self-defense is seen as the opposite of a war of aggression. Murray further explained: "There is no indication that this reaffirmation of the traditional principle of defensive warfare, to which Pius XII was driven by the brutal facts of international life, extends only to wars conducted by so-called conventional arms."[62] The right of self-defense was reaffirmed by Vatican II's *Gaudium et Spes* as well: "As long as the danger of war remains and there is no competent and sufficiently powerful authority at the international level, governments cannot be denied the right to legitimate defense once every means of peaceful settlement has been exhausted." At the same time, however, the Pastoral Constitution morally dismissed nuclear warfare as "far exceeding the bounds of legitimate defense."[63]

In his historical and moral analysis of the Just War Theory, James Turner Johnson, a moral theologian, reads recent Catholic teaching this way: "The development of contemporary Catholic doctrine has not, in spite of strong statements against contemporary war, been in the direction of out-of-hand rejection of war in this era but rather along the lines taken in the just war tradition."[64] Nevertheless, the bishops evolved "a set of rigorous conditions which must be met if the decision to go to war is to be morally permissible."[65] Catechist John Hardon outlined the implications: "In order for a war to be just, it must be on the authority of the sovereign; the cause must be just; . . . the belligerent should have a rightful intention [and the] war must be waged by 'proper means.' "[66] In more specific terms, the just-war criteria fall into two categories: *Jus ad Bellum,* which refers to why and when recourse to war is permissible, and *Jus in Bello,* which pertains to the actual conduct of war.

In the first category, *Jus ad Bellum,* the bishops included: (1) "just cause"; (2) "competent authority"; (3) "comparative justice"—"Do the rights and values involved justify killing?"; (4) "right intention"— "pursuit of peace and reconciliation"; (5) "last resort"; (6) "probability of success"; and (7) "proportionality." The last criterion, proportionality, was asserted as relevant both to the decision to begin warfare and to the conduct of war. The same was true for the question of discrimination which "prohibits directly intended attacks on non-combatants and non-military targets."[67] Both of these principles took on great importance in the bishops' discussions of nuclear warfare and weaponry.

In his survey of just war theology and politics William O'Brien writes: "The history of attempts to limit the conduct of war reveals a third category of restrictions, namely, prohibited means (that is, means that by definition are considered disproportionate and cannot be used even if they can be discriminatory)."[68] Not surprisingly, this principle was applied by some observers to nuclear arms. This standard emerged in the bishops' discussions, but, as Bishop Gumbleton informed me, it did not become a part of the final document. Allowing for it would have been tantamount to declaring nuclear weapons evil *in themselves* and would have pointed indisputably toward unilateral disarmament. This was a step the majority of bishops were not prepared to take.

In the section which followed "The Just War Criteria" in the peace pastoral the bishops treated "The Value of Non-violence." They opened their discussion this way: "Moved by the example of Jesus' life and by his teaching, some Christians have from the earliest days of the Church committed themselves to a nonviolent life-style." Chronicling pacifist tendencies among some early Christians, as well as the work of twentieth-century figures such as Mahatma Gandhi, Dorothy Day, and Martin Luther King, Jr., the bishops said they "support . . . a pacifist option for individuals." And they called this vision of Christian nonviolence a means to resist injustice which is not passive.[69] A key phrase here is "option for individuals." The bishops stopped short of granting legitimacy to a pacifist stance for a nation; to do otherwise would have put them in the exceedingly difficult position of undermining if not completely subverting the just war framework.

The bishops were thus very conscious of how they handled the relationship between the Just War Theory and the option of pacifism—nonviolence. In the end they chose to call these "distinct but interdependent methods of evaluating warfare. They diverge on some specific conclusions, but they share a common presumption against the use of force as a means of settling disputes." And the bishops concluded the section by saying: "Finally, in an age of technological warfare, analysis from the viewpoint of non-violence and analysis from the viewpoint of the just-war teaching often converge and agree in their opposition to methods of warfare which are in fact indistinguishable from total warfare."[70] Here we see in corporate rhetoric a response to the need to harmonize divergent positions that are ineradicable from the organization's traditions.

In more metaphoric (and perhaps ambiguous) ways the bishops used the symbol of the "new moment" as a reason for linking just war and pacifist thought. As I have said elsewhere, "The bishops' rhetorical strategy was to unite both just war adherents and pacifists under the bold symbolic banner, the 'new moment,' thereby bringing together otherwise divergent groups."[71] The Just War Theory was the official teaching of the Church, "in possession for the past 1,500 years of Catholic thought,"[72] while the pacifist–nonviolent perspective was previously owned by groups considered to be on the periphery of mainstream Catholicism. Therefore, the bishops had to take great care in managing these "distinct but interdependent" interests, as they called them.

Their rhetorical strategy of symbolic transcendence is important. Other types of organizations also use it to redefine what they are or to respond to changes in their organizations. In image advertising, for example, conglomerates with diverse interests (such as United Technologies) employ techniques to bring all of their concerns under a single, broad symbolic banner. This rhetorical strategy is necessary, though not always effective. Large corporations today develop "mission" or "value" statements to orient all of their divisions toward central concerns. For example, in the early 1980s General Motors announced that its primary concern would henceforth be quality; presumably the pursuit of quality would serve as a superordinate value premise guiding the decisions of employees. After the Bhopal, India, disaster of 1984 Union Carbide sought to redefine itself, subordinating the corporate logo to divisional names, in a move to distance the corporation from the negative publicity that persisted long after the lethal gas leak. In 1989 Sears Roebuck redefined itself as a "discount store" but also christened itself "Brand Central." Subsequently a lawsuit against the corporation alleged that it did not actually lower prices but only *said* it was doing so. These and other "new moments" in organizational experience occur as responses to changing circumstances and as attempts to reshape rhetorically what an organization *is* or what particular audiences are to believe about the organization. In the case of the bishops reconciling the differences, even contradictions, of the just war tradition and the less institutionalized nonviolence option required a new, powerful, and embracing rhetorical symbol.

It is of no small importance that the bishops' pastoral letter gave serious and sustained attention to the pacifist-nonviolent option. This in itself made the peace pastoral something of a revolutionary document in Catholic social teaching. As Sr. Casey observed, "The committee and ultimately the letter itself gave the nonviolent position a genuine hearing and a significant measure of respect. This made the pastoral a more *authentic* document." Bishop Gumbleton, in crediting the final draft for being "clear, persuasive, and fairly precise," elaborated by saying: "The document sets forth two positions in Catholic teaching on war and peace: working through justice to bring peace—the option of nonviolence—and the option of just war." And Bishop Sklba praised the accepted document for allowing "both just war and pacifism to stand legitimately within its shelter."

Critics examined the "shelter" very carefully. For example, Bishop Reilly related to me the interesting story of how the sequence of the bishops' treatments of just war and nonviolence came to be. In the second draft pacifism was discussed first. Because of this, "people said we were elevating pacifism over the Just War Theory. But that was not so. We discussed pacifism first; we adopted a historical perspective which presented pacifism as the option of many Christians in the earliest days of the Church." Nonetheless, as a result of rather strident criticism, particularly from more conservative organizations within the U.S. Church, the Just War Theory was moved to the first position. Yet Bishop Reilly stressed the need to see just war and nonviolence as "balancing one another."[73]

Beyond the issue of the order of presenting the two approaches the bishops still faced the problem of how the Just War Theory and pacifism went together, if at all. They took a somewhat equivocal position in treating the two as "distinct but interdependent." But there were other options for managing the positions, some of which were taken up by critics and observers. One way to treat just war and nonviolence is to see them as irreconcilable. This was clearly the position of James Finn, one who testified before the ad hoc committee. He argued that "in the document the two traditions open to Catholics—pacifism and just war—are joined in such a way that they corrupt each other." Pointing to pragmatic difficulties raised by the two positions, Finn further argued: "Adherents of the two options do share an overall moral vision of peace, but on how best to incarnate that vision in the world they differ. They no longer travel together on one broad path but go in decidedly different directions." Accordingly, Finn called for the individual to choose *either* just war or pacifism, or *neither*.[74]

Norbert Rigali acknowledged that Just War Theory and pacifism are difficult to reconcile, and he faulted the bishops for giving insufficient attention to their mutually contradictory implications. His conclusion also addressed pragmatic justifications for the legitimacy of both positions: "Just-war theory and the pacifist option, with their attendant opposite choices regarding arms, must coexist in the church, not because they complement one another, but because in the church and even among those with teaching authority there is not complete agreement about objective Christian morality regarding war."[75] Thus, Rigali turned his argument to support the legitimacy of different beliefs within the Church.

There are, of course, many in the Church and in the larger society who adopt pacifism as an absolute or a nearly absolute stance. This was the case with the so-called "Mennonite caucus" of bishops mentioned earlier. Bishop Raymond Hunthausen of Seattle told an audience in late 1981:

> I heard Bishop Gumbleton say that he is a total pacifist. I've never said that about myself. I've always said that I'm a nuclear pacifist; but given our present world, it is unrealistic to talk about conventional war. So maybe it's time for me to say I am a total pacifist, in our current global context.[76]

Such a position was taken by an increasing number of Catholic bishops in the United States; estimates range from thirty to sixty. This fact seemed to justify James Douglass's earlier statement that "the pacifist conclusion has eclipsed the just-war norm."[77]

Still another position open to argument derived from asserting the legitimacy of only *one* official teaching within the Catholic framework. This was clearly the choice of Michael Novak, who held: "So in matters of war and peace there is more than one vocation, yet one common teaching about justice in war and peace." That teaching was the Just War Theory. Novak extended his argument to say: "As there are wars which are unjust, so also there is peace which is unjust." Nevertheless, he acknowledged the right of individuals to choose pacifism for themselves, "particularly the calling of the clergy not to take up arms."[78] Novak argued that his position was supported by the Vatican memo issued after the January 1983 meeting with the U.S. bishops in Rome. He quoted it to the effect that the second draft "in speaking about nonviolence and just war seems to propose a double Catholic tradition: a tradition of nonviolence and a tradition along the lines of the just-war theory that existed throughout the history of the Church." The memo continued: "Other participants [at the meeting] indicated that nonviolence has never been seen in the Church as an alternative to the just-war theory."[79]

It is clear that the bishops did change some of their language on the two positions between the second and the final drafts. They dropped their introductory remark: "We may now examine the content of two legitimate modes of Christian witness on issues of war and peace." Gone also were these words describing the nonviolence option: "Essentially this position holds that any use of military force is incompatible with the Christian vocation."[80] But in their final draft the bishops seemed to affirm a single-teaching stance when they declared: "The Church's teaching on war and peace establishes a strong presumption against war which is binding on all; it then examines when this presumption may be overridden, precisely in the name of preserving the kind of peace which protects human dignity and human rights."[81]

Nevertheless, the bishops called the two approaches—just war and nonviolence—"distinct but interdependent methods of evaluating warfare." This view, shared by some theologians, is obviously a difficult one to articulate without undermining just war analysis or weakening the pacifist stance. But some observers, such as moral theologian David Hollenbach, argued that it could be done. "The pacifist and just-war approaches to the morality of warfare are complementary and . . . both are needed as the Christian community approaches the nuclear debate." Hollenbach acknowledged the tension between the two positions but saw the just war approach enriched by considering the importance of nonviolence. He said this complementarity brought forward the basic just war question: whether a Christian may take part in violence. Hollenbach went further than the bishops, expressing "the conviction that violent warfare should be presumed to be morally unacceptable and even sinful."[82]

Spokespersons for corporate bodies usually cannot eliminate tensions between diverse points of view that exist within their organizations. Their normal rhetorical need is to find means by which to minimize differences or to legitimize one view but not others. The bishops chose the first course. With respect to the biblical vision of war and peace and the tension between just war and pacifist theories, they chose embracing strategies. Their positions were intended to be transcendental and inclusive, encouraging the faithful to find unity within the "new moment" and a revised, "covenantal" vision of peace. Because their conceptualizations were broad and their arguments abstract, their final document seemed equivocal and uncertain at a number of points. The bishops tried to be *both* "priestly" and "prophetic." Perhaps inevitably, their rhetoric was not convincing to all of the audiences they addressed. The outcome was so well summarized by Ed Doherty of the bishops' staff that I quote extensively from our interview:

> One tension from the start was between those who wanted a prophetic document based on scripture and certain Church traditions and the strict natural-law theorists who focused on the Soviet threat and therefore preferred the Just War Theory and the right of legitimate self-defense. . . . I must acknowledge after reading the document carefully that the Just War Theory carried the day. You might even ask, as you get into the document, "What happened to the scripturally based prophetic tradition?" Another place where the tension arose was with respect to pacifism and Christian thought. This was analyzed, of course, in the Rome meeting [of January 1983]. In the final analysis, the bishops' position doesn't totally satisfy the view expressed in Rome—the supremacy of the Just War Theory. The peace pastoral, in its final form, stresses both pacifism and just war, but recognizes the Just War Theory as the authoritative position of the Church.

Such problems of managing multiple identities, interests, positions, and the tensions among them are certainly not unique to the bishops nor to the Roman Catholic Church, although the role of a sacred tradition surely complicates the problems. With the Church's sanctification of tradition, the NCCB could not declare Augustine and Aquinas mistaken or irrelevant. On the other hand, by inserting the nonviolence option into their pastoral letter, the bishops were trying to recognize changed historical circumstances. Within the Church, identity and the sacred are closely linked.[83] The bishops had need to create a "new moment" to justify new interpretations of scripture and tradition. They could not alter tradition without altering the Church itself. They had to find new meanings in that tradition and argue for their legitimacy. They had also to make exceedingly subtle—but inevitably arguable—distinctions such as "distinct but interdependent."

Other groups, organizations, and nations face the same problem when trying to be true to "sacred" texts yet adapting to the specific challenges of the day. The debate over gun control in the United States is a political instance of the same problem. The Constitution guarantees the right to bear arms, but there seem to be pressing reasons today for limiting that right. The tension lies between the absolute character of a "sacred" text and the specific situations in which that text must be applied. Any organization that claims to have true doctrines, moral certainties, or absolute guarantees is bound to have trouble reconciling those views with countervailing pressures or choices. The Roman Catholic Church, because it has in effect so many "charters" or "constitutions," continually faces monumental rhetorical challenges of this sort.

154

CONCLUSION

The U.S. Catholic bishops' peace pastoral is about many things, as testified to by a number of my interviewees when asked to indicate "the moral core of the letter." What follow are a few of their comments. Archbishop Thomas Kelly: "No one can destroy human life." Auxiliary Bishop Richard Sklba: "[The peace pastoral] put a laser beam on civil government, addressing its moral responsibility." Archbishop John Quinn: "Raising the nuclear arms issue and embedding it firmly in a moral context." Joseph Cardinal Bernardin: "There should be no areas of life that escape moral scrutiny." Monsignor Daniel Hoye: "That we must reverse the trend, making a moral analysis of the arms race and saying 'no' to it." Professor Bruce Russett: "That a radically intensive reflection on defense policies is necessary." Staff member Ed Doherty: "There is virtually no use of nuclear weapons that could be morally justified." Bishop Leroy Matthiesen: "The statement by Pope John Paul II at Hiroshima that war has to be ruled out." John Cardinal Krol: "The right of self-defense and how much force you can use in repelling an unjust aggressor." Father Richard Warner: "The value of human life, the dignity of human life." Sister Juliana Casey: "It is twofold. First, there's a responsibility of the faithful and leaders to speak to issues of life and death. Second—and this is the *real* core—there's the principle that life is extremely valuable and cannot be handled lightly." Father Bryan Hehir: "I'm not too sure. I wouldn't try to isolate it that way."[84]

What is clear, however one sums up or "essentializes" (as Burke would put it[85]) *The Challenge of Peace,* is that it says something about who the bishops are, how complex organizational problems are to be confronted, and what specific symbolic associations are to be used in developing and articulating their churchly doctrine and rhetorical strategy. Indeed, the processes of finding ways to maintain a unifying identity for the NCCB, the Church, and its communicants required the bishops to re-create ideas and rhetorical expressions of themselves: that action in fact "changed" the bishops from what they had been at the start of the process. The entire task of the bishops may be usefully described as "the management of multiple identities." We have seen how the *The Challenge of Peace* developed in its social, political, and religious contexts. The NCCB cut a winding and broad path through the territory of multiple identifications, making terminological and social connections at important points. In making the needed connections between and among disparate doctrines and choices, they exploited ambiguity as a potent, and actually necessary, rhetorical resource. They used terms like "collegiality," "community," "the new moment," and "peace" as versatile symbolic means of identifying themselves as united spokespersons for a unified and stable institution. The bishops' response to the situation has been fairly characterized as "structured ambiguity."[86] Father Bryan Hehir invoked the notion of "a centimeter of ambiguity" in his many lectures on the peace pastoral's somewhat equivocal position on deterrence.[87] And during the drafting process Archbishop John Roach called ambiguity "a legitimate, treasured part of the whole moral tradition of the church."[88] Ultimately the bishops postured themselves in a number of different ways simultaneously. This was both a rhetorical achievement in their managing issues and identities and a weakening of the presumed authoritativeness of their discourse.[89]

Through their struggle to work out a cogent stand on arms control the bishops came to share a new collective identity as a body. Such collegiality is often, but not inevitably, the consequence of working out details of corporate rhetoric. The result for the bishops is illustrated vividly in this anecdote from the Chicago meeting where the peace pastoral was ultimately approved. At one point, as amendments to the document were considered, Auxiliary Bishop Patrick Ahern of New York moved to change certain references to "we" and "us" to read: "those of us who listened to the testimony" (that is, only the members of the drafting committee). The motion "failed resoundingly,"[90] indicating a desire on the part of the bishops to share equally and responsibly in their corporate "we." Indeed, as Bishop Fulcher told me, "Through an amazing process of conversion the peace pastoral came to be *owned* by all the bishops."

In a very real sense, then, the peace pastoral became a "constitution" for the bishops. When any body frames a "constitution," there will have been a formative process, resulting in a structure with certain presumably authoritative qualities and conclusions.[91] The peace pastoral was such a constitution. The details reviewed here show us that, as spokespersons for a great institution, the bishops *had* to struggle to align in a consistent and persuasive fashion tradition, sacred texts, responses to immediate circumstances, and their own identity as authoritative representatives of the institution. To some degree they succeeded. In some cases they were not successful, at least not with all of their churchly audiences. That their rhetorical achievement was mixed is not remarkable. If there were no grounds for doubt, then no argument, no rhetoric, would be needed. As Aristotle put it, the object of composing rhetoric is "to discover the means of coming as near . . . success as the circumstances of each particular case allow."[92] What is important for this study is not so much how fully the bishops attained their objectives but rather the kinds of rhetorical problems that confronted them because they were spokespersons for an institution and because they needed to speak both to "insiders" and "outsiders." Speaking as *individual citizens*, even bishops would have been far more free in composing persuasive discourse, and the same applies to anyone contributing to or constructing corporate rhetoric. What is also important is how the bishops as rhetors were changed—in effect, reconstituted—as a result of their rhetorical efforts and how they and their audiences came to understand this "re-constitution." As is the case with any organization constructing an important statement, the bishops came to say as much about themselves as they did about the issues.

NOTES

1. Oliver F. Williams, "The Making of a Pastoral Letter," in *Catholic Social Teaching and the United States Economy: Working Papers,* ed., John W. Houck and Oliver F. Williams (Washington: University Press of America, 1984), 17–18.

2. Tim Unsworth, "Bishops' Letter on War and Peace: Prescription for Pastoral Leadership," *National Catholic Reporter,* 11 May 1984: 17.

3. *The Challenge of Peace: God's Promise and Our Response* (Washington: USCC, 1983), 2, 3, 4.

4. Robert J. Roth, "The Bishops' Pastoral and the Individual Conscience," *America,* 31 Mar. 1984: 239.

5. J. Bryan Hehir, "From the Pastoral Constitution of Vatican II to *The Challenge of Peace,*" in *Catholics and Nuclear War: A Commentary on The Challenge of Peace, The U.S. Catholic Bishops' Pastoral Letter on War and Peace,* ed Philip J. Murnion (New York: Crossroad, 1983), 74, 86.

6. See, e.g., "World Church in the Making," editorial, *Commonweal,* 24 Oct. 1980: 579–80.

7. James Malone, "A Look Back at Collegeville," *Origins,* 7 Oct. 1982: 261.

8. John Cardinal Dearden, "Collegial Sharing in Ministry," address at Collegeville, MN, June 1982, in *Origins,* 15 July 1982: 116.

9. Avery Dulles, *Models of the Church* (Garden City, NY: Doubleday, 1974), esp. 22.

10. Avery Dulles, *A Church to Believe In: Discipleship and the Dynamics of Freedom* (New York: Crossroad, 1983), 6–18.

11. Pope John Paul II, *Redemptor Hominis* (The Redeemer of Man), as quoted in *The Challenge of Peace,* 85.

12. *The Challenge of Peace,* 86

13. Robert J. Doolittle, "Speech Communication as an Instrument in Engen-

dering and Sustaining a Sense of Community in Urban and Poor Neighborhoods: A Study of Rhetorical Potentialities" (Ph.D. diss., Pennsylvania State University, 1972), 171–73.

14. Dearder., "Collegial Sharing"; William Borders, "What Makes the Church a Community?" address at Collegeville, MN, June 1982, in *Origins,* 16 Sept. 1982: 210–14.

15. Peter Henrici, "The Church and Pluralism," *Communio* 19 (1983): 128–32.

16. Claude Dagens, "Hierarchy and Communion: The Bases of Authority in the Beginning of the Church," *Communio* 9 (1982): 67–78, esp. 74.

17. J. Bryan Hehir, "The Implications of Structured Pluralism: A Public Church," address at the Catholic University of America, Washington, 19 May 1984, in *Origins,* 31 May 1984: 42. "Subsidiarity," a related term in Catholic tradition, refers to participative decision making and a degree of local control that are fostered within a centralized administrative structure.

18. Dagens, "Hierarchy and Communion," 74.

19. St. Cyprian, as quoted in Dearden, "Collegial Sharing," 115.

20. John L. Hanson, "When the Bishops Speak, Can the People Understand?" *Catholicism in Crisis,* Oct. 1983: 9–10.

21. Michael Novak, *Moral Clarity in the Nuclear Age* (Nashville: Thomas Nelson, 1983).

22. George A. Kelly, *The Battle for the American Church* (Garden City, NY: Doubleday, 1981), 27.

23. Webster F. Patterson, "Nuclear War, the Bishops, and the *Sensus Fidelium:* A New Process for Consensus?" *Chicago Studies* 22 (1983): 151–62, esp. 152.

24. See, e.g., Robert N. Bellah, R. Madsen, W. M. Sullivan, A. Swidler, and S. M. Tipton, *Habits of the Heart: Individualism and Commitment in American Life* (Berkeley: University of California Press, 1985); Peter Berger and Richard Neuhaus, *To Empower People: The Role of Mediating Structures in Public Policy* (Washington: American Enterprise Institute, 1977); Richard Bernstein, *Beyond Objectivism and Relativism: Science, Hermeneutics and Praxis* (Philadelphia: University of Pennsylvania Press, 1983); Philip Berryman, *Liberation Theology* (New York: Pantheon, 1987); and Larry Lyon, *The Community in Urban Society* (Philadelphia: Temple University Press, 1987).

25. George Cheney and Steve Goldzwig, "Peacemaking and Social Process: The Rhetorical, Organizational and Critical Implications for 'Base Communities' as Mediating Structures-in-Action" (Paper delivered at the annual conference of the International Communication Association, New Orleans, May 1988).

26. See, e.g., George Cheney, "Leadership and Management in the Academic Department: How Can Community and Bureaucracy Be Reconciled?" *Bulletin of the Association for Communication Administration,* no. 61 (August 1987): 14–18.

27. *The Challenge of Peace,* 73.

28. *The Challenge of Peace*, 89, emphasis deleted.

29. *The Challenge of Peace*, 73, 89.

30. As quoted in Jim Castelli, *The Bishops and the Bomb* (Garden City, NY: Doubleday, 1983), 41.

31. *The Challenge of Peace*, 89.

32. *The Challenge of Peace*, 83–84.

33. Joseph Cardinal Bernardin, "A Consistent Ethic of Life: An American-Catholic Dialogue," in *The Seamless Garment* (Kansas City, MO: *National Catholic Reporter*, 1984), 3.

34. Bernardin, "An American-Catholic Dialogue," 5, 6, 7.

35. Bernardin, "A Consistent Ethic of Life: Continuing the Dialogue," in *The Seamless Garment*, 10.

36. Bernardin, "An American-Catholic Dialogue," 7; "Continuing the Dialogue," 12–13.

37. Bernardin, "Continuing the Dialogue," 11.

38. As quoted in Jim McManus, "Pastoral Teaching Links Abortion, Nuclear Threat in Call for 'Ethic of Life,'" *National Catholic Reporter*, 11 May 1984: 8.

39. Richard J. O'Connor, "Nuke, Abortion Link Called 'Grotesque,'" *National Catholic Reporter*, 6 Apr. 1984: 13.

40. Joseph Allegretti, "Critics of Consistent Life Ethic Exhibit Disdain for Bishops," *National Catholic Reporter*, 6 Apr. 1984: 3.

41. David R. Carlin, Jr., "Patchy Garment: How Many Votes Has Bernardin?" *Commonweal*, 10 Aug. 1984: 422.

42. "The 'Seamless Garment': No Solid Constituency?" editorial, *Our Sunday Visitor*, 7 Oct. 1984: 3.

43. Andrew M. Greeley, "Selective Catholicism: How They Get Away with It," *America*, 30 Apr. 1983: 333–36.

44. Francis Schüssler Fiorenza, "The Church's Religious Identity and Its Social and Political Mission," *Theological Studies* 43 (1982): 197–225.

45. Peter Henriot, "Toward a Seamless Garment: Connecting the Pastorals," *Center Focus*, no. 65 (March 1985): 1.

46. See George Cheney and Phillip K. Tompkins, "Coming to Terms with Organizational Identification and Commitment," *Central States Speech Journal* 38 (1987): 1–15.

47. See Phillip K. Tompkins and George Cheney, "Communication and Unobtrusive Control in Contemporary Organizations," in *Organizational Communication: Traditional Themes and New Directions*, ed. Robert D. McPhee and Phillip K. Tompkins (Beverly Hills: Sage, 1985), 194.

48. Castelli, *Bishops and the Bomb*, 87.

49. John O'Grady, in a collection of responses to the first draft of the peace pastoral (obtained through permission of the office of the late Bishop George Fulcher).

159

50. William N. Matthews, Staff Associate of Pax Christi, USA, personal letter to members of the bishops' ad hoc peace committee, 1 Dec. 1982 (obtained through the office of the late Bishop Fulcher).

51. George Weigel, "Beyond *The Challenge of Peace: Quaestiones Disputatae*," *Center Journal* 3 (Winter 1983): 108–11.

52. As quoted in James M. Rhodes, "The Kingdom, Morality and Prudence—The American Bishops and Nuclear Weapons," *Center Journal* 3 (Winter 1983): 54.

53. Jan Schotte, summary of proceedings of the Rome meeting, as quoted in Rhodes, "The Kingdom," 54.

54. Rhodes, "The Kingdom," 55.

55. As quoted in Rhodes, "The Kingdom," 55.

56. As quoted in *The Challenge of Peace*, 19.

57. *The Challenge of Peace*, 9.

58. Sandra M. Schneiders, "New Testament Reflections on Peace and Nuclear Arms," in Murnion, *Catholics and Nuclear War*, 91–105, esp. 91.

59. *The Challenge of Peace*, 9–10.

60. Juliana Casey, address to the Campaign for Human Development National Committee Meeting, Washington, Oct. 1983, in *Proceedings*, 17–22.

61. *The Challenge of Peace*, 26.

62. John Courtney Murray, "Remarks on the Moral Problem of War," *Theological Studies* 20 (1959): 45–49.

63. *The Documents of Vatican II*, ed. Walter M. Abbott, trans. Joseph Gallagher (New York: Guild Press, America Press, Association Press, 1966), 293.

64. James Turner Johnson, *Just War Tradition and the Restraint of War: A Moral and Historical Inquiry* (Princeton, NJ: Princeton University Press, 1981), 344.

65. *The Challenge of Peace*, 27.

66. John A. Hardon, *The Catholic Catechism* (Garden City, NY: Doubleday, 1975), 348.

67. *The Challenge of Peace*, 28–34.

68. William V. O'Brien, *The Conduct of Just and Limited War* (New York: Praeger, 1981), 37.

69. *The Challenge of Peace*, 34–37.

70. *The Challenge of Peace*, 37.

71. Steve Goldzwig and George Cheney, "The U.S. Catholic Bishops on Nuclear Arms: Corporate Advocacy, Role Redefinition, and Rhetorical Adaptation," *Central States Speech Journal* 35 (1984): 19.

72. *The Challenge of Peace*, 37.

73. See J. Michael Hogan, "Managing Dissent in the Catholic Church: A

Reinterpretation of the Pastoral Letter on War and Peace," *Quarterly Journal of Speech* 75 (1989): 400–415, where he argues that the bishops suppressed the influence of the pacifist group Pax Christi in drafting the peace pastoral. Hogan criticizes scholars, including the present author, who have described the peace pastoral in "revolutionary" terms by using broad, secular political standards to consider the letter's content. However, Hogan largely neglects the institutional context of the Roman Catholic Church, within which *The Challenge of Peace* was indeed revolutionary in terms of (1) the participative process of its development, (2) its explicit recognition of individual pacifism, and (3) its alignment with the secular nuclear freeze movement. See also George Cheney and Steve Goldzwig, " 'Locating' the Bishops' Advocacy: A Response to Hogan," *Quarterly Journal of Speech*, 76 (1990): 307–309.

74. James Finn, "Pacifism and Just War: Either or Neither," in *Catholics and Nuclear War*, 132–45, esp. 142–43.

75. Norbert J. Rigali, "Just War and Pacifism," *America*, 31 Mar. 1984: 236.

76. Raymond Hunthausen, in "Converting to Peace: Four Bishops Speak about Their Journeys and Their Church," *Sojourners*, Jan. 1982: 11.

77. James W. Douglass, *The Non-Violent Cross: A Theology of Revolution and Peace* (London: Macmillan, 1966), 156.

78. Novak, *Moral Clarity in the Nuclear Age*, 32, 35.

79. "Vatican Memo to the U.S. Bishops on the Peace Pastoral," *Origins*, 7 Apr. 1983: 691–95.

80. The Challenge of Peace, 2nd draft, rpt. in *National Catholic Reporter*, 5 Nov. 1982: 12.

81. *The Challenge of Peace*, 22.

82. David Hollenbach, *Nuclear Ethics: A Christian Moral Argument* (New York: Paulist Press, 1983), 3, 14.

83. See Hans Mol, *Identity and the Sacred* (New York: Free Press, 1976).

84. These quotations are also printed in George Cheney and Phillip K. Tompkins, "On the Facts of the 'Text' as the Basis of Human Communication Research," in *Communication Yearbook* 11, ed. James A. Anderson (Newbury Park, CA: Sage, 1988), 476–77. See the same article for a detailed textual analysis of the peace pastoral that is adapted slightly from the present author's dissertation.

85. See Kenneth Burke, *A Grammar of Motives* (1945; rpt., Berkeley: University of California Press, 1969), 249–50.

86. Joseph A. Varacalli, *Toward the Establishment of Liberal Catholicism in America* (Washington: University Press of America, 1983), 73–74.

87. J. Bryan Hehir, "The Challenge of Peacemaking," lecture on audiocassette (New York: Paulist Press, 1983), 60 min.

88. As quoted in Kenneth A. Briggs, "Bishops Support Letter on Nuclear Arms," *New York Times*, 19 Nov. 1982: A-14.

89. The connection between authority and identity is discussed by Roland

Robertson and Burkhart Holzner, *Identity and Authority: Explorations in the Theory of Society* (New York: St. Martin's Press, 1979).

90. Castelli, *Bishops and the Bomb,* 163.

91. Burke, *A Grammar of Motives,* 338.

92. Aristotle, *Rhetoric,* trans. W. Rhys Roberts (New York: The Modern Library, 1954), 23, 1355b.

6

CONCLUSIONS, LESSONS, IMPLICATIONS

Here it remains to make the point that both in the most ancient societies as well as in the most modern societies one can observe a variety of identities on a variety of levels, such as social (national, tribal), group (clan, adulthood, community, family, club, sect, etc.), and individual. The whole and the parts may not be well attuned to one another in modern dynamic societies: Individuals may be at cross purposes with their families, and families may demand loyalties that the state . . . wants to usurp. Yet however much conflict or congruence there may be, it is important that each unit of social organization is analyzed as such and not just as a derivation of the individual. The effect of religion [or any other social institution] can only be understood if we relate it to a variety of identities rather than [to] one, as happens much too often in the scholarly literature.

Hans Mol, *Meaning and Place:*
An Introduction to the Social Scientific Study of Religion

Elegantly and conveniently this epigraph spans my concerns in the final chapter of this book. Mol's comments address both the central question: What does it mean to speak with a collective voice? and the thematic answer I have consistently offered: the management of multiple identities. In fact, the problem that Mol finds in many analyses of religion—the tendency to treat collective phenomena purely as derivative from individual ones—also typifies much of the research conducted under the rubrics of organizational communication and rhetorical criticism. Scholarship in these areas has for the most part failed to come to terms with the corporate rhetor, the corporate message, and the corporate audience. In organizational studies generally, the growing trend toward *institutional* analysis has remedied this deficit to some degree and has thereby begun to reclaim the tradition established by such seminal thinkers as Marx, Weber, and Durkheim. Mary Douglas, in *How Institutions Think,* shows how organizations and other collectivities do in effect make "corporate" decisions *for* individuals: organizations set categories for thought and action and they "fix" identities.[1] In rhetorical criticism the increasing influences of Burkean, Marxist, and post-structuralist forms of analysis have provided important clues to what scholars should examine with respect to organizational and institutional rhetoric.[2] However, there is still a great need to wrest these areas of study from their strictly individualistic moorings; to appreciate the workings of social structure and process as much as we do the attitudes and actions of individual, natural persons. This book has aimed in part to address that need.

Through the elaboration of a theoretical framework and its application to a significant case I have shown how organizational rhetoric in contemporary postindustrial society works to manage multiple identities. In this concluding chapter I shall offer twelve principles which organize and articulate the lessons of my study for organizational rhetoric generally. But first, I wish to make a few observations on what the method of this study has shown.

The case study described in this book is detailed and extensive so as to account fully for the organizational, rhetorical, and identity-related aspects of a series of events: the development of a historic "corporate" document. Organizational rhetoric is by nature complex. To understand what is "beneath" as well as what is "within" a text such as *The Challenge of Peace,* the researcher must consider carefully an array of factors, including the hierarchical relationships entailed; both stated and obscured purposes; the process of message construction; and the interests and involvements of audiences or publics. In sum, one must know the complete history of a corporate "voice" to understand its message deeply. As a framework for analysis the "management of multiple identities" compels a researcher to assess the interplay of individuals, interests groups, and symbols in the study of organizational rhetoric. In communication studies there is a felt need for comprehensive and significant case studies of organizational life which can also contribute to the theoretical development of the discipline. This book addresses that need and offers the following summarizing principles.

1. *Complex organizations and their "associates" (i.e., individuals and groups) must manage multiple identities; some of these identities will be in harmony with one another; others will be in conflict.* This fact of

164

organizational life was dramatically and consistently demonstrated in the experience of the U.S. Catholic bishops. As I have shown, they *had* to try to manage an extensive array of sometimes conflicting identities in order to develop their historic peace pastoral. They needed to create a rhetorical document that reflected or seemed to reflect diverse interests of groups within the Church and at the same time appeal to outside groups. At the minimum they had to produce what Charles Curran has called "a complex document for a 'big church.' "[3] In the process the bishops forged a new collective identity for the National Conference of Catholic Bishops as an entity within the larger Catholic hierarchy and organization. This too was important, because the domains of national conferences of bishops were still evolving as the NCCB devised its peace pastoral. Their deliberative product offered fairly expansive definitions of these domains—definitions that pleased some within the Church and displeased others.

How successful were the bishops in persuading others? Father Andrew Greeley, sociologist and popular author, wrote me in May 1984 saying, "My own feeling is that the Peace Pastoral will have no effect whatsoever." Greeley defended this claim by arguing that the bishops had merely "caught up" with the majority of American Catholics (74 percent in one 1982 Gallup Poll) who already favored a nuclear freeze.

Greeley had a different judgment a year later. In a 1985 article, "Why the Peace Pastoral Did Not Bomb," he said: "The American Bishops' pastoral on nuclear weapons appears to be the most successful intervention to change attitudes ever measured by social science." He added: "This astonishing discovery raises fascinating questions about how church leadership should teach and about what American Catholics are really like." Greeley justified his change of opinion by citing the findings of one of his employing organizations, the National Opinion Research Center (NORC). One survey, taken just before the peace pastoral was issued in May 1983, reported that 32 percent of both Catholics and Protestants thought that "too much" money was being spent on arms. A year later another NORC survey found 32 percent of Protestants responded in the same manner but revealed a much higher figure for Catholics: 54 percent. According to Greeley, this shift represented "a change in attitude by perhaps 10 million Catholics." In explaining the change, Greeley focused on the kinds of groups for whom the greatest attitudinal shift occurred: Democrats, liberals, and those who did not vote for Ronald Reagan in 1980. "The stand of the bishops, at just the right time (mostly a matter of good fortune), provided for uneasy Catholics a focus for their concern which was not available to Protestants. . . . Astonishingly, [the bishops] had said the right thing at the right time."[4]

Although Greeley's second appraisal of the bishops' rhetorical effectiveness was probably overstated, his data did suggest that the bishops had managed issues and identities in ways that suited a wide segment of U.S. Catholics' perceptions of the political situation concerning war and peace in the mid-1980s.[5] Moreover, the experience of the years 1983 to 1986 suggests that the bishops' efforts encouraged other religious denominations, as well as other Catholic conferences, to issue statements either influenced by or directly modeled on *The Challenge of Peace*.[6] Of course, when one organization of a particular type "speaks" on an issue, it is common to find others of the same type speaking. So it is for corporations, labor unions, professional associations, and other collectivities.

The question of how or if the bishops influenced public policy is more perplexing. Clearly, *The Challenge of Peace* opposed most features of U.S. defense policy during Reagan's first term of office.[7] In the face of this opposition Reagan appears to have attempted to minimize the differences between the Church's stand as defined by the bishops and the Administration's identity. At his press conference of 4 May 1983 Reagan said: "[The bishops] are looking for a way toward peace and promoting world peace. And that's what we're also looking for."[8] Eric O. Hanson suggests strongly that the Administration was employing its own rhetorical strategy: "to coopt the [peace pastoral's] lofty sentiments" and "to bury the document with polite praise for peace."[9] As a strategy this was probably more effective than provoking even greater publicity for the bishops by highlighting discrepancies between their stance and that of the Administration. At the very least, the Reagan Administration saw a need to reckon with the NCCB as a political actor in the arena of public opinion.

But the bishops' influence on the development of defense and arms control policy must also be considered in the larger context of the freeze movement of the early 1980s. Certainly that effort as a movement lost energy and momentum in 1984 and 1985, the two years following the publication of the peace pastoral. And during the same period the anti-nuclear effort lost much of the organized character it had when the freeze was a hot topic. Furthermore, Americans witnessed a dramatic change in posture toward arms control during the latter years of the second Reagan term. This shift, along with the celebrated openness of the Soviet party chief Mikhail Gorbachev, produced two historic summit meetings—in Reykjavik, October 1986, and in Washington, December 1987—and the first-ever agreement by the superpowers to eliminate a class of nuclear weapons (in this case, the intermediate-range nuclear missiles positioned in Eastern and Western Europe). From 1986 to the time of this writing actions and promises of further de-escalating the arms race have been main features of U.S.–Soviet relations, although the arms race has by no means been halted. It is probably not an overstatement to say that the freeze movement (with the NCCB among its leaders) left a legacy of a wider acceptance of arms control initiatives. "The 'new moment' that the bishops saw in 1983, largely as a result of public alarm over the accelerating arms race, begins to have a more positive content."[10] After all, by 1987 the only visible constituency in opposition to the U.S.–Soviet cutback was, ironically, the far right, those who felt abandoned by Reagan in his negotiations with Gorbachev.[11]

The bishops reviewed their efforts and their impact in a 1988 statement, *Building Peace: A Pastoral Reflection on the Response to* The Challenge of Peace *and a Report*. Among other things the bishops noted how "the letter launched an unprecedented process of prayer, preaching, education, reflection, discussion, and action." The NCCB also described the pastoral letter as part of a larger process, the Church's ongoing commitment to peacemaking. The statement recognized the progress in U.S.–Soviet relations in the late 1980s, but at the same time reaffirmed the need for "urgent and persistent efforts to move more decisively toward effective arms control and mutual disarmament." The bishops continued to evaluate nuclear deterrence policy in terms of "strictly conditioned moral acceptance." They also continued their earlier practice of commenting on specific weapons systems by concluding that "proposals to press deployment of SDI [the Strategic Defense Initiative, or 'Star Wars'] do not measure up to the moral criteria outlined in this report."[12] *Building Peace* thus represented a postscript to *The Challenge of Peace;* together the documents "provide a summation of the Catholic bishops' contribution to the nuclear debate of the 1980s. . . . The bishops and other participants in the nuclear debate of the past decade need to assess the changes which are shaping the political, strategic and moral questions of the 1990s."[13]

My analysis indicates that the bishops had at least some success in their efforts to influence their many audiences, although their decision to deal with some of the details of nuclear arms control meant that portions of the peace pastoral would soon be outdated. It also reveals that in managing multiple identities the bishops produced a politically moderate, although somewhat left-leaning, document, for the time and for the exigencies of their rhetorical situation. Both right and left could find their interests represented to some degree in the pastoral. As it does for most corporate rhetors, the management of multiple identities tends to yield centrist messages if the messages are to speak for the commonly understood interests of the many. This highlights a distinctive feature of organizational communication. Corporate messages, particularly messages having a constitutional nature, tend to be—perhaps *have* to be—conservative if they are to reflect the full range of salient and dominant interests. (Radical challenges to the established order usually must be "non-constitutional," at least in their initial formulations.) The NCCB observed this principle, though it required much travail and rhetorical creativity, as I have shown. The result was a message that could be accepted, at least in part, by groups as diverse as U.S. Catholics, the Vatican, the Reagan Administration, and the general public.

2. *For a constituency or a group of stakeholders to criticize an organization and be heard, they must be recognized to some extent as insiders, or at least as sharing in the organization's identity and interests.* The bishops were able to criticize and engage in debate with Washington only when "fortress" Catholicism had sufficiently deteriorated and the U.S. Catholic Church had lost much of its sectarian character. The full integration of U.S. Catholics into the mainstream of American society, to which my interviewees referred, meant in practical terms that the bishops could relax their customary nationalistic stance. In drafting the peace pastoral the bishops generally perceived themselves as a constituency of the U.S. government and as sharing the national interest. As reasonably credible political commentators the bishops could effectively exercise their option of advocacy, in this case offering a critique of U.S. defense and foreign policies.

This second principle applies to a whole range of social contexts: family, organization, ethnic group, social movement, nation. In general, only those who can lay claim to the group's identity can effectively launch criticisms against it. This is why "boundary role persons," such as field representatives, official spokespersons, and ambassadors, often experience severe tensions on the job.[14] Because they are not at the "center" of the organization,[15] boundary-role persons are subject to questions about their loyalty. And if their loyalty is in question, their attempts to criticize, adapt, and improve the organization are necessarily suspect.

In his famous study of individual responses to organizational problems, *Exit, Voice, and Loyalty,* Albert O. Hirschman contends that the option of voice, or open criticism of the organization, is pragmatically favored when two conditions are met: (1) when the dissenter *has* some degree of loyalty to the organization, and (2) when the dissenter is *perceived* as being sufficiently loyal to merit a hearing. "Voice," as the articulation of a special interest, requires a "blending of apparent contradictions": on one hand, the dissenter must express his or her view so that organizational leaders know and can be responsive to what the person or group seeks; but on the other hand, the leaders must be allowed to make decisions with a substantial degree of autonomy. Therefore, the dissenter must "be in turn influential and deferential."[16]

The bishops managed this practical contradiction even as they managed their emerging interest-group identity. Other dissenters who seek to remain loyal must do the same. This is why the position of the organizational "whistle-blower" is so problematic: to go public with criticisms of the organization is usually interpreted as an act of disloyalty toward it, even when the case is otherwise.[17]

3. *For a part of an organization to assert its autonomy successfully and remain within the organization, it must avoid challenging the basic or "true" identity of the organization as a whole.* With respect to the bishops this principle applied directly to their relationship with the universal Catholic Church, particularly as represented by the Vatican. Not only did the bishops need to adhere to the specific constraints of Church tradition (in the form of conciliar and papal pronouncements); they also had to declare explicitly their Catholic allegiance at several points during the drafting of the peace pastoral. Here was the delicate balance: to nurture an emerging identity for the group as a national conference without threatening the "authorized" identity of the Church.

An analogous problem faces any organization when a subunit (e.g., a department, division, branch, etc.) asserts its interests and its distinctiveness. This is why the promotion of competition between departments—say, sales and engineering—in a business firm is so insidious from the whole organization's "point of view." If the controlling members of the organization encourage or allow such a competition to develop, they can unwittingly permit the interests of the entire organization to become subordinate to those of constituent groups. The same reasoning explains why some organizations are sensitive about the consistent use of their logo and other identifying symbols: they seek to keep the *total* organizational identity supreme. For example, California Polytechnic State University, in San Luis Obispo, issued in 1986 an elaborate set of guidelines for use of the University's name, mandating that every printed piece of material that goes off campus have complete identification on it. Herbert Simon's theory of organizational identification recognizes these issues and problems. In arguing from an administrative standpoint, Simon asserts that decisions must be "allocated" and made in such a way as to promote the interests of the organization as a whole.[18] This prescription is designed to counteract the tendency to identify with local interests, what Edmund Burke called "the little platoon" in society to which we belong.[19]

In making their own statement about war and peace, the bishops could not pursue their "local" interests beyond the point at which they would begin to violate the interests of the "universal" Church. Rhetorically sensitive advocates in similar positions—academic department heads, divisional business managers, regional coordinators for governmental agencies—work within the same constraints.

4. *Organizations must, in one way or another, speak to outsiders, individuals and groups in their environment. In doing this effectively they must not adapt so thoroughly that their authority with insiders or their basic identity is jeopardized.* Rhetoric, by its very nature, involves adaptation to one or more audiences. Aristotle held that the successful rhetor must adapt by drawing upon the premises already held by audience members.[20] In Kenneth Burke's view the rhetor must foster some type of identification or association between his or her interests and those of the audience addressed.[21] Any organization that seeks to speak to one or more publics must observe these complementary principles. That means that in organizational settings an entity or an individual must find ways to adapt to others' views while maintaining the distinctiveness claimed by the rhetor. If this is not accomplished, people associated with the rhetorical agent and/or people outside the organization might see what is proposed as "untrue," easily changed, or illegitimate. Within these constraints it remains true, as Jill J. McMillan points out in her analysis of organizational rhetoric, that organizations must "plausibly align themselves to a changing environment."[22]

Organizations today that engage in "corporate advocacy," or attempts at powerful but indirect political influence, face at least two significant challenges with respect to the preservation of their identities: (1) to appeal to widely held value premises yet say something unique, and (2) to behave politically without being labelled as political actors.[23] This is the case for businesses, labor unions, and social-action groups.

To the bishops who sought to make a statement on issues of war and peace, both challenges were salient. To be persuasive at all beyond the organizational boundaries of the Church the NCCB had to connect with the pragmatic concerns of many Americans. The bishops did this by locating themselves and their pastoral letter within the larger nuclear freeze campaign; however, they explicitly distanced themselves from the merely secular concerns of most of these activists. Too, the bishops stressed the indirect nature of their political involvement so as to avoid being branded "political" by the press, by the Reagan Administration, or by conservative citizens. The bishops styled themselves as "citizens" who were making their case both to Catholics and to the larger public. Their audiences were defined as those who had or could have a direct impact on the political process through voting and advocacy. According to several of the bishops I interviewed, this model now guides the NCCB in its treatment of an array of social issues; they acknowledged, however, the delicate nature of this balance. (In 1990, for example, a heated controversy arose over the NCCB's decision to retain the United States' largest public relations firm, Hill & Knowlton, and the Reagan Administration's pollster, The Wirthlin Group, in an effort to market widely the Church's opposition to abortion.) As George Weigel explained, in reflecting four years after *The Challenge of Peace,*

> The bishops' critique, which reflected the movement teaching that the arms race resulted from a failure of American morality and will, eventually led to the National Conference of Catholic Bishops' 1983 pastoral letter, "The Challenge of Peace." The letter, which drew front-page attention in the *New York Times* and a *Time* cover story, was much less a theology and politics of peace than a commentary on weapons and nuclear strategy. The bishops' final proposals were shaped by conventional arms control theory and aimed at political Washington. Here the Catholic prelates followed the pattern set by their Protestant colleagues during Vietnam: church-as-lobbyist model took precedence over religious leaders' classic task of culture formation through moral education.[24]

Weigel expanded this commentary into a full-blown critique in his 1987 book, *Tranquillitas Ordinis: The Present Failure and Future Promise of American Catholic Thought on War and Peace.* There he blasted *The Challenge of Peace* as "a tragically lost opportunity," arguing that in being unduly influenced by the secular debate over nuclear arms in the early 1980s, the bishops produced not a "peace pastoral" but "a weapons pastoral."[25]

From a sharply contrasting viewpoint Ronald G. Musto argued forcefully that *The Challenge of Peace* "has produced a revolution in American Catholic thinking on war and peace equal to that of Vatican II and the Pastoral Constitution *Gaudium et Spes.*"[26] He believed that the peace pastoral represented an important moment in the U.S. Catholic Church's development of "a theology and practice of peace." The peace pastoral formalized the trend toward a more vigorous and explicit stand on peacemaking by the U.S. bishops. Musto continued:

> The pastoral epitomizes the history and scope of the American Catholic dialogue of peacemaking. It is the first attempt at a synthesis of and compromise between the just-war and pacifist traditions within Catholic history, between the church's recognition of the nation-state and the international system and its defense of the rights of individual conscience, between its functions of prophetic denunciation and education and its role as an institution in American society. It combines the wisdom of the gospels, the Catholic tradition of positive peacemaking, *Pacem in Terris,* Vatican II, recent papal teaching, and the experience of recent American history.[27]

The peace pastoral thus embodied both permanence and change, both priestly and prophetic voices, both an adaptation *to* and an intended adaptation *of* the wider society.

The NCCB's dilemma in developing the peace pastoral was enormously complex. Their possible strategies were several. They could maintain a broad position which retained what Father Bryan Hehir called "a centimeter of ambiguity." They could unflinchingly condemn deterrence and leave application of this position to political actors. On a case-by-case basis they could address specific weapons systems and plans for their use. They could opt fully for the nuclear freeze alternative. They could let the peace pastoral speak for itself as a complex, nuanced call for disarmament and peace. Each such possibility carried with it a potentially fatal risk. Too much ambiguity could yield unresolved uncertainties, vitiating the normal functions of pastoral letters. The bishops settled for the "centimeter of ambiguity." Sweeping condemnation could arouse the hostility of the audiences the bishops hoped to persuade. Too much specificity would carry them beyond their credited expertise and authority and would undermine their credibility as theological and moral teachers. Endorsing the freeze would render their document excessively political and oriented toward a single issue. The bishops chose, wisely as it turns out, to allow some ambiguities to remain, to distinguish between the doctrinal and the political aspects of their document, and to offer the latter as bases for further study and discussion. This was their strategy for adapting to special interests without abandoning their claims to moral, churchly authority. By conceding the legitimacy of differing opinions on a number of matters, they wedded churchly authority to citizenly inquiry and debate.

5. *Organizations, like individuals, must struggle with the dialectic of permanence and change; the more traditional an organization is, the*

more difficulty it has in adapting to different times or situations. Con-versely, to effect substantial change in a traditional organization threat-ens its consistency, its "true" and lasting identity. Clearly this principle is related to the fourth principle, although the fourth is broader in its applicability. The identity of an individual or a collectivity is defined in practical terms as continuity in contrast to change. This is particularly the case for an individual or an organization that declares consistency and coherence to be of value. For an organization or a family or a nation to emphasize tradition is to suggest a test of identity by which its actions can be judged. Innovative or uncharacteristic actions call into question an organization's "essence." So it is for governments that make major policy shifts (as nations in the former Eastern Bloc are struggling with presently) and corporations that try to adopt a new image (as is the case for various U.S. defense contractors in the post-Cold War age).

As Brian Smith observes, the Roman Catholic Church is always in danger of losing its identity in part because it is so traditional.[28] And as Francis Schüssler Fiorenza explains, the Church's integrity as an institu-tion depends on its ability "to hold fast to two elements, the religious identity and the socio-political mission, without reducing one to the other."[29] The bishops' political advocacy clearly jeopardized that identity and that tradition, although a complex historical argument can be made to show that the bishops were consistent with the Church's central con-cerns. For example, Francis Winters argues that

> the bishops' challenge . . . should come as no surprise. For over a millen-nium, the church has sought to hobble wayward governments in just this fashion, by denying them the personnel necessary to carry out unwarranted military campaigns. Not content simply to counsel the King against unwar-ranted use of force, the church has also spoken to his subordinates and commanded them to lay down their arms.

In even more philosophic terms Winters goes on to explain:

> This intransigence in criticizing security policies arises from a world view that has taken shape over two millennia and that rests on a minimalist view of the state. In the eyes of the Catholic Church, the legitimate role of government is limited by the competing rights of other, nongovernmental members of society, including the individual, the family, and the Church itself. The person is prior—in his individuality as well as in his chosen associations—to the state. It is precisely this priority—metaphysical and moral—which established the tradition of inalienable rights delimiting the competence of the state. Secure within this tradition, the Church feels confident in challenging the state's competence to order citizens to support

or execute military policies that the Church views as irremediably perverse.[30]

While most of the interviewees for this study probably would have agreed with Winter's placement of the peace pastoral in the sweeping context of Catholic history, they typically did not discuss the moment in such grand terms. In treating what the peace pastoral says about church–state relations, most of them highlighted the clear emergence of the moral argument in the debate on nuclear arms. Father Bryan Hehir, responding to a question about "the mission" suggested by *The Challenge of Peace,* said: "The bishops demonstrated the utility of the religious-moral argument in a public policy debate and opened up the debate for others." There were, of course, complaints that the bishops diminished tradition, but the general response to the peace pastoral within the Church suggested that with such devices as the moral hierarchy and their emphasis on the dignity of human life, they successfully portrayed themselves as change agents still firmly aligned with the Church's traditions.

6. *If leaders or controlling members of an organization wish to alter the organization's identity in significant ways, they must ground their call for change in the interests of at least some considerable parts of the organization.* This principle poses yet another challenge for organizations in managing multiple identities. Organizational policy makers who move too far from the interests of their internal constituencies can threaten both the leaders' authority and the organization's cohesiveness. Innovators in any organization must in some way link the intended changes to the ongoing or traditional concerns of organizational members. For example, when the perfection of the polio vaccine in the late 1950s essentially eliminated the organizational rationale for the March of Dimes, that organization widened its scope and broadened its identity to include the fight against birth defects, thereby preserving the organization. This change in organizational identity, however, was consistent with the traditional interests of members; thus the organization effected the transition smoothly.

Instances where organizational leaders depart from, violate, or eschew the interests of members are referred to as "organizational transcendence." James Wood describes this as "an organization's use of its name and other resources in actions not predictable from its members' attitudes toward those actions."[31] In studying social action by mainline Protestant churches during the 1970s, Wood found that a number of their leaders were able to espouse positions considerably more liberal than those held by their congregations when those positions were tied to the core values of the organization. In this way church leaders exploited the ambiguities of terms such as "social justice," using organizationally held values to warrant individually chosen actions.

The U.S. Catholic bishops were and are somewhat left of center with respect to American Catholics on political issues, such as nuclear arms control and aid to the poor, but they have generally been to the right of the majority of Catholics on issues of personal morality, such as abortion and birth control. In developing the peace pastoral the bishops grounded their arguments in the Church's traditions, notably the dignity of human life, while moving the U.S. Church toward greater political advocacy.

7. *To allow for genuine pluralism and widespread participation in decision making necessarily challenges the authority of those in control of a centralized, hierarchical, autocratic, or doctrinaire organization.* As I have shown, the bishops sought to embrace simultaneously two conflicting images, hierarchy and community. Any synthesis of these two must be tentative because of the differences between them. Of course, to promote community is not necessarily to evoke a tension between hierarchical structure and democratic participation. What the bishops struggled with was their particular conception of community and its implications for the authoritative organization from which and for which they spoke. To some extent the bishops recognized the difficult rhetorical problem here: to open channels of communication at all levels of the organization is to invite challenges to institutional authority and hierarchical identity. With respect to the Roman Catholic Church in general Brian Smith framed the rhetorical problem this way: "Leaders at the top of the Church must balance [the] increased sharing of responsibility among lower clergy, religious, and laity with maintenance of effective episcopal authority necessary for decisions on issues not subject to change by popular consensus."[32]

Indeed, it is difficult for any hierarchical organization to allow for many voices while privileging one voice from the top, even though it is widely understood that greater participation in decision making often yields increased commitment to the implementation of decisions. Thus, many organizations (for example, large corporations) that take a step toward allowing greater member participation often step back when the leadership's authority is in question. Labor unions, although they have been largely effective in enacting egalitarian ideals, sometimes retreat into the privileged discourse of their leaders.[33] To embrace "community" fully as an organizational identity requires that "hierarchy" be largely abandoned or at least minimized; there is no other way.

175

8. *For transnational and transcultural organizations the management of multiple identities is especially difficult: cultural, ethnic, and national identities must be balanced with the identity of the entire organization.* I have made much of this point already. The Roman Catholic Church, the European Parliament, multinational corporations, United Nations agencies, and various other international organizations face this problem in its full complexity. The problem lies in rooting an institution in each national context while maintaining strong support linkages to the organization's center.[34] The United Nations has had great difficulty with this problem, suffering criticisms from many of its members for being insufficiently "universal." As the number of international organizations proliferates, particularly in the non-governmental category, this dilemma will become commonplace.[35] For instance, the growing number of transnational organizations for the protection and promotion of human rights will contend with multiple cultural contexts and varying conceptions of justice while seeking to advance universal ideals and practices.[36]

In developing their new advocacy position, the U.S. Catholic bishops faced special problems along these lines. Numerous articles have appeared in recent years questioning the very coherence, identity, and viability of Catholicism, particularly in a secularized and pluralistic United States. For example, a series of commentaries were issued in *Commonweal* magazine in late 1984 under the ominous heading "The End of Catholicism?" And a *Time* cover story in early 1985 discussed as one of the Pope's probing themes for clergy and religious the idea of *identity*.[37] In an essay published as the NCCB embarked on the peace pastoral historian David O'Brien, who has written extensively on contemporary Catholicism, put the question plainly to the faithful of this country: "American Catholics: Just Who Do You Think You Are?"[38] Edward K. Braxton, a frequent contributor to Catholic publications, posed the question again in late 1987, almost five years after the peace pastoral's publication. His pondering over "Is there an American Catholic Church?" was evoked by the Pope's second visit to the United States, in September 1987. "Pope John Paul's declaration that there is no 'American church' seems to be in striking contrast with statements that were being made in the weeks before his arrival and during his visit."[39] Indeed, in their presentations to the Pope in Los Angeles during his visit, four bishops, including Joseph Cardinal Bernardin, stressed the need for the Catholic Church in the United States to respond to the distinctive cultural and political challenges while maintaining the church's universal character. As late as March of 1989 a group of bishops was invited to

176

Rome to justify the U.S. Church's "Americanness." The problem of melding local identities with transnational and transcultural structures and mores is not new, and it seems likely to grow—for the Roman Catholic Church and for virtually all transnational corporations and agencies. As businesses, industries, and agencies expand, how local identities are to be balanced against "higher" identities is increasingly a conceptual and rhetorical problem for all but decidedly local organizations.

9. *The key texts, messages, and symbols of an organization reveal important aspects of how the organization is constituted; this is particularly true for organizations that celebrate "sacred" symbols.* Kenneth Burke's metaphor of "constitution" is instructive here: the term is powerfully ambiguous in that it refers to a "sacred" text, an authoritative body of principles, a state of being, the structure or form of an organization, and an organizational process of formation.[40]

In my interview with him, I asked Cardinal Bernardin if he was comfortable in describing the peace pastoral as a "constitution."

> I think that's a fairly good way to describe it. The peace pastoral is a new style of teaching. . . . But, it's [also] a style that's endorsed by the Second Vatican Council in *Gaudium et Spes*. *Gaudium et Spes* stated a number of things: first, that the Church cannot be separate from the world because it is incarnated in the world. Moreover, there should be no areas of life that escape moral scrutiny. Second, it's not just Church authorities that should deal with these questions but the whole citizenry. And, number three, when it comes to addressing societal problems, you have to depend on facts, research, interpretations, so things are not always as clear as they might be in other areas. . . . Now this points up another question—that by allowing people to react in exchanging drafts and comments, we somehow undermine our own authority. But I submit that we *enhance* our authority, especially on social issues.

As a "constitution" of sorts the peace pastoral was a nexus for managing multiple identities. I have shown in some detail how the corporate statement interwove these identities with the sacred symbols of the Church. Identities were managed conceptually and rhetorically to achieve a corporate voice; the voice was strengthened through participation and particularly by the retreat which united the bishops in their call for action. The metaphor of "constitution" can thus provide a starting point for an observer or researcher who wants to find out what any organization perceives itself to be—what it believes its truly important facets are. By analyzing what identities are managed in corporate statements, one can discern what special identities and interests are encompassed by messages from an organization. This discernment enables discrimination between genuinely important identifications and peripheral ones. Doctrinal statements, policy statements, charters, resolutions, and the like are open to this kind of analysis—especially where organizations have and celebrate "sacred" symbols, as most do either explicitly or implicitly.

10. *In organizational relations, as in interpersonal matters, different identities are associated with different fields of argument or domains of discourse—for example, theological, moral, political, popular, technical, scholarly.* This principle was understood deeply by the U.S. Catholic bishops drafting *The Challenge of Peace.* They struggled to speak both as moral-theological leaders and as technical–political leaders without embracing the "identity" of technical–political spokespersons. As the bishops participated in both domains of discourse—using terms of the Church as well as those of secular interest groups—they were pushed and pulled by groups who wanted them either to stick to one set of terms (in the case of the political right) or work with both sets (in the case of the left). Ultimately the bishops argued in both fields but clung to their moral-theological identity when they were challenged by critics.

Organizations of all types exert power by defining the nature of, relevance of, boundaries of, and participants in particular domains of discourse. This is one of the central themes in Michel Foucault's analyses of various institutions: criminal justice, psychiatry, the social sciences, and so forth.[41] Certainly much of the Reagan Administration's success in promoting the Strategic Defense Initiative ("Star Wars") from 1983 to 1988 can be explained in these terms. By shifting the domain of the argument from the *moral*–political arena to the *technical*–political one, Reagan induced critics to focus on the question "Will it work?" rather than on "Is it right?" Reagan and his supporters persuaded many Americans to identify Star Wars as a technical–political issue, thus excluding most citizens ("as non-experts") from the debate. As Bruce Russett explains, this strategy has often been employed to delimit the discussions of nuclear arms and nuclear power.[42] Speaking on a more general level and following both Marx and Weber, Jürgen Habermas has shown how technical or instrumental rationality in the modern world has overshadowed a "communicative" form that centers on human relationships and mutual understanding.[43]

The tenth principle I am enunciating applies even to relatively loose and informal communities of interest that we do not ordinarily think of as organizations. Lawrence J. Prelli sets forth in detail the informal rhetorical logic that must operate in discourse if it is to be accepted by scientific communities as "scientific." He shows that criteria such as accuracy, replicability, relevance to communally recognized problems of knowledge, and the credibility of sources and methods are applied as measures of all that purports to be scientific. For failing to meet such tests, creationism has in some state courts been legally declared non-scientific, whereas evolution has been declared to be scientific.[44] My point is that in a variety of domains such as the domain of scientific discourse, there are informal as well as formal rules that either legitimate or deny identification for particular communities of interest.

11. *Organizations, as rhetors, exploit the resource of ambiguity to manage multiple interests and multiple identities.* Ambiguity is an inherent resource of language. Burke explains its importance for analysis and criticism this way: "What we want is not *terms that avoid ambiguity,* but *terms that clearly reveal the strategic spots at which ambiguities necessarily arise.*"[45] Here is a powerful insight about organizations and about human relations in general. Organizations, like individuals, will use strategic points of ambiguity[46] to reconcile differences, to unite members under one symbolic banner, to "stretch" an interpretation of the organization's mission, to establish common ground with outsiders, but also sometimes to deceive. The term "efficiency," for example, connotes an array of meanings, including individual performance, organizational performance, the ratio of input to output, speed, effectiveness, etc. So the value of efficiency can be invoked and manipulated in organizational decisions to justify many different courses of action while being celebrated as an American ideal.[47]

As I have shown, the NCCB drew upon and even cherished the resource of ambiguity. They brought together disparate traditions under the "new moment"; they embraced diverse groups with a "theology of peace"; they articulated a hierarchy of moral "authority"; and they argued for a "seamless garment" of life-related positions. All of these rhetorical moves were tentative, however, with the last being perhaps the most problematic in its practical capacity to bring together widely variant perceptions, interests, goals, and groups.

12. *The management of multiple identities necessarily involves the use of power: in any situation particular identities may be celebrated, incorporated, coopted, suppressed, or rejected.* In other words, in the management of multiple identities not all identities are treated equally. This I have shown in the case of the bishops. While making their discourse more catholic, the bishops held to positions that were Catholic. They granted some legitimacy to the identity of pacifist elements within the Church, but in the end the bishops incorporated those into an expanded interpretation

of the Church's central tradition on war and peace. The bishops declared their own identity as a national conference, but they did not locate their interests outside the universal concerns of Rome. The bishops identified to some extent with the secular nuclear freeze movement, but they distanced themselves from its complete political identity. These rhetorical strategies entail the use of power: the power to define, the power to authorize, the power to associate or alienate one group with/from another.[48] Whenever a group or an organization succeeds in setting labels, the terms for debate— as the Reagan Administration did for some years in calling the Nicaraguan opposition "freedom fighters"—the profound relationship between power and language invites analysis.[49]

The workings of power in the management of multiple identities are also apparent if we consider individual persons. Of the various identifications and commitments that an individual has or shares, some are inevitably more influential than others. For example, Abrahamson and Anderson note how individuals' commitments to particular institutions either "transcend an institutional realm and affect other institutional commitments or are compartmentalized."[50] They report specifically that North Americans' economic, political, and educational commitments are tightly interconnected in everyday thought and speech, tending to reinforce one another, while familial and religious commitments usually function more independently.

In sum, management of multiple identities is the rhetorical challenge facing all individuals and institutions in a complex, organizational society. This overarching principle explains the central activity of organizational rhetoric: the "corporate" voice reflects, effects, and affects the management of multiple identities. Taking this point of view enables a student of organizations to view the individual from the perspective of an organization and the organization from the perspective of an individual.[51] The latter perspective is of particular importance today: while participating in and analyzing organizational life, one should keep in mind the life and the interests of the individual, the natural person. The management of multiple identities as a guiding concept helps us to appreciate the full power of language in shaping the "worlds" of both individuals and groups. As Burke says so well:

> Are things disunited in "body"? Then unite them in "spirit." Would a nation extend its physical dominion? Let it talk of spreading its "ideals." Do you encounter contradictions? Call them "balances." Is an organization in disarray? Talk of its common *purpose*. Are there struggles over means? Celebrate agreement on ends. Sanction the troublously manifest, the incarnate, in terms of the ideally, perfectly invisible and intangible, the divine.[52]

Of course, these and other rhetorical exercises, however eloquent or initially compelling, should always be assessed with the loftiest human interests in mind: peace, justice, equality, and the opportunity for self-expression. Mere "management," however complex and masterful it may be, is not enough for a world which still suffers from violence, exploitation, inequality, and oppression. Organizations should serve the interests of their creators, all individuals.

NOTES

1. Mary Douglas, *How Institutions Think* (Syracuse, NY: Syracuse University Press, 1986).

2. See, e.g., the overview provided in Raymie R. McKerrow, "Critical Rhetoric: Theory and Practice," *Quarterly Journal of Speech* 56 (1989): 91–111. See also the excellent overview of contemporary rhetorical criticism in Roderick P. Hart, *Modern Rhetorical Criticism* (Glenview, IL: Scott, Foresman, 1989).

3. Charles A. Curran, "A Complex Document for a 'Big Church,'" *Commonweal*, 13 Aug. 1982: 438–40. The interrelations of identities can in some cases evoke paradox. For example, as the Solidarity labor union of Poland took control over much of the government in late 1989, many observers in the United States called the step a triumph for capitalism at the same time that they argued for limiting labor power in their own country.

4. Andrew Greeley, "Why the Peace Pastoral Did Not Bomb," *National Catholic Reporter*, 12 Apr. 1985: 11.

5. While at work on my dissertation in 1984–85, I conducted a questionnaire survey of 100 lay Catholics in five parishes of the Diocese of Lafayette, Indiana. Of those surveyed, 82 percent agreed with the position of the bishops on nuclear arms control, and a similar proportion, 76 percent, believed that the bishops' efforts had made arms control a more salient issue for Americans as a whole. It should be noted that the bishops' follow-up program for the peace pastoral was the most extensive they had ever employed, although it was inconsistently pursued across the nation. See NCCB, *Building Peace: A Report on The Challenge of Peace and Policy Developments, 1983–1988* (Washington: USCC, 1988).

6. See, e.g., James E. Wood, Jr., "The Nuclear Arms Race and the Churches," editorial, *Journal of Church and State* 25 (Spring 1983): 219–29; Kermit D. Johnson, "The Illusion of Unilateral Security," *Christianity and Crisis*, 17 Nov. 1986: 410; Eric O. Hanson, *The Catholic Church in World Politics* (Princeton, NJ: Princeton University Press, 1987), esp. 321. See also William A. Au, *The Cross, the Flag, and the Bomb: American Catholics Debate War and Peace, 1960–1983* (Westport, CT: Greenwood Press, 1985), 253. Among statements by other religious groups that were inspired by *The Challenge of Peace* was the United Council of Methodist Bishops' *In Defense of Creation: The Nuclear Crisis and a Just Peace* (Nashville: Graded Press, 1986), in which they condemned nuclear deterrence as a policy.

7. F. H. Knelman, *Reagan, God and the Bomb: From Myth to Policy in the Nuclear Arms Race* (Buffalo, NY: Prometheus Books, 1985), esp. 184.

8. *New York Times,* 5 May 1983: A-1.

9. Hanson, *Catholic Church in World Politics,* 300–301.

10. Phillip Berryman, *Our Unfinished Business: The U.S. Catholic Bishops' Letters on Peace and the Economy* (New York: Pantheon, 1989), 176.

11. Strobe Talbott, "The Road to Zero," *Time,* 14 Dec. 1987: 18ff. For an assessment of the freeze movement's overall impact see Douglas C. Walker, *Congress and the Nuclear Freeze: An Inside Look at the Politics of a Mass Movement* (Amherst: University of Massachusetts Press, 1987), esp. 301. For a focus on the bishops see Mark R. Amstutz, "The Challenge of Peace: Did the Bishops Help?" *This World,* Spring/Summer 1985: 22–35. For a discussion of the various groups involved in the freeze movement see Elise Boulding, "The Early 1980s Peak of the Peace Movement," in *Peace Action in the Eighties: Sociological Views,* ed. Sam Marullo and John Lofland (New Brunswick, NJ: Rutgers University Press, in press).

12. *Building Peace,* 4, 7, and 72. It should be noted that the bishops established an Ad Hoc Committee on the Moral Evaluation of Deterrence to review policy developments between 1983 and 1988. The final report, consistent in spirit with *Building Peace,* was issued on 25 June 1988. See *Origins* 18 (21 July 1988): 133–48.

13. J. Bryan Hehir, "The Catholic Bishops and the Nuclear Debate: A Case Study of the Independent Sector" (Paper delivered at the Symposium on Religion, War, the Independent Sector, and American Culture, Indiana University, 19 Oct. 1989).

14. J. Stacy Adams, "The Structure and Dynamics of Behavior in Organizational Boundary Roles," in *Handbook of Industrial and Organizational Psychology,* ed. Marvin D. Dunnette (Chicago: Rand-McNally, 1976), 1175–99.

15. John Kenneth Galbraith, *The New Industrial State,* 3rd ed. (Boston: Houghton Mifflin, 1978).

16. Albert O. Hirschman, *Exit, Voice, and Loyalty: Responses to Decline in Firms, Organizations and States* (Cambridge, MA: Harvard University Press, 1970), 32.

17. See, e.g., Robert Perrucci, Robert M. Anderson, Dan E. Schendel, and Leon E. Tractman, "Whistle-Blowing: Professionals' Resistance to Organizational Authority," *Social Problems* 28 (1980): 149–67.

18. Herbert A. Simon, *Administrative Behavior,* 3rd ed. (New York: Free Press, 1976). Many different types of organizations are sensitive about their identities, names, and logos. See "Dept. of Higher Education: Identity Crisis Division," *New Yorker,* 8 Sept. 1986: 89–90.

19. As quoted in Peter L. Berger and Richard N. Neuhaus, *To Empower People: The Role of Mediating Structures in Public Policy* (Washington: American Enterprise Institute, 1977), 4.

20. Aristotle, *The Rhetoric*, trans. W. Rhys Roberts (New York: The Modern Library, 1954).

21. Kenneth Burke, *A Rhetoric of Motives* (1950; rpt., Berkeley: University of California Press, 1969).

22. Jill J. McMillan, "Institutional Plausibility Alignment as Rhetorical Exercise: A Mainline Denomination's Struggle with the Exigence of Sexism," *Journal for the Scientific Study of Religion* 27 (1988): 326–44. Cf. Peter L. Berger, *The Sacred Canopy* (Garden City, NY: Doubleday, 1967).

23. George Cheney and Steven L. Vibbert, "Corporate Discourse: Public Relations and Issue Management," in *Handbook of Organizational Communication: An Interdisciplinary Perspective,* ed. Fredric M. Jablin, Linda L. Putnam, Karlene H. Roberts, and Lyman W. Porter (Newbury Park, CA: Sage, 1987), 165–94.

24. George Weigel, "A Long March," *The Wilson Quarterly* 11 (New Year's, 1987): 139.

25. George Weigel, *Tranquillitas Ordinis: The Present Failure and Future Promise of American Catholic Thought on War and Peace* (Oxford: Oxford University Press, 1987), esp. 257–85.

26. Ronald G. Musto, *The Catholic Peace Tradition* (Maryknoll, NY: Orbis Books, 1986), 262.

27. Musto, *Catholic Peace Tradition,* 262.

28. Brian H. Smith, *The Church and Politics in Chile: Challenges to Modern Catholicism* (Princeton, NJ: Princeton University Press, 1983). See also Carol J. Jablonski, "*Aggiornamento* and the American Catholic Bishops: A Rhetoric of Institutional Continuity and Change," *Quarterly Journal of Speech* 75 (1989): 416–32. See also the more general discussion by Stuart Albert and David A. Whetten, "Organizational Identity," in *Research in Organizational Behavior,* vol. 7, ed. L. L. Cummings and Barry M. Staw (Greenwich, CT: JAI Press, 1985), 263–95.

29. Francis Schüssler Fiorenza, "The Church's Religious Identity and Its Social and Political Mission," *Theological Studies* 43 (1982): 205; see also 197–225.

30. Francis X. Winters, "The American Bishops on Deterrence—'Wise as Serpents: Innocent as Doves,'" *Science, Technology, and Human Values* 8 (1983): 26.

31. James R. Wood, "Legitimate Control and 'Organizational Transcendence,'" *Social Forces* 54 (1975): 199–211.

32. Smith, *Church and Politics,* 21.

33. Richard B. Freeman and James L. Medoff, *What Do Unions Do?* (New York: Basic Books, 1984).

34. Smith, *Church and Politics,* 22.

35. Elise Boulding, *Building a Global Civic Culture: Education for an Interdependent World* (New York: Teachers College, Columbia University, 1988). Of

course, "globalization" can refer to disparate phenomena: compare, e.g., the identification of a person as a world citizen with the domination of a world market by a multinational corporation.

36. See, e.g., Jack Donnelly, *Universal Human Rights in Theory and Practice.* Ithaca, NY: Cornell University Press. A discussion of this issue from a rhetorical-communicative perspective can be found in George Cheney and Cynthia Stohl, "Communicating about Human Rights: An Advocacy Model," (Paper delivered at the 25th anniversary conference of the International Peace Research Association, Groningen, The Netherlands, July 1990).

37. Richard N. Ostling, "Discord in the Church," *Time,* 4 Feb. 1985: 50–55, esp. 53.

38. David O'Brien, interview, "American Catholics: Just Who Do You Think You Are?" *U.S. Catholic,* Apr. 1981: 6–11.

39. Edward K. Braxton, "Is There an American Catholic Church?" *America,* 5 Dec. 1987: 424. Also see "U.S. Catholics: A Feisty Flock Awaits the Pope," *Time,* 7 Sept. 1987, cover story.

40. Kenneth Burke, *A Grammar of Motives* (1945; rpt., Berkeley: University of California Press, 1969), 338.

41. See, e.g., Michel Foucault, *The Foucault Reader,* trans. Paul Rabinow (New York: Pantheon, 1984).

42. Bruce Russett, *The Prisoners of Insecurity: Nuclear Deterrence, the Arms Race, and Arms Control* (San Francisco: Freeman, 1983).

43. See, e.g., Jürgen Habermas, *Toward a Rational Society,* trans. Jeremy J. Shapiro (Boston: Beacon Press, 1970).

44. Lawrence J. Prelli, *A Rhetoric of Science: Inventing Scientific Discourse* (Columbia: University of South Carolina Press, 1989).

45. Burke, *Grammar of Motives,* xviii. See also William Empson, *7 Types of Ambiguity* (New York: New Directions, 1947).

46. See, e.g., Eric Eisenberg, "Ambiguity as Strategy in Organizational Communication," *Communication Monographs* 51 (1984): 227–42.

47. See, e.g., George Cheney and Greg Frenette, "Persuasion and Organization: Values, Logics, and Accounts in Contemporary Corporate Public Discourse," in *Values, Arguments, and Organizational Decisions,* ed. Charles Conrad (Norwood, NJ: Ablex, in press); and George Cheney and James Brancato, "Scientific Management's Rhetorical Force and Enduring Impact," unpublished manuscript, the University of Colorado at Boulder, 1990.

48. See, e.g., Roland Robertson and Burkart Holzner, eds., *Identity and Authority* (New York: St. Martin's Press, 1979); See also Carol J. Jablonski, "Rhetoric, Paradox, and the Movement for Women's Ordination in the Roman Catholic Church," *Quarterly Journal of Speech* 74 (1988): 164–83; Hervé Carrier, *The Sociology of Religious Belonging* (New York: Herder, 1965), 186–94; and Kenneth Burke's discussion of autonomy in *A Rhetoric of Motives,* where he explains how scientists often try to distance themselves from the morally questionable uses to which their discoveries are put.

49. See, e.g., Norman Fairclough, *Language and Power* (London: Longman, 1989).

50. Mark Abrahamson and William P. Anderson, "People's Commitments to Institutions," *Social Psychology Quarterly* 47 (1984): 371–81.

51. This is the dual perspective taken by Stanley Seashore in his classic study, *Group Cohesiveness in the Industrial Work Group* (Ann Arbor: Institute for Social Research, University of Michigan, 1954).

52. Kenneth Burke, "Rhetoric—Old and New," in *New Rhetorics*, ed. Martin Steinmann (New York: Scribner's, 1967), 76.

APPENDIX A
RECORD OF ELITE INTERVIEWS AND CONTACTS

Name	Position	Relevance	Contact(s)	Time(s)	Date(s)
George Fulcher	Bishop of Lafayette, IN	Member, drafting commitee; initial head of follow-up	PI PI	60 min. 60 min.	21 July 1983 14 Dec. 1983
Joseph Fichter	Sociologist, Loyola University, New Orleans	Reacted to project proposal	PL	———	8 Nov. 1983
Russell Shaw	Director of Public Affairs, USCC, Washington	Provided access to other offices	PI	30 min.	10 Nov. 1983
Brian McCullough	Director of Peace Pastoral Clearinghouse	Explained follow-up program	PI	50 min.	10 Nov. 1983
John Tracy Ellis	Professor of	Offered historical	PI	60 min.	11 Nov. 1983

		perspective			
	Church History, Catholic University, Washington				
James Malone	Bishop of Youngstown, OH; President of NCCB	President during follow-up	PI TI	60 min. 30 min.	22 Dec. 1983 8 Feb. 1985
John Roach	Archbishop of St. Paul–Minneapolis	President of NCCB during pastoral development	TI	40 min.	12 Mar. 1984
Daniel Reilly	Bishop of Norwich, CT	Member, drafting committee	TI	75 min.	14 Mar. 1984
Theodore Hesburgh	President, University of Notre Dame	Spokesman on various issues	PI	90 min.	5 Apr. 1985
John Gilligan	Professor of Law, Notre Dame; Former Governor of Ohio	Coordinator of peace studies	PI	90 min.	5 Apr. 1985
M. Desmond Ryan	Executive Director, Indiana Catholic Conference	Explained perspective of one state's Catholics on the peace pastoral	PI	60 min.	8 May 1984

APPENDIX A (continued)

Name	Position	Relevance	Contact(s)	Time(s)	Date(s)
Thomas Gumbleton	Auxiliary Archbishop of Detroit	Member, drafting committee; President, Pax Christi, USA	PI	60 min.	12 May 1984
William McCready	Center Director, Cultural Pluralism Research Center,National Opinion Research Center (NORC), Chicago	Offered information on surveys of Catholics; speculated on letter's impact	PI	25 min.	16 May 1984
Joseph Cardinal Bernardin	Archbishop of Chicago; President, NCCB	Chaired drafting committee	PI	45 min.	16 May 1984
Raymond Rufo	Diocesan Consultant for Parish Services, Lafayette, IN	Described grass-roots response to peace pastoral	PI	2 hours	22 May 1984

Name	Affiliation	Role	Type	Duration	Date
Bill Whalen	Director of Publications, Purdue	Representative for Indiana on pastoral follow-up	PI	30 min.	25 May 1984
Andrew Greeley	Sociologist at NORC	Commented on impact of pastoral	PL	——	29 May 1984
John Quinn	Archbishop of San Francisco; Former President NCCB	Influential in development of pastoral	TI	35 min.	8 Aug. 1984
Juliana Casey	Leadership Conference of Women Religious, Detroit	Representative to drafting committee	TI	50 min.	23 Aug. 1984
John O'Connor	Archbishop of New York	Member, drafting committee	TI	45 min.	24 Aug. 1984
Bruce Russett	Professor of Political Science, Yale	Principal consultant to drafting committee	TI	60 min.	17 Sept. 1984
John Cardinal Krol	Archbishop of Philadelphia	Spokesman for NCCB at 1979 Senate testimony on SALT II	TI	45 min.	7 Oct. 1984

Name	Position	Relevance	Contact(s)	Time(s)	Date(s)
Richard Sklba	Auxiliary Bishop of Milwaukee	Consultant to bishops on scriptural matters	TI	55 min.	22 Oct. 1984
Thomas Kelly	Archbishop of Louisville	General secretary of NCCB during pastoral's development	TI	50 min.	26 Oct. 1984
William Lewers	Office of Justice and Peace, USCC	Overseer of follow-up as of May 1984	TI	20 min.	29 Oct. 1984
Edward Doherty	Office of Justice and Peace, USCC	Staff member, drafting committee	TI	75 min.	29 Oct. 1984
Philip Hannan	Archbishop of new Orleans	Voiced opposition to peace pastoral	PL	—	6 Nov. 1984
Richard Warner	Representative, Conference of Major	Representative to drafting committee	PI	50 min.	13 Nov. 1984

Name	Affiliation	Description	Interview type	Duration	Date
	Superiors of Men, South Bend, IN				
Leroy Matthiesen	Bishop of Amarillo	Led Texas bishops in opposition to arms race	TI	60 min.	19 Nov. 1984
J. Bryan Hehir	Director, Office of International Justice and Peace, USCC	Staff member, drafting committee	TI	40 min.	21 Nov. 1984
William Higi	Bishop of Lafayette, IN	Discussed diocesan perspective on peace pastoral	PI	60 min.	29 Nov. 1984
Michael Novak	Researcher, American Enterprise Institute, Washington	Represented lay Catholic critics of peace pastoral	TI	55 min.	19 Dec. 1984
Daniel Hoye	General Secretary, NCCB	General secretary during follow-up	TI	35 min.	20 Dec. 1984
Bob Williams, Ron Voss, Craig Davis	Members, Lafayette Diocesan Peace Committee;	Developed program for implementing peace	Group discussions, individual	Varied	Numerous occasions between

APPENDIX A (continued)

Name	Position	Relevance	Contact(s)	Time(s)	Date(s)
Ed Lammert Ray Rufo Don Reichert	Bob Williams, chair	pastoral		conversations	Sept. 1984 and Feb. 1985

PI = Personal Interview
PL = Personal Letter
TI = Telephone Interview

APPENDIX B
COMPOSITE INTERVIEW SCHEDULE

QUESTIONS

I. Personal Role in the Development of the Peace Pastoral
   A. What contributions did you make to the formation or development of the bishops' peace pastoral?
   B. During the process of the letter's development, did you ever feel the need to distinguish between your *official* role and your *personal* one?

II. The Development of the Peace Pastoral in General
   A. What factors were considered in selecting members for the drafting committee?
   B. In your view, what were the main problems faced by the bishops during the formulation of the various drafts of the letter?
   C. What were the significant triumphs of the bishops during this process?
   D. In your opinion, what were the most important changes in the letter during the progression from draft to draft? Why were they made?
   E. The peace pastoral was directed at several audiences. How were their various concerns weighed during the development of the letter?
   F. What role did input from the Vatican and the Western European bishops play in the formation of the peace pastoral?
   G. How important were exchanges between the bishops and officials of the Reagan Administration during the development of the letter?
   H. What were the major contributions to the pastoral which came from the general meetings of the bishops?
   I. Were the views of some interest groups represented more in the process than those of other groups? If so, which groups had the greatest influence?
   J. What role did the Collegeville, Minnesota, retreat of June 1982 play in helping the bishops to forge a consensus?

K. How were the prophetic and "priestly" functions balanced during the development of the letter?.

L. How did you feel about the publicity accorded the bishops during the formation of the letter?

III. The Significance and Meaning of the Peace Pastoral

A. Do you believe that the final draft of the peace pastoral fairly represents the pluralism of or the diversity of opinion within the U.S. Catholic Church?

B. How consistent is the letter with the position of the Vatican on war and peace issues?

C. How consistent is the letter with the current defense policies of the United States?

D. What do you think about the relationship of the just war theory and the pacificist or nonviolent option in the letter?

E. In your view, what is the moral *center* or *core* of the pastoral?

F. What kind of *mission* does the peace pastoral suggest for the U.S. Catholic Church?

G. Would you agree with the commentators who have said that the *process* of the letter's development is as important as the *product,* the document itself? Why or why not?

H. Do the development and expression of the peace pastoral indicate anything about increasing democratization within the Church? How so?

I. Is the Catholic Church best represented by the *community* metaphor invoked in the letter?

J. Do you agree with the assessment by Msgr. John Tracy Ellis that the peace pastoral is a sign that Catholics have "arrived" in the mainstream of American society?

K. Because of the consultative and democratic process by which the peace pastoral was developed, the way in which it echoes the Pastoral Constitution on the Church in the Modern World, the tremendous publicity accorded it, and its widespread dissemination and discussion, the document might be called a "constitution" of the U.S. Catholic Church today. How do you react to such a characterization?

IV. Follow-up on and Implementation of the Peace Pastoral

A. What is being done in your ministry to implement the pastoral?

B. What is your personal involvement in these programs?

C. When preaching/teaching about the peace pastoral, what parts or aspects of it do you emphasize?

D. In your view, what are the greatest challenges to stimulating discussion and acceptance of the letter among U.S. Catholics?

E. How does the diversity of views among clergy, religious, and lay educators affect the implementation of the pastoral?

F. What are the key issues with which clergy, religious, and lay educators must wrestle in teaching the peace pastoral?

G. In your view, what are the best strategies for promoting the peace pastoral?

H. In your opinion, will the "seamless garment" approach to linking life-related issues be persuasive for the majority of American Catholics? Why or why not?

I. In your opinion, will the linkage of the peace letter to social justice concerns be persuasive for the majority of American Catholics? Why or why not?

J. What effect are interest groups in opposition to the bishops having on the peace pastoral follow-up?

K. How is the question about the *authority* of the NCCB affecting the follow-up on the peace pastoral?

V. The Impact and Effects of the Peace Pastoral

A. What kind of long-term impact will the peace pastoral have in shaping public opinion on U.S. defense policy?

B. How will/has the peace pastoral affect(ed) the bishops' self-image?

C. How will/has the peace pastoral affect(ed) the image of the bishops held by American Catholics?

D. How will/is the peace pastoral affect(ing) subsequent actions by the bishops?

E. As a result of the peace pastoral and the accompanying follow-up, will peace advocacy or a distinct orientation toward peacemaking become a visible part of U.S. Catholic identity? Why or why not?

F. How will/is the peace pastoral affect(ing) the balancing of devotion to the Church and loyalty to the nation on the part of U.S. Catholic laypersons? How are the faithful weighing their Catholicity and their Americanness?

G. How is the peace pastoral being received in your ministry?

INDEX OF NAMES

Abrahamson, Mark, 180
Abrams, Elliot, 100
Ahern, Patrick, 156
Allegretti, Joseph, 136
Anderson, William P., 180
Andropov, Yuri, 63
Aristotle, 8, 11, 156, 170

Barnard, Chester I., 3, 20, 123n.91
Bausch, William, 37
Beres, Louis, 89
Berger, Peter L., 158n.24, 183n.22
Bernardin, Joseph Cardinal, 64, 65, 68, 70,
    74, 87, 99, 100, 102, 103, 105, 106, 107,
    108, 114, 134–137, 140, 155, 176, 177,
    188
Berrigan, Daniel, 53
Berrigan, Philip, 53
Berryman, Phillip, 124
Bitzer, Lloyd F., 119n.19
Blake, William, 12
Booth, Wayne, 18
Boulding, Kenneth, 2, 36
Bozeman, Barry, 9
Braxton, Edward K., 176
Brezhnev, Leonid, 63
Brown, Richard Harvey, 29n.70
Bryant, Donald C., 15
Bundy, McGeorge, 92
Burke, Edmund, 12, 170
Burke, Kenneth, 1, 10, 11, 12, 13, 15–18,
    19, 155, 164, 170, 180

Carter, Jimmy, 63
Carroll, John, 37, 41
Casaroli, Agostino Cardinal, 116
Casey, Juliana, 66, 72, 140, 141, 142, 144,
    145, 146, 147, 151, 155, 189
Castelli, Jim, 66, 73, 75, 80n.55, 83, 100,
    106, 143
Clark, William, 75, 99, 100, 107
Cogley, John, 37
Coleman, James S., 7
Cooke, Terence Cardinal, 68
Cuddy, Edward, 91
Curran, Charles, 38, 165

Dagens, Claude, 112
Davis, Craig, 191
Day, Dorothy, 53
Dearden, John Cardinal, 127
Defois, Gerard, 115
Dingman, Maurice, 71, 75
Diocletian, 111
Dohen, Dorothy, 37, 38
Doherty, Edward, 66, 91, 92, 100, 154,
    155, 190
Douglas, Mary, 164
Douglass, James, 53
Drinan, Robert, 59, 78n.38
Dulles, Avery, 34, 85, 116, 127, 128
du Preez, Peter, 17, 30n.80
Durkheim, Emile, 164
Durkin, Mary Greeley, 39

Eagleberger, Lawrence, 98
Edwards, Richard, 7
Ellis, John Tracy, 38, 75, 96, 186
Erikson, Erik, 10

Falwell, Jerry, 97
Ferraro, Geraldine, 97
Fichter, Joseph, 186
Finn, James, 151
Fiorenza, Francis Schussler, 173
Fogarty, Gerald P., 113
Foote, Nelson N., 18
Forsberg, Randall, 60
Foucault, Michel, 10, 178
Freud, Sigmund, 10, 11
Fulcher, George A., 65, 70, 105, 110, 115,
    116, 141, 143, 156, 186

Gandhi, Mohandas, 149
Gergen, Kenneth J., 29n.70
Gibbons, John Cardinal, 38
Gilligan, Carol, 28n.38
Gilligan, John J., 60, 187
Goldzwig, Steve, 75
Gorbachev, Mikhail S., 43, 166, 167
Greeley, Andrew, 39, 138, 165–166, 189
Gremillion, Joseph, 48, 49

Gumbleton, Thomas, 63–64, 65, 96, 108, 116, 140, 142, 149, 151, 152, 188
Gunn, Giles, 31n.88

Habermas, Jürgen, 178
Hanna, Mary, 35, 39
Hannan, Philip, 91, 108, 190
Hanson, Eric O., 166
Hanson, John L., 130
Hardon, John A., 148
Harré, Rom, 30n.85
Hatfield, Mark, 60
Hehir, J. Bryan, 66, 74, 87, 88, 97, 100, 114, 126, 129, 131, 132, 142, 155, 156, 172, 174, 191
Hennesey, James, 53
Henriot, Peter, 139
Hesburgh, Theodore, 88, 94, 100, 126, 146, 147, 187
Higi, William, 191
Hirschman, Albert O., 168
Hitchcock, James, 117
Höffner, Joseph Cardinal, 115
Hogan, J. Michael, 160–161n.73
Holland, Norman, 17
Hollenbach, David, 153
Holzner, Burkart, 161–162n.89
Hook, Sidney, 91
Hoye, Daniel, 108, 131, 137, 155, 191
Hunthausen, Raymond, 66–67, 91, 152

Iacocca, Lee, 22
Ireland, John, 38
Irving, Washington, 12

James, William, 10, 11, 20
Jegen, Mary Evelyn, 82
Jesus Christ, 85, 86, 108, 128, 146, 149
John XXIII, Pope, 34, 49, 50, 85, 92
John Paul II, Pope, 41, 49, 50, 59, 66, 74–75, 101, 102, 112, 115, 116, 127, 128, 145, 146, 155, 176
Johnson, James Turner, 148
Johnson, Paul, 34

Kaufmann, Franz-Xaver, 43
Keats, John, 12
Kelly, George A., 39, 117, 130
Kelly, James R., 124
Kelly, Thomas, 63, 71, 108, 143, 155, 190
Kennan, George, 90, 92
Kennedy, Edward, 60
Kennedy, John F., 39, 96
Kenny, Michael, 71
King, Martin Luther, 149

Krol, John Cardinal, 57, 88, 101, 102, 142, 155, 189

Lammert, Ed, 192
Lampert, Michael A., 26n.8
Lapham, Lewis H., 1
Lasswell, Harold, 10, 11
Lehman, John, 72
Lehman, Joseph, 100
Lehman, Ronald, 100
Leo XIII, Pope, 38, 48
Lewers, William, 190

MacKenzie, W. J. M., 1, 11, 12, 13, 14, 18
Mahony, Roger, 107
Malone, James, 90, 98, 105, 106, 114, 137, 143, 157n.7, 187
Marty, Martin, 41
Marx, Karl, 11, 164, 178
Matthews, William N., 144
Matthiesen, Leroy, 67–68, 71, 137, 155, 191
McBrien, Richard, 35, 39
McCready, William, 109, 188
McCullough, Brian, 186
McFarlane, Robert, 100
McMillan, Jill J., 31n.88, 170
McNamara, Robert, 92
McSorley, Richard, 66, 71
McSweeney, William, 41
Mead, George H., 10, 11
Mead, Margaret, 10
Mechling, Elizabeth W., 41
Merton, Thomas, 53
Miller, Richard, 103
Mol, Hans, 163
Murnion, Philip J., 82
Murphy, P. Francis, 63, 64
Murray, John Courtney, 38, 148
Musto, Ronald G., 171–172
Nichols, Peter, 35, 85
Novak, Michael, 47, 72, 73, 75, 81n.83, 91, 109, 117, 130, 137, 152, 191

O'Brien, David, 40, 176
O'Brien, William, 149
O'Connor, John Cardinal, 65, 90, 91, 96, 97, 102, 103, 105, 106, 131, 136, 140, 142, 143, 189
O'Connor, Richard, 136
O'Grady, John, 143
Ostling, Richard N., 75, 82

Palmer, Parker J., 47
Patterson, Webster T., 124

Index of Names

Paul VI, Pope, 49, 50, 55, 85, 86, 92, 132
Pilla, Anthony, 68
Pius XI, Pope, 48
Pius XII, Pope, 49, 148
Powaski, Ronald E., 121
Prelli, Lawrence J., 178

Quinn, John, 64, 107, 108, 118, 155, 189

Ratzinger, Josef Cardinal, 116, 145
Reagan, Ronald, 63, 118, 165, 166, 167
Reichert, Don, 192
Reilly, Daniel, 65, 96, 102, 115, 131, 143, 151, 187
Rhodes, James, 146
Rigali, Norbert, 151
Roach, John, 64, 65, 68, 98, 99, 106, 114, 133, 156, 187
Robertson, Roland, 161–162n.89
Rostow, Eugene, 98
Rowny, Edward, 98
Rufo, Raymond, 73, 97, 129, 188, 192
Russett, Bruce, 66, 73, 100, 104, 108, 121n.44, 142, 155, 178, 189
Ryan, M. Desmond, 187

St. Augustine, 48, 94, 147, 154
St. Bernard of Clairvaux, 15
St. Peter, 112
St. Thomas Aquinas, 48, 49, 147, 148, 154
Schattschneider, E. E., 31n.89
Schell, Jonathan, 79n.42
Schlafly, Phyllis, 91
Schreier, Howard N., 41
Seashore, Stanley, 185n.51
Shaw, Russell, 186

Shotter, John, 29n.70
Simon, Herbert A., 8, 18, 110, 169–170
Simons, Herbert W., 27n.36, 41
Sklba, Richard J., 70, 108, 131, 139, 143, 151, 155, 190
Smith, Brian H., 34, 36, 40, 42, 173, 175
Smith, Craig R., 46n.31
Smith, Gerard, 92
Spalding, John Lancaster, 38
Stohl, Cynthia, 184n.90
Sullivan, Walter, 72
Szoka, Edmund, 106

Tompkins, Phillip K., 8, 26n.8, 30n.86, 46n.31, 161n.84

Unsworth, Tim, 125

Vacek, Edward, 117
Varacalli, Joseph A., 56
Voss, Ron, 191

Walzer, Michael, 104
Warner, Richard, 1, 66, 74, 88, 94, 96, 137, 140, 155, 190
Weber, Max, 2, 7, 21, 164, 178
Weigel, George, 145, 171
Weinberger, Caspar, 69, 98, 99, 107
Whalen, Bill, 189
Whyte, John H., 39
Williams, Bob, 191
Winters, Francis X., 73, 173–174
Wohlstetter, Albert, 120n.34
Wood, James, 62, 63, 174

Yzermans, Vincent, 39, 47, 48

INDEX OF SUBJECTS

abortion, 55, 69, 94, 99, 132; linked to the issue of nuclear arms, 68–69, 132, 133–134, 137
accountability, 4
advertising, strategies in, 23
"advertorials," 6
aggiornamento, 42, 49
alienation and division, 13, 16
ambiguity in language, 56, 82–83, 102, 129, 133, 136, 155–156, 172, 179
"American Catholic Liberalism," 38
American Catholics (Hennesey), 53
American-Catholic tension, 40, 43, 108–109
"anonymous society," 4
anti-Catholic prejudice, 38, 96
argument, fields of, 178–179
audience, nature of, 6
audiences, rhetor's relationship to, 59
authority, apostolic, 111
authority, nature of, 53–54, 161–162n.89

Bible, 127, 143–147
biblical basis for peace, 143–147, 153
bishop, authority of, 111
boundary-role persons, 39, 168
Building Peace (NCCB), 167, 181n.5
Bulletin of the Atomic Scientists, 103
bureaucracy, 2–3, 7, 8, 14–15

"Call to Action," 55–56
capital punishment, 55
casuistry, 104, 135
Catholic America (Cogley), 37
Catholic Biblical Association, 144
catholicus (universalis), 85
Catholic Worker, The, 69
centralization, in organizations, 118
Challenge of Peace, The (NCCB), 1, 2, 10, 17, 24, 40–41, 43, 47, 54, 60–76, 82, 83, 84, 87, 94–95, 100, 104, 112, 113, 116, 124, 125, 126, 128, 129, 130, 132, 133, 134, 147, 148–149, 151, 154, 155–156, 164, 165, 166, 167–168, 171, 172,

173, 174, 177, 178; criticism of, 71–73, 90–92, 96–97, 143–144, 151–154, 171; final draft, 91, 105–107, 144, 153, 156; first draft, 69–7, 143–144; responses to, 165–168; second draft, 63, 69, 73–75, 99, 144, 153; vote on, 62–63
Church and Politics in Chile (Smith), 34, 40
A Church to Believe In (Dulles), 127
Collegeville, Minnesota (retreat of bishops in 1982), 70–71, 88, 126–127, 128
collegiality, 41, 70, 81n.78, 112, 125–127, 156
Commentary, 72
Commonweal, 176
community: ideal of, 128–129, 131–132, 175; model of Church, 125, 127–130
"congregation" and "segregation," 13
Congregation for the Bishops, 111
conscientious objection, 55
"constitution," idea of a, 86, 139, 147, 154, 156, 168, 177–178
constraints, rhetorical, 72, 75–76, 83–84, 119n.19, 124
"corporate" advocacy/"corporate" issue management, 7, 9, 22, 51, 87, 170
"corporate" messages, 2, 3, 4–6
corporation, legal, 4
corpus, 4
covenant, idea of, 146–147

"de-centering" of the self, 5
Decree on the Apostolate of the Laity (Vatican II), 58
Decree on the Bishops' Pastoral Office in the Church (Vatican II), 113
deterrence, nuclear, 50, 56, 57, 68, 74, 99–107, 115, 167
dignity of human life, 48, 55, 113–137
Dramatism, 15

ecclesiology, 36
emotional attachment, 10
encyclicals, papal, 48–50
enthymeme, 8

199

ethos, 58, 76
Exit, Voice, and Loyalty (Hirschman), 168
Ezekiel, 143

Foreign Affairs, 92
"freeze," nuclear, 58, 60, 61, 62, 63, 74, 75, 98, 104–107, 141, 165, 166, 167, 170–171
Freeze! (Kennedy and Hatfield), 60
Functions of the Executive, The (Barnard), 20

Gaudium et Spes (Vatican II), 49, 51, 85, 86, 87, 88, 126, 148, 171
global identity, 184n.35
Gospel of Peace and the Danger of War, The (NCCB), 57
Gospel of Peace and Justice, The (Gremillion), 48
gun control, 154

"hierarchical communion," 112, 175
hierarchy, idea of, 175
hierarchy of moral authority, 114–117, 130, 131, 136
History of Christianity, A (Johnson), 34
How Institutions Think, 164
Human Life in Our Day (NCCB), 55

identification, 11, 15–20, 140; with organizations, 12, 14, 18–20, 140, 169
identitas, 11
identities, management of, 2, 9, 14–15, 16, 20–24, 36, 37, 40–44, 75, 82–181
identity: changes in, 17; collective, 10, 13–15, 18, 111, 129, 163, 173, 174; nature of, 9, 10–13, 19, 140, 180
"image/identity management," 22
In Defense of Life (O'Connor, John J.), 65
individualism, 11
interdependence of nations, 49, 92–93, 134
interest groups, 35, 42, 58, 140–143, 179
interests, shared, 13, 18, 140–141, 174
interviewing, method of, 32–33n.95, 193–195
Isaiah, 146

Jeremiah, 143
Jus ad Bellum and *Jus in Bello*, 148
Justice in the World (Synod of Bishops), 50
Just War Theory, 48–49, 53, 65, 143, 147–154

Kingdom of God, idea of, 145–146, 147

labor unions, 175
laity, role of, 58, 73, 125, 129, 130, 131
logos, 6
Lumen Gentium (Vatican II), 85, 111–112

Magisterium, 145
management, concept of, 9, 31n.91
mandatum docendi, 116
Mater et Magistra (Pope John XXIII), 50
Meaning and Place (Mol), 163
media, nature of, 5–6
message, structure of, 5
Models of the Church (Dulles), 127
moral argument, 57, 66, 69, 76, 79n.51, 93–94, 95, 99, 102, 134–137
Moral Clarity in the Nuclear Age (Novak), 117, 130
multinational corporations, 37, 118
MX missile, 63, 102–103
mystery, hierarchical, 15

National Catholic Reporter, 61, 115
National Catholic Welfare Council, 54, 110, 113
National Council of Churches, 51, 61
nationalism, 38, 54, 108, 110, 168
Nationalism and American Catholicism, 38
National Opinion Research Center, 109, 165
national security, 108
neutron bomb, 67
"new moment," the, 150, 167
New Religious Right, 62
Newsweek, 97
New Yorker, The, 97
New York Times, The, 67, 68, 75, 99, 105, 107
Nichomachean Ethics (Aristotle), 11
nuclear arms, 66; possession of, 66, 71, 100, 101, 144; summits, 166–167; use of, 56, 57, 63, 65, 71, 93, 101, 103, 107, 144, 149; and economic deprivation, 56, 69, 134; nuclear arms control, 49, 55, 56, 60, 64, 82, 94, 167; linked to other issues, 132–140
nuclear strategy, 100, 102, 103, 107
nuclear war, danger of, 92–93

Octogesima Adveniens (Pope Paul VI), 50, 55

organization, definition of, 3, 19, 20
organizational control, 7
organizational environment, 7
"organizational personality," 19
organizational rhetoric, nature of, 2–10, 15, 20–24, 163–164
organizational theory, 2–3, 20, 163–164
organizations, history of, 7; personification of, 21–22
Our Sunday Visitor, 137
Our Unfinished Business (Berryman), 124
Oxford English Dictionary, 12

Pacem in Terris (Pope John XXIII), 49, 92, 172
pacifism and nonviolence, 53, 143, 147–154
"partial inclusion," 17
participative decision making, 41, 129, 175
pastoral letter, nature of, 125
Pastoral Letter on Marxist Communism (NCCB), 125
pastoral letter on the U.S. economy (NCCB), 98, 139
pathos, 6
Pax Christi USA, 60, 64, 65, 66, 140, 144, 161n.73
peace, 90, 92–94; theology of, 66, 94, 145–147, 171
peace movement, 42, 53, 54–55
"People of God," 130
Pershing II missile, 103
pluralism, 39, 41, 96, 130, 151–152, 175
polis, 8
political argument, 69, 75, 79n.51, 88, 95, 99
Political Identity (MacKenzie), 1, 11
pope, authority of, 111
Populorum Progressio (Pope Paul VI), 50, 92
post-structuralism, 27n.36, 164
poverty, linked to the issue of the arms race, 94–95, 132–137
power, nature of, 179–180
pragmatic argument, 52, 57, 63, 66, 68, 69, 75, 95, 137–139
premises (for decisions and persuasion), 8, 19
priesthood, nature of, 111
priestly stance, 144–145, 153
pro-life position, 55

prophetic stance, 83, 144, 153
Protestantism in the U.S., 37, 174–175

Quadragesimo Anno (Pope Pius XI), 48

rationality, types of, 178
Reagan Administration, 14, 15, 22, 60, 61, 62, 63, 67, 69, 75, 76, 98, 99, 100, 102, 105–108, 166, 171, 178, 180
religion, nature of, 47, 97, 163
religious organizations that supported the nuclear freeze, 61–62
Rerum Novarum (Pope Leo XIII), 48, 50
rhetoric, nature of, 14, 19, 20, 156, 170
Rhetoric of Motives, A (Burke), 1
rhetorical criticism, 164
"rhetorical situation," 4
role, concept of, 17
Roman Catholic Church, 9, 15, 34–36, 83, 84–86, 110, 118, 124, 129, 132, 133, 169, 173–174; advocacy by, 42, 48–52, 54–59, 68, 72, 75, 87, 88, 89, 96–97, 98, 168; as organization, 35, 43–44, 85; challenges to, 36, 40–44; identity and mission of, 36, 40, 42, 70, 88, 89, 138, 147, 154, 176–177; in the U.S., 37–40, 47, 52–54, 95–110, 165, 168, 176–177; mystery of, 85–86, 127

"sacred" texts and symbols, 177–178
SALT II, 57, 60, 63
"seamless garment," 134–139
sectarian posture, 145
"selective Catholicism," 39, 138
separation of church and state, 38, 51, 75
socialization, 19
social justice, 41, 48–52, 69, 71, 87, 132, 134, 175
social movements, general, 40, 41–42
Sojourners, 61
"sound bite," 6
source (of message), 7
Soviet Union, 43, 99, 132, 147; as a threat, 60, 90–92, 109
"stakeholder," 6
"stateless" corporations, 23
Strategic Defense Initiative ("Star Wars"), 62, 167, 178
"structured pluralism," 129
subsidiarity, 158n.17
Survival of Dogma, The (Dulles), 34
synods of bishops, 126, 127

Index of Subjects

tautotes, 11
Time, 21, 60, 74, 75, 79n.50, 176
technical argument, 178
To Live in Christ Jesus (NCCB), 56, 57
topoi, 69, 139
tradition, 172–173
Tanquillitas Ordinis (Weigel), 171
transcendent terms, 85, 150
transnational organizations, 176–177
Trident nuclear submarine, 66
Trinity, idea of the, 11

United Council of Methodist Bishops, 181n.6
United Nations, 49, 61, 101, 176
United Nations Second Special Session on Disarmament, 61
U.S., relationship to the world, 89–95
U.S. Catholic bishops—National Conference of Catholic Bishops (NCCB), 2, 10, 17, 24, 25n.2, 35, 40, 43, 47, 51, 52, 54–59, 82, 83, 106, 113, 116–117, 118, 125, 126, 127, 128, 141–142, 143, 145, 148, 150, 152, 165, 166, 167, 168, 169, 170, 171, 172, 174, 175, 176, 178, 179, 180; authority of, 57–59, 63, 73–76, 89, 95, 110–118, 138, 141–142, 156, 172, 177, 178; identity of, 59, 63, 70–73, 89,

97, 100, 106, 110–118, 125, 141–142, 155–157, 165, 169, 178; meeting of 15–18 November 1982, 74–75
U.S. Catholic Conference (USCC), 25n.2, 39, 98, 117
U.S. Congress, 60, 102
U.S. Constitution, 4, 6, 154
U.S. defense build-up, 60–62, 90
U.S. News & World Report, 91
U.S. Presidential election: 1980, 60, 63; 1984, 62, 97; 1988, 6

Vatican, 76, 110, 113–116, 133, 152
Vatican Council: First, 86, 113; Second, 34, 36, 39, 42, 49, 50, 51, 58, 85, 86, 87, 96, 112, 128, 130, 148
Vietnam War, 39, 53, 54, 68
"Voice," option of, 168–169

Wanderer, The, 62, 91
war, conduct of, 147–149
War and Peace Committee (NCCB), 65–66, 69–70, 73–74, 82, 96, 97, 98, 101, 140–141, 156
Washington Post, 117
Western European bishops, 76, 114–116
"whistle-blower," 109, 169

202